Small Works

Small Works

Poverty and Economic Development in Southwestern China

John A. Donaldson

Cornell University Press
ITHACA AND LONDON

First published 2011 by Cornell University Press

Printed in the United States of America

Library of Congress Cataloging-in-Publication Data

Donaldson, John A., 1970–
Small works : poverty and economic development in southwestern China / John A. Donaldson.
p. cm.
Includes bibliographical references and index.
ISBN 978-0-8014-4968-0 (cloth : alk. paper)
1. Poverty—China—Yunnan Sheng. 2. Poverty—China—Guizhou Sheng. 3. Economic development—China—Yunnan Sheng. 4. Economic development—China—Guizhou Sheng. 5. Yunnan Sheng (China)—Economic conditions. 6. Guizhou Sheng (China)—Economic conditions. I. Title.
HC428.Y8D65 2011
339.4'6095134—dc22 2010053587

Cornell University Press strives to use environmentally responsible suppliers and materials to the fullest extent possible in the publishing of its books. Such materials include vegetable-based, low-VOC inks and acid-free papers that are recycled, totally chlorine-free, or partly composed of nonwood fibers. For further information, visit our website at www.cornellpress.cornell.edu.

Cloth printing 10 9 8 7 6 5 4 3 2 1

To my wife

Contents

Figures, Tables, and Maps

Figures

Tables

MAPS

Acknowledgments

Like raising a child, raising a monograph requires a village. Acknowledging adequately the contributions made by the many people who have assisted me would require nearly as much space as the book itself. A few short sentences will have to suffice.

I have received sage counsel from numerous people throughout the academic world, including my community at Singapore Management University and colleagues at George Washington University and University of Toronto. I thank my advisors, Bruce Dickson, Harry Harding, and Hal Wolman, and also Michael Mochizuki and Daniel Wright. These scholars were indispensable, providing me with patient advice and guidance. Nearly all the other professors in the Political Science Department at George Washington University have also helped me directly or indirectly—including the much-missed Lee Sigelman. In addition, the founders of the extraordinary Asian Network for the Study of Local China (ANSLoC), including founders Tao-chiu Lam, Philip Hsu, Tse-kang Leng, Lai Hongyi, and especially the organizer, Jae Ho Chung, deserve my heartfelt thanks.

The China Scholars group of my George Washington University classmates, including Injoo Sohn, Phillip Stalley, Yisuo Tzeng, and Jaime Reilly, provided a supportive community for feedback and support, as did Stephanie McNulty, Lee Ann Fujii, Mark Teel, and Jessica Lieberman. I especially thank Hal Wolman, Kris Ramsay, Wang Shufen, Tom Holyoke, Luan Shenghua, Liu Tian, Nicholas Harrigan, Joel Ng, and Aurobindo Ghosh for their advice on quantitative methods. Among the many other scholars who provided sage advice, Dorothy Solinger, David S. G. Goodman, Lin Kun-Chin, Chen Shaohua, and Li Qiang deserve special mention.

In China, I benefitted from the advice of scholars from Tsinghua University in Beijing and from a number of universities in Guizhou and Yunnan, where individual scholars supported this project with their full commitment, to the point of nearly adopting it as their own. Professors Cheng Housi and Yu Minxiong deserve special mention. I hope that I have used their cooperation and assistance wisely. In addition, I learned a great deal from local officials and residents in Guizhou and Yunnan, who provided frank and insightful opinions about what is happening in the Chinese countryside and what, if anything, has helped improve local economies and the lives of poor people.

The Fulbright Foundation and the research office at Singapore Management University both provided vital funding. In addition, sections of chapter 2 are based on material from my 2009 article "Why Do Similar Areas Adopt Different Developmental Strategies?: A Study of Two Puzzling Chinese Provinces," *Journal of Contemporary China* 18(60): 421–44, and portions of chapter 5 are based on material from my 2007 article "Tourism, Development and Poverty Reduction in Guizhou and Yunnan," *China Quarterly* 190: 333–51.

Many undergraduate research assistants from Singapore Management University helped with various aspects of this book. Zhou "Premier" Chuanyi, Guo Xin, and Zhong Ke served as a core research group. Wilson Loke, Elvin Ong, and Phoebe Luo also deserve special mention. Other research assistants included Nicholas Chia, Abdul Shariff Bin Aboo Kassim, Ethan Tong, Lim Feng Lin, Eugene Kwok, Gokul Sahni, Isaac Chee, Li Jing, Nupur Bhargava, Yves Yeo, Zhang Xuefeng, and many others whom I may have unintentionally omitted. Among those helping with editing were Jennifer Milewski, Rajan Rishyakaran (greatly missed), Hazel Tan, Mark E. Donaldson, Madhu Chaubey, and Chan Ying Xian.

My wife and family have been critical as my supporters, data enterers, and last-minute editors. It is sometimes not easy—even for other scholars—to live with someone in the midst of this kind of project. Many friends and loved ones have prayed over this book, and I thank them and God for help and encouragement.

Finally, I thank the rural residents whom I met in China. Invariably, they supported the research I was conducting, and without their help, this book would have been impossible. Although I can never adequately repay my debt to them, I hope one day to do them some good.

Abbreviations

CCP	Chinese Communist Party
GDP	gross domestic product
GMD	Guomingdang
LDC	less-developed countries
NBS	National Bureau of Statistics
NGOs	nongovernmental organizations
NRHS	National Rural Household Survey
NRPMS	National Rural Poverty Monitoring Survey
PRC	People's Republic of China
RMB	renminbi ("the people's currency"); Chinese currency. The exchange rate was until recently fixed at RMB 8.2 for US$1. It is also known as the yuan.
SARS	severe acute respiratory syndrome
SOE	state-owned enterprise
TVE	town and village enterprise
UNDP	United Nations Development Programme
UNESCAP	United Nations Economic and Social Commission for Asia and the Pacific
UNESCO	United National Educational, Scientific and Cultural Organization
UNWTO	United Nations World Tourism Organization

Chinese Terms

Diannan Bang	southern Yunnan clique
hexie shehui	Harmonious Society
kexue fazhan guan	Scientific Development Concept
laoxiang	people from one's hometown
li	unit of measure; 1 li = 0.5 kilometer
mu	unit of measure is equivalent to 0.16 acre.
nongjiale	tourism involving traveling and staying in the countryside, often in a peasant's home
nongye guanguang lvyou	agricultural sightseeing and tourism
xianxiang gonglu	village-to-market roads (literally county-to-township roads)
Yigong-Daizhen	food-for-work (public works) program
yuan	Chinese currency, also known as Renminbi (RMB)
zhen	town

Small Works

Introduction

> But while there comes the reek of wines and meats that rot inside the gates of these rich, the bones of the starving and cold are strewn along the roadsides.
>
> —Du Fu, "Song on the Road—Going from the Capital to Feng County" (translated by Hu Kaimei, 2001)

Is economic growth good for the poor? In theory, yes. With increasing wealth, the poor should benefit along with everyone else. This argument has long prevailed in the thinking of scholars of development and poverty. Back in the eighteenth century, Adam Smith emphasized the benefits for the poor of a growing economy (Gilbert 1997). The arguments of this lonely voice have now been widely accepted, and by the mid-twentieth century, development scholars of most ideological stripes agreed that economic growth was necessary for the long-term reduction of poverty. Many took this idea further, maintaining that such growth was the most central factor. The voices supporting this position are both powerful and prominent. In 2006, Michael Spence, Nobel Prize–winning economist, launched the Commission on Growth and Development, a group of notables convicted that global challenges such as poverty are "best met in conditions of rising and sustained prosperity, and expanding economic opportunities" (Commission on Growth and Development 2010). Although the World Bank has on occasion moderated a sometimes dogmatic commitment to economic growth, its recent World Development Report (World Bank 2009) is a classic statement of a growth-first development strategy. Although the strategy has provoked substantial resistance from a wide range of scholars and policymakers, the belief that economic growth and poverty reduction are tightly linked remains dominant.

In few places has this argument has been more starkly presented than in a paper penned by a pair of World Bank economists, David Dollar and Aart Kraay. After analyzing worldwide and historical data they conclude,

"It should come as no surprise that the general relationship between growth of income of the poor and growth of mean income is one-to-one" (Dollar and Kraay 2000, 27). The controversial idea in Dollar and Kraay's research is not the hypothesized relationship between economic growth and poverty reduction. In fact, few critics argue that this relationship is entirely spurious (Weisbrot et al. 2000). Instead, the most contentious conclusions of Dollar and Kraay's broad empirical study are that the relationship between economic growth and poverty reduction is one to one; that economic growth alone can be sufficient to reduce poverty; and that, because market-based decisions spur growth best, the state should interfere in the economy as little as possible. Dollar and Kraay provide a powerful empirical argument to support a liberal state approach to poverty reduction. Although it has sparked controversy in both the academic and policy communities, with many supporting it (e.g., Bigsten and Levin 2001) and others criticizing it (e.g., Weisbrot et al. 2000; Rodrik 2000; Oxfam 2007), Dollar and Kraay's contention embodies the enduring idea that growth is crucially important for poverty reduction.

Indeed, recent scholarship suggests that absolute poverty rates worldwide appear to decline during periods of global economic expansion (Ravallion 2009; Narayan, Walker, and Trathen 2009); however, important exceptions cast doubt. Regarding India, Amartya Sen (1981) notes that during the Great Bengal Famine (in 1943) 1.5–3 million people died of starvation despite a booming economy. More recently, the Bharatiya Janata Party (BJP) in 2004 suffered a stunning election defeat despite an economy growing in excess of 8 percent per year. The BJP lost, analysts argue, because this historic expansion, which the BJP highlighted with the sunny campaign slogan "India Shining," had done little to benefit hundreds of millions of poor and working-class citizens (e.g., Wilkinson 2005). Newspaper stories about farmers driven to suicide in the face of hunger, mounting debt, and callous moneylenders made the slogan appear bitterly ironic. Meanwhile, in regions such as the Indian state of Kerala, poverty declined rapidly despite only modest economic growth and little development (Singh forthcoming). In China, the reform of agriculture between 1978 and the mid-1980s sparked both rapid growth and poverty reduction. But, since then, rural poverty rates in China have fallen much more slowly, and have actually increased in some years, despite the record-breaking pace of economic growth (e.g., Park and Wang 2001; Chen and Ravallion 2007). In the United States, despite an impressive 89 percent increase in real GDP per capita between 1973 and 2007, poverty rates also increased from a historic low of 11.1 percent to 12.5 percent (updated from Freeman 2003, data from Johnston and Williamson 2010, and U.S. Census Bureau 2008). Exceptions such as India, China, and the United States during these specific periods suggest that a divergence between economic growth and poverty rates is neither rare nor trivial (Donaldson 2008). Throughout the world, some areas grow, but poverty persists; other areas are stagnant, yet poverty diminishes.

What factors impede poverty reduction when economic growth is robust? Conversely, what explains poverty reduction in areas with modest rates of economic growth and development? In this book, I examine the connection between economic growth and poverty reduction by analyzing two exceptions to the correlation. Doing so reveals more about the relationship between growth and poverty, including factors that reduce poverty despite low rates of economic growth and those that prevent economic growth from reducing poverty.

Discovering what has caused this pattern may illuminate pathways, other than economic growth, that can reduce poverty. Identifying such pathways is, as always, pressing. The problem of poverty is inherently important, contributing to severe political and social problems such as low life expectancy, malnutrition, starvation, and oppression (Sen 1999), as well as domestic disturbances (Dunbabin 1974), civil war, and international conflict (e.g., Holsti 1999).[1] As Gro Harlem Brundtland, former director general of the World Health Organization, reminded the United Nations World Summit for Social Development, "Poverty is still the gravest insult to human dignity. Poverty is the scar on humanity's face" (Brundtland 1995). Finding solutions other than economic growth that are effective in reducing poverty can bring hope to areas that, due to geographical, demographic, or other factors, are unlikely to see rapid economic expansion. Despite centuries of effort involving incalculable amounts of money and determined commitments to end poverty (or halve it, or some other goal) by some arbitrary specific date, we have failed to make sufficient progress. Most governments since the industrial revolution have made poverty reduction a priority (Lipton and Ravallion 1995), yet they have had, at best, modest success. In 2005, more than 1.37 billion people, nearly one out of every five on the planet, lived below the international poverty line, earning less than $1.25 per day (Chen and Ravallion 2008). Despite industrialization, urbanization, technological advance, and economic growth, poverty endures. Policymakers must identify effective methods that permanently eliminate poverty. More growth may indeed be necessary to achieve this goal, yet economic growth alone is not enough.

In this book, I examine the relationship between economic growth and poverty reduction by analyzing two regional economies that violate the conventionally accepted relationship. On the Chinese mainland, two neighboring poor provinces—Guizhou and Yunnan—face similar challenges and

1. It is probably true that "deprivations, alone, are insufficient to reproduce revolutionary upheavals" (Lasswell 1936, 237), an argument with which many social scientists agree (Tilly 1978; Skocpol 1979). Nevertheless, poverty has contributed to many serious social revolutions and civil conflicts throughout history, most recently in Tunisia, Egypt, and elsewhere.

conditions while sharing key demographic and geographical characteristics (see map 1).[2] As I describe more fully in chapter 1, the two provinces are strikingly similar. Both are remote and mountainous. Farming on tiny rocky plots deep in the mountains, many rural families in the two provinces subsist on what they can produce from these harsh agricultural conditions. Ethnic minorities make up a large proportion (approximately one-third) of the populations of both provinces. The Chinese central government has implemented different policies in each of the three main Chinese regions (coastal, center, and western) and so treats these two western provinces similarly (Fan 1997). Moreover, most areas of these two provinces, unlike those in northwest China, normally enjoy abundant water resources.

Despite these similarities, the economy of one of these provinces grew sluggishly while poverty declined, whereas the economy of the other province grew rapidly with few people emerging from poverty. Guizhou is the first province, a poor remote province, with an area about one-third larger than Greece (176,000 km^2 vs. 132,940 km^2) and a population in 2007 larger than that of Poland (almost 40 million people). In 1991, Guizhou performed poorly as measured both by its GDP per capita (RMB 890,[3] ranking last among the thirty provinces considered[4]) and by the percentage of its population living below the international poverty line (59 percent, ranking twenty-eighth out of thirty). Throughout the 1990s and beyond, the Guizhou economy grew sluggishly and was among the slowest growing Chinese provinces. Nevertheless, starting in the early 1990s, the rate of severe poverty in Guizhou declined from 41.9 percent in 1990 to 24.5 percent in 1996 to below 20 percent by the end of the decade—the third fastest decline in poverty among the provinces.

By contrast, neighboring Yunnan, with an area slightly larger than Japan (394,000 km^2 vs. 377,835 km^2) and with a population nearly that of Spain (approximately 45 million people in 2006), experienced rapid economic growth but little decline in poverty. Also a poor province, it ranked twenty-fifth out of thirty in per capita GDP and in 1991 ranked twenty-third in the proportion of the population living below the international poverty line (44 percent). But Yunnan saw its GDP increase rapidly in the 1990s, thanks in large part to its booming tobacco, tourism, and export industries. In spite of this (and using the same statistics), the poverty rate in Yunnan actually

2. For convenience, the terms *China* (where, due to the Taiwan question, even stating the number of provinces in the country is politically controversial) and *Chinese* here refer to the Chinese mainland and exclude statistics for Taiwan, Hong Kong, and Macao.

3. The exchange rate was for many years pegged at approximately RMB 8.2 per U.S. dollar before being allowed more flexibility. RMB and yuan are both used to refer to China's currency. The population and area statistics for Guizhou and Yunnan are from statistical yearbooks for China (State Statistical Bureau various years-b, various years-c).

4. In addition to the exceptions already mentioned, these statistics exclude Chongqing, which became a provincial-level municipality in March 1997.

Map 1 Administrative divisions of the People's Republic of China. Guizhou and Yunnan are circled.
Source: http://en.wikipedia.org/wiki/File:China_administrative.g

increased from 30.3 to nearly 33 percent in 1996.[5] Not only did the rapid economic growth not benefit the poor of the province, the economic expansion in Yunnan left a higher proportion of its people poor. According to one measure, during this period approximately 2.2 million more people became impoverished in Yunnan, whereas 2.4 million people emerged from poverty in Guizhou.[6] Although the Yunnan poverty rate subsequently declined slowly throughout the rest of the decade and into the next, this indicator consistently remained higher than that of the slower-growing Guizhou. Today, the much faster-growing Yunnan still appears to contain more poor people than its slower-growing neighbor, despite the lower initial Yunnan poverty rate in the 1990s.[7]

Other indicators suggest a similar pattern. The National Bureau of Statistics (NBS) publishes statistics on per capita rural net income, which form the basis for calculating the income levels of the poor and nonpoor counties in Guizhou and Yunnan.[8] As shown in figure 1, the average net rural income of the Guizhou nonpoor counties started at a lower level in 1990 and, as of 2007, had yet to catch up to that of the Yunnan nonpoor counties. As it happens, the income of the Yunnan nonpoor counties exceeds the average per capita net rural income of the Guizhou nonpoor counties by a wide margin. The story for the poor counties of these provinces, however, is markedly different. In 1992, average per capita net rural incomes of the poor counties of Yunnan and Guizhou were nearly identical (RMB 466 vs. RMB 464). By 1995, however, the average annual per capita net rural income for the Guizhou poor counties had exceeded that for the Yunnan poor counties, despite the much higher overall Yunnan GDP growth rate. In spite of an economic growth rate in Yunnan that dramatically outpaced that in Guizhou, the nominal net rural incomes in the Yunnan poor counties increased on average 2 percentage points slower than in the Guizhou poor counties every year between 1992 and 2007. In fact, between 1996 and 2007, the net rural income of the Guizhou poor counties exceeded that of the Yunnan poor counties by an average of more than 16 percent. Both the World Bank and official Chinese statistics indicate a similar pattern. Sometime in the early 1990s, rural net incomes in the Guizhou poor counties increased rapidly, overtaking the rural income of the Yunnan poor counties by 1996 and continuing to exceed it until at least 2007. Most of the economic growth in Yunnan apparently

5. The change in the Yunnan poverty rate was the second worst of all the Chinese provinces during this period.

6. These statistics are based on the official poverty line of China (RMB 206 per capita net income in 1985, equivalent to RMB 625 in 2000), which is a fraction of the international poverty line.

7. The figures for differences in the actual number of poor people can be somewhat deceptive because much of the poverty in China is transitional, with a large proportion of people moving into and out of poverty (Jalan and Ravallion 2000). Nonetheless, the contrast between the two provinces is striking.

8. Starting in 1986, the Chinese State Council classified each of the county-level regions as either poor or nonpoor.

benefitted its nonpoor residents, whereas the poor in Guizhou seemed to have done better despite the lower economic growth rate.

What factors might explain the puzzling patterns of economic growth and poverty reduction found in these two provinces? Variation in provincial policies and strategies is one possible explanation; it is also possible the key explanatory factors are unaffected by human plans. Nonetheless, it is helpful to develop a framework to analyze the array of governmental strategies that other scholars suggest have reduced poverty. These vary on several dimensions, including the relationship that the state adopts toward the market, the goal of the intervention, the development strategies used, the scale of the intervention, and the specific mechanism through which the poor are helped. The strategies are summarized in table 1.

Although many of these strategies rely on economic growth to help increase the income of the poor, advocates of each strategy also argue that the poor will benefit through mechanisms other than economic growth—potentially explaining the pattern in Guizhou in which poverty reduction outpaced economic growth. Similarly, advocates of each strategy maintain that not adopting theirs will be especially harmful to the poor and could, therefore, create the problem we find in Yunnan, in which the income of the poor did not grow as quickly as the economy. In addition to examining nonpolitical factors such as geographical, cultural, economic, and demographic differences, I use this framework to explore whether the patterns found in Guizhou and Yunnan might have been caused by the implementation of one or more of these approaches.

Table 1, although far from exhaustive, makes it clear that approaches to poverty reduction are numerous. One group of scholars has argued that the policies implemented by an open, liberal state will reduce poverty (e.g., Krueger 1995; Bates 1981; Bhagwati 1988; Lal and Myint 1996; World Bank 2009). States reduce poverty by proactively building institutions and implementing policies that support the market while allowing most economic decisions to be made by private actors via the market. Through the market, increasingly efficient modes of production will emerge. Production will scale up, providing job opportunities to a wider range of workers, many of whom will shift from agricultural production to manufacturing and service industries. In addition to contending that the poor generally benefit from this economic growth, many supporters of this approach argue that a pro-market set of policies implemented by an active, but limited, state will be especially beneficial to the poor.[9] Advocates of a second approach, the developmental

9. Some advocates of the liberal state model echo Kuznets's familiar argument that economic growth can for a time increase inequality. Nevertheless, inequality and poverty are separate concepts. Most advocates of this approach maintain that the poor will benefit from growth, even though the rich benefit to a greater extent, thus increasing inequality. Moreover, some contemporary scholars, such as Dollar and Kraay (2000), reject Kuznets, arguing that the poor will benefit from economic growth just as much as other segments of the population (Kanbur 2000).

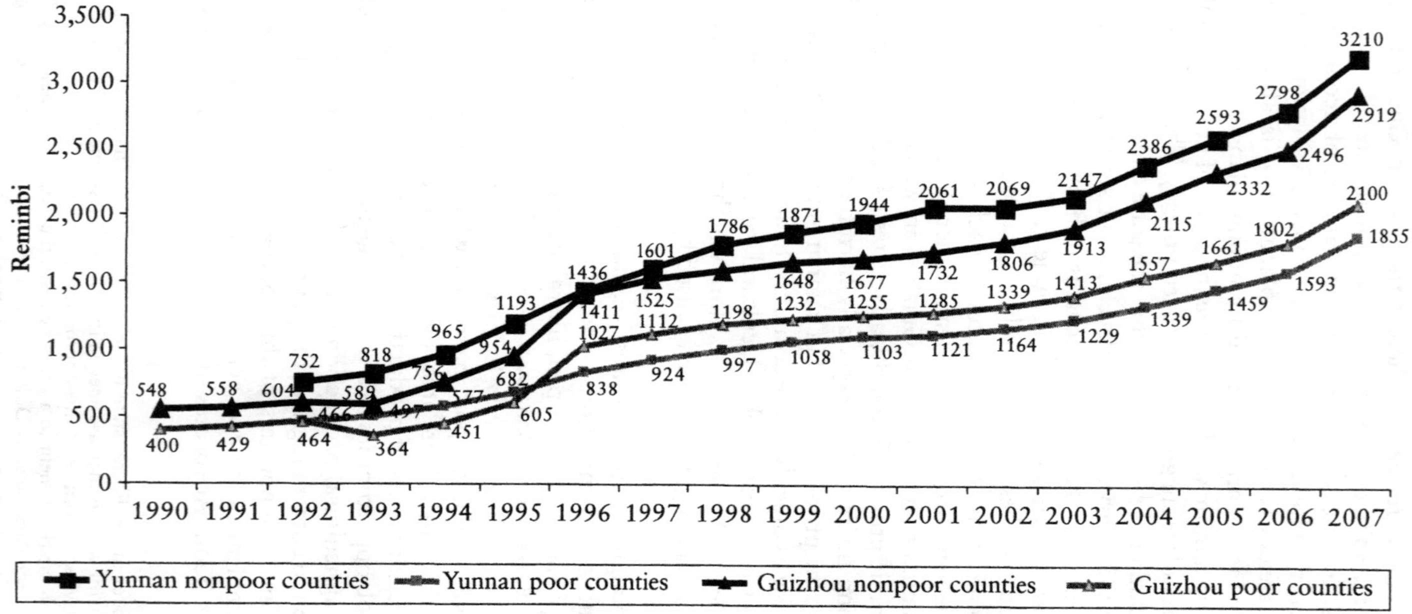

Fig. 1 Per capita net incomes—nonpoor versus poor counties in Guizhou and Yunnan, 1990–2007.
Source: State Statistical Bureau (various years-b, various years-c).

Table 1. State strategies for poverty reduction

	State type						
Characteristic	Liberal state	Developmental state	Welfare state	Protectionist state	Agriculture-oriented state	Progressive state	Micro-oriented state
Primary relationship with market	Market facilitation	Market alteration	Market alteration	Market replacement	Market alteration	Market replacement	Multiple relationships
Primary goal	Growth	Growth	Growth	State-led industrialization	Agricultural development	Poverty reduction (redistributive justice)	Poverty reduction (technical issue)
Primary development strategies	Deregulation Opening economy Legal infrastructure Reducing public expenditures	"Triple alliance" among domestic state, domestic industrialists, and foreign capital State investments in key industries Investment in large-scale infrastructure Urban development	Protecting the poor from the market Establishing safety nets based on unforeseen shifts in markets/ readjustment policies	Import-substitution industrialization State-led industrialization Urban development	Investing in rural infrastructure Guaranteeing rural inputs Implementing micro-credit programs Land reform	Investing in education, health care Redistributing wealth	Enhancing rural livelihoods Strengthening local, rural markets
Trickling effect	Top-down	Top-down	Top-down	Top-down	Bottom-up	Bottom-up	Bottom-up
Scale of industry	Market decides	Large	Market decides	Large	Small	Varies	Small
Mechanisms for poverty reduction	Growth Trickle down Shifting labor from agriculture to industry Controlling inflation, government interference	Promoting manufacturing industry, shifting labor from agriculture to industry	Protecting the poor	Shifting labor from agriculture to industry	Enhancing agricultural production and income	Direct aid (education, health care)	Stimulating opportunities for the poor
Examples	United Kingdom, India (postreform)	Asian tigers, Israel	United States	Egypt, Turkey	Taiwan, South Korea	Kerala, Cuba, Botswana	Guizhou

state, argue that reducing poverty necessitates all-encompassing state involvement in the process of development and industrialization (e.g., Evans 1979; Cardoso and Faletto 1979; Amsden 1985; Woo-Cumings 1999). By adopting a primary role in investing in and nurturing large-scale export industries, the state alters the market to generate opportunities for the poor in the more modern industrial sector. A third approach protects the poor through weaving and anchoring the safety nets of the welfare state, reducing poverty by providing benefits, programs, or opportunities to people classified as poor through a means test or some other mechanism (Conway and Norton 2002; Devereux 2002). A fourth and more radical approach, the protectionist state, is founded on the mistrust of the concealed power held by those who dominate and benefit from freer markets (Frank 1969; Amin 1974). These dependency theorists (as they were known) argue that to reduce poverty the state must replace the market by closing the economy to some degree and focusing on (usually large-scale) industries that can manufacture goods that substitute for imports.

The first four approaches to poverty reduction, although based on fundamentally different strategies, share common ground. In particular, they share a commitment to the pursuit of development, usually involving increasing overall productivity and scale of production. The first four are also top-down approaches that echo the ideas of economists such as Paul Rosenstein-Rodan (1957) and Ragnar Nurkse (1953), who suggest that a modern manufacturing sector will shift labor from traditional agriculture—a classic aspect of development, as conceptualized by Walt Rostow and others (e.g., Lewis 1954; Rostow 1960).

Other scholars advocate strategies that are more consistent with the basic needs approach that became popular among nongovernmental organizations (NGOs) and even in the World Bank for a brief period during the 1970s (International Labour Organization 1976; Chenery et al. 1974; Streeten 1982).[10] Advocates of the agriculture-oriented state ("farmer first"[11]) approach argue that, because more than three-quarters of the world's poor are involved in agriculture and earn an estimated 70 percent of their cash and

10. In the early 1970s, World Bank President Robert McNamara shifted the strategy of the institution away from large-scale infrastructure projects and toward rural lending, focusing on the reduction of poverty and provision of basic needs. By the early 1980s, neoclassical economic theory, with its liberal state approach, began to dominate development thinking. The office of World Bank chief economist changed hands from the long-tenured Hollis B. Chenery, who had overseen the World Bank research on the basic needs approach to poverty reduction, to Anne Krueger, a neoliberal economist (Lipton and Ravallion 1995). Subsequently at the World Bank, as elsewhere, the popularity of the basic needs approach declined in favor of neoclassical approaches to poverty reduction (Uitto 2006), as exemplified by the 2009 World Development Report (World Bank 2009). Nevertheless, some of the aspects of the basic needs approach have been institutionalized, for instance in the United Nations Development Programme (UNDP) Human Development Index (Haq 1995).

11. The term *farmer first* is associated with Robert Chambers (Chambers, Pacey, and Thrupp 1989).

noncash income from growing food, governments should concentrate on bolstering agriculture (e.g., Dorward et al. 2004; Adelman 1986; Chambers, Pacey, and Thrupp 1989; Mellor 1995; Bezemer and Headey 2008). Through investing in rural infrastructure, guaranteeing or subsidizing rural inputs, implementing micro-credit programs, and guaranteeing grain purchases, the state reduces poverty in a cost-effective manner, one that stimulates industrialization over the long term, in part by creating demand from below. In cases of severe landlessness, comprehensive land reform is also needed to ensure a fairer distribution of land resources (Berry and Cline 1979).

Another bottom-up strategy, the progressive state, reduces poverty through social activism and redistributive justice. Progressive state policies, such as those implemented in the Indian state of Kerala, ensure that the poor benefit directly from sizable public investments in grassroots education, health care, and food provision, as well as the redistribution of wealth through land reform or nationalization of industry (e.g., Duncan, Jefferis, and Molutsi 1997; Mehrotra 1997; Franke and Chasin 1992; Parayil 2000).

Despite important disagreements among the advocates of all these approaches, they share two positions. First, their advocates agree that economic growth often benefits the poor, even though they recognize numerous exceptions to the relationship between economic growth and poverty reduction. Nevertheless, they rarely go as far as Dollar and Kraay in suggesting that the poor benefit from growth on a one-to-one basis. Second, advocates of these positions promote an active role for the state.

The framework I present here encourages an attitude toward the interaction of the state and the market that improves significantly on the tired and flawed state-market debate that too often views the economic roles for the state and the market as zero-sum.[12] Scholars have for decades recognized this weakness (Toye 1987; Evans 1995; Killick 1989; Streeten 1993; Martinussen 1997), but the search for ways to reconcile the roles of the state and the market has only recently begun. Rather than focusing on this debate in terms of state versus market, I analyze the effects of the varying relationships between the state and the market on economic growth and poverty reduction (Killick 1989), classifying them based on the role adopted by the state, such as market facilitation, market alteration, and market replacement (see table 1).[13]

12. Even when they temper their work with terms such as *state-led* or *market-led,* advocates from both sides of the state-market debate often consider the economic roles of the state and market to be trade-offs, a view that obscures the inevitable involvement of both the state and the market in nearly every antipoverty policy.

13. The state here is seen as a fragmented actor, although often one with sufficient autonomy from social groupings to allow it independent action. This is consistent with Theda Skocpol's view of states as "organizations claiming control over territories and people [that] may formulate and pursue goals that are not simply reflective of the demands or interests of social groups, classes, or society" (1985, 9). The state is not as empty as it seems to pluralists. Although often not unified, the state nevertheless acts. The market here is seen as a mechanism

Analyzing poverty and antipoverty policies allows us to compare and evaluate the effectiveness of alternative strategies for development and poverty reduction, helping us understand why some efforts have been effective in reducing poverty without growth and others have not. I do this by disaggregating poverty data, not just relying on averages, and by seeking causal factors, not just correlations.[14] As Martin Ravallion, World Bank economist, argues, "People are often hurting behind the averages. Panel data and observations from the ground can reveal this, but the aggregate statistics cannot. It is important to know the aggregate balance of gains and losses, but it will be of little consolation to those suffering to be told that poverty is falling on average" (2001, 1811).

Aggregated statistics reveal generalities but conceal important exceptions that, when studied, may deepen our understanding of the relationships between factors. Many economists have fruitfully studied individual or comparative cases of poverty by combining qualitative and quantitative methods (e.g., Bhagwati 1985; Sen 1999; Kanbur 2002). Moreover, the research of development economists has generated numerous ideas about how policy can affect poverty (e.g., Lipton and Ravallion 1995; Lal 1985; Ravallion 2001; Hemmer and Wilhelm 2000; Klasen 2001). What we lack are comparative studies of systematically selected economies that are exceptions to the hypothesized relationship between economic growth and poverty reduction. As Ravallion argues, the next step is for "more micro, country-specific, research on the factors determining why some poor people are able to take up the opportunities afforded by an expanding economy—and so add to its expansion—while others are not." To do so requires looking beyond the aggregates, the traditional terrain of economists, by examining the "diversity of impacts underlying the averages" (Ravallion 2001, 1813). My examination of two Chinese provinces, exceptions to the conventionally

through which individuals, households, firms, and other economic actors make decisions on how to allocate, spend, and save the resources they control (this is similar to the conception in Przeworski 2003, 12). By mediating exchanges, this structure unleashes forces that alter not only people's welfare by affecting incomes but also economic, political, and social relations. On the surface, the market facilitation and market replacement relationships might seem to be slight modifications of the pro-market and pro-state positions, respectively. Nevertheless, even though supporters of the liberal state model castigate state planning, we should not see such attacks as inherently antigovernment. As one neoliberal scholar, economist P. T. Bauer, stresses, "Criticism of central planning or of the policies pursued in its name must not obscure the importance of the essential tasks of government. The adequate performance of these tasks *is indeed helpful to the effective operation of the market, if not necessary for it*" (1984, 28).

14. For instance, a strong correlation might tempt a researcher to conclude a study, perhaps prematurely, when instead an exploration of the exceptions would lead to a deeper understanding of the underlying dynamics of the relationship (Miller 1996; Ravallion 2001). The predominant view of poverty as primarily an economic problem, as well the leading role economists have had in studying the problem, tends to crowd out potentially insightful interdisciplinary and qualitative analysis (Samad 1994).

assumed economic growth–poverty reduction relationship, contributes to this agenda.

Despite the importance of China as a model for poverty reduction, scholarship on China has contributed only modestly to our theoretical understanding of the effects of local approaches to poverty reduction. To be sure, scholars from a variety of fields have researched the causes of poverty in China as a whole (e.g., Rozelle, Zhang, and Huang 2000; Chen and Ravallion 2007; Piazza et al. 2001; Khan and Riskin 2001), as well as in individual Chinese communities (e.g., Lyons 1994; McCulloch and Calandrino 2002). But little comparative work has been conducted on the role of local governments in reducing poverty in China (see chap. 2). Even when we broaden the focus to the economic effects of reform efforts in China, we find that surprisingly little work—especially comparative research—has been conducted in the poorest Chinese provinces, areas benefitting less from China's rapid economic growth.

Research Design

This book is based on a within-country research design. Focusing on a single country with local government units that possess a degree of regional autonomy provides sufficient variation in key variables for a comparative analysis while, at the same time, controlling for factors (such as national policy, macro culture, history, and geography) that multicountry designs leave uncontrolled.[15] Examining provinces within China is optimal because the Chinese central government permits this degree of regional autonomy and provincial governments have sufficient political power and autonomy to design and implement their own policies. There is a scholarly consensus about the rise of regional power in China that says, in part, the central government intentionally devolved a degree of power, authority, and resources to the provincial and other levels of local government. As Barry Naughton argues, this shift occurred from the early days of the post-1978 reform. "But, significantly, Deng has seen authentic decentralization of authority as the fundamental principle of economic reform. As early as 1978 he said: 'whoever is given responsibility should be given authority as well'" (Naughton 1993, 503; see also Chung and Lam 2009). In addition, China has many millions of poor people, and poverty rates vary from region to region. Despite this variation in poverty rates, China has seen a dramatic drop in its overall rate of poverty. The country also faces many of the typical problems (overpopulation, corruption, and so forth) that other developing countries encounter.

15. Although these factors can vary within even small countries, such as Sri Lanka, Switzerland, and Belgium, they typically do so less than they do from country to country.

By performing a regression analysis of the economic growth rates and other related variables with the changes in poverty rates in Chinese provinces and selecting the outliers for further study (see the appendix for details), we can identify exceptions to the conventionally accepted relationship between the two rates. Even in tightly correlated relationships, most data points in a regression model are a certain distance away from the regression line. The further away a point is, the lower the chances that its position is the result of random factors and the greater the chances that it is caused by one or more specific factors not included in the model. I develop a regression model using three independent variables (changes in GDP, geographical location, and initial levels of poverty) that economists commonly expect to be related to poverty reduction (the dependent variable). Through this process, Guizhou and Yunnan emerge as the most extreme of the outlier provinces on each side of the regression line.

I focus here on rural poverty. Although urban poverty in China is also a serious and growing problem (Meng, Gregory, and Wan 2007), it is distinct from rural poverty, having different causes and solutions. Moreover, although data on rural poverty in China are rare, they are plentiful compared to data on urban poverty.[16]

In addition, I focus on absolute, as opposed to relative, poverty measured by income. Scholars define *absolute poverty* as a condition in which resources are insufficient to meet basic nutrition and other crucial needs, whereas *relative poverty* is the lack of resources that the society as a whole accepts as necessary. Even families that have enough to survive may not have access to items that their specific society considers necessary. Because, by most reasonable standards, these families remain quite poor, relative poverty is an important issue. Nevertheless, absolute poverty, the lack of access to resources needed to maintain life, is at the heart of poverty research. Other forms of poverty are only indirectly related (if at all) to income and include oppression and discrimination (e.g., Lipton and Ravallion 1995; Webster and Engberg-Pedersen 2002; Kanbur and Squire 1999). Such forms of poverty are important, but they can be difficult to study and are beyond the scope of this book.

My analysis is based on ten months of fieldwork conducted between September 2003 and July 2004, with follow-up visits each year until 2010. Overall, I used five methods of data collection. First, I assessed Western and Chinese secondary sources. Second, I interviewed informants in Beijing and

16. The Chinese government does not report disaggregated comparable urban poverty data (Park and Wang 2001) and frequently underestimates related statistics, such as urban unemployment. One major study by Khan and Riskin (2001) reports urban poverty, but the authors do not survey each of the provinces nor (as they readily admit) do they take samples large enough to generate reliable provincial-level data. The Chinese statistical bureau does not report urban poverty. The available rural poverty data are also flawed but in ways that do not mar my analysis (see the appendix to this book).

the two provincial capitals, Kunming (Yunnan) and Guiyang (Guizhou). These included both Chinese academics—a source of educated guesses on what could explain this puzzling relationship between growth and poverty rates—and provincial government officials. Third, I conducted extensive fieldwork in the countryside in both Yunnan and Guizhou, involving numerous trips exploring several counties in both provinces in search of evidence both for and against candidate factors. Fourth, I conducted dozens of interviews in the countryside. In some counties, I traveled, often on foot, from village to village and township to township, interviewing residents. In these semi-structured interviews, I asked broad questions about changes in residents' lives (and what had caused those changes), as well as more pointed questions about the factors that could potentially explain the puzzle, such as farming conditions, local infrastructure, government support, taxes, and migration. In other counties, I met with local government officials who not only accompanied me to rural development projects they had implemented but also detailed the development and poverty reduction strategies that they were implementing locally. Finally, I collected descriptive statistics on candidate explanatory factors. Each of these methods has its biases and point of view. Despite these limitations, by using five different data collection methods, I was able to cross-check my sources. When my sources agreed, I considered the conclusions more reliable. When they diverged, I analyzed the reasons for the discrepancy.

Explaining the Puzzle

I found that five broad categories of factors could potentially explain the puzzle: demographic, geographical, cultural, economic, and political. My data show that most of the factors I examined, such as government spending and growth in the agriculture sector, do not explain the puzzling relationship (see chap. 1). But compelling evidence from multiple sources supports the importance of four factors: roadways, migration, tourism, and coal mining. First, road building in Guizhou helped its poor people more than road building in Yunnan. Guizhou leaders focused on constructing inexpensive dirt roads that poor farmers used to transport their surplus goods to local markets and to learn more about them. Concurrently, Yunnan leaders concentrated their resources on building six modern costly highways linking the provincial capital, Kunming, with three other provincial capitals and three bordering countries. These highways enhanced economic growth in the province, but did not benefit poor people very much.

Second, the patterns of rural-to-urban migration in Guizhou and Yunnan contribute to our understanding of the puzzle. In Guizhou, starting in the late 1980s and early 1990s, large numbers of rural residents migrated from the province to seek work in other provinces. Once there, most sent back substantial portions of their salaries to their hometowns. Although these funds were generally too small to invest in sustainable productive activities, they still helped improve the incomes and livelihoods of those back home. Therefore, these remittances reduced poverty in Guizhou while the labor force that had emigrated helped increase economic development in the host provinces. In contrast, the rural residents of Yunnan migrated at a much lower rate, and when they did, they tended to migrate only within the province, where their labor contributed to the economic growth of Yunnan.

Third, the modest tourism industry in Guizhou employed and benefited more poor people in the 1990s than did the much larger one in Yunnan. The Chinese central government, in concert with the Yunnan provincial government, made an overt decision to concentrate limited resources on developing a handful of tourist sites, dedicating fewer resources to other, often economically poor areas of potential interest to tourists. By the late 1980s, these few chosen areas had been lifted out of poverty, and additional resources were dedicated to increase tourism there, further enhancing the local economy but creating few additional benefits for poor people. By contrast, almost all the tourist spots in Guizhou, although not as popular as those in Yunnan, are in poor counties and are structured such that poor people can benefit by participating in the industry.

Finally, Yunnan and Guizhou both possess abundant coal resources. Yunnan leaders established policies that encouraged the development of larger-scale coal mines; by doing so, they inadvertently limited the participation of the poor in this labor market. In contrast, the coal mines in Guizhou were more informally and less efficiently exploited (as well as being extraordinarily dirty and dangerous), but they raised incomes of the Guizhou poor more directly.

These four factors appear to be almost completely unrelated to one another. How can such an assortment generate generalizable, testable hypotheses? As a final step, I analyze the state strategies (from table 1) that best fit Guizhou and Yunnan and develop theoretically and empirically useful conclusions.

Taken together, these four factors suggest that in many ways Yunnan resembles a developmental state. Under this approach, the state, by adopting a primary role in economic decision making, attempts to promote industrialization. The state does this not by replacing market forces entirely but by altering them, seeking to produce marketable products. The Yunnan government focused on tobacco, heavy industry, and tourism. Although developmental states often try to reduce poverty by absorbing surplus rural labor into the industrial sector, this tactic can fail to generate opportunities that are positioned and structured so that poor rural residents can take advantage of them. In Yunnan, these policies benefited the urban areas of the province and some of its wealthier rural areas but (due to the structure of the economic opportunities) excluded its poorest residents from the benefits of growth.

By contrast, Guizhou traversed none of the first six paths listed in table 1. Instead, from the late 1980s and early 1990s Guizhou implemented yet another approach, the micro-oriented state (see table 1). This approach tends to reduce poverty by increasing economic opportunities for poor people without contributing to rapid increases in productivity through economies of scale. The smaller-scale structures in Guizhou allowed poor people access to the benefits of transportation, coal mining, and tourism, facilitating participation in economic activities even by those lacking education, start-up capital, experience, and training. Like the agriculture-oriented (farmer-first) state, this strategy focuses on increasing the income of rural residents; however, it does not do so by directly promoting agricultural development (the per capita agricultural production of Yunnan, even in poor areas, exceeds that of Guizhou). Like the progressive state, the micro-oriented state focuses primarily on poverty reduction in a bottom-up fashion, but the micro-oriented state does not seek empowerment or redistributive justice for its citizens (there was little evidence of higher spending or a concentration on education and health care in Guizhou, nor is there evidence that Guizhou residents were remarkably empowered). Instead, the micro-oriented state views poverty more as a technical problem and focuses on the specific issue of how poverty can be reduced. For this reason, at various times and in different sectors, the state chooses to either facilitate, alter, or replace the market, depending on practical issues or on its judgment of which relationship will be successful.

To the extent that the micro-oriented state has a development strategy (as opposed to a poverty reduction strategy), it attempts to enhance rural livelihoods and strengthen local rural markets, thereby organizing villages around an accessible market town. One of the key features of this strategy is its focus on small-scale, low-tech development, choosing to develop industries that are accessible to poor rural workers (e.g., Max-Neef 1991). Because it does not aim to increase productivity by adding economies of scale, the micro-oriented state tends to reduce poverty but not stimulate much economic growth. Finally, in contrast with the direct approach to poverty reduction of the progressive state, the micro-oriented state focuses on developing indirect opportunities for poor people to increase their incomes.

In addition to detailing a possible alternative to poverty reduction in poor areas, the experience of Guizhou also provides insights into ideas about and approaches to development held by the provincial leaders. In the case of Guizhou, this is especially important because Hu Jintao, current president and general secretary of China, served as the top provincial party leader in Guizhou just as many of these policy decisions were being made and implemented. As it turns out, these decisions presaged one of Hu's most important policies—the Scientific Development Concept (*kexue fazhan guan*)—which years later was promoted as national policy. Exploring the various political factors that influenced the decision making thus helps us understand more about the thinking of the current Chinese Communist Party (CCP) general secretary. When Hu became general secretary of the Central Committee of the CCP in 2002, he was a "mystery man," somewhat reclusive and mistrustful of the United States (Tkacik 2002; Li and Lye 2005). Compared to other top Chinese leaders, such as Premier Wen Jiabao or any of Hu's predecessors, Hu remains obscure to Western scholars.

By the time Hu became the provincial party secretary of Guizhou, even though he was the youngest provincial party secretary in the history of the People's Republic of China (PRC) (Ewing 2003), he had had extensive firsthand experience with grinding rural poverty. Hu Jintao spent much of his postcollege life (1968–1981) in the northwestern province of Gansu, which, like Guizhou, was home to some of the most impoverished farmers in China. While he was there, Hu worked much of the time as an engineer for the Ministry of Hydraulic Engineering, a position that provided extensive experience in the often desolate Gansu countryside. Hu was no recluse there—he gained a reputation for visiting rural areas throughout Gansu and was lauded by his local patron as a "walking map" of the province.[17] Hu Jintao's subsequent three-year appointment to Guizhou (1985–1988) was designed by Hu's central patron, General Secretary Hu Yaobang (no relation). At the time, Hu Jintao was under pressure in Beijing, facing criticism for his position as the head of the China Youth League Secretariat from conservatives opposed to the reforms being implemented by Hu Yaobang and other top leaders. A provincial appointment not only removed Hu Jintao from the tense Beijing palace intrigue (Hu Yaobang was forced to resign from his position in 1987) but also gave the young protégé useful executive experience as a top provincial party official (Tkacik 2002; Lam 2006).

The accounts of Hu's achievements in Guizhou conflict. Some scholars are dismissive. For instance, Richard Ewing suggests that "Hu Jintao did not distinguish himself and instituted no major reforms" (2003, 21), and Li Cheng suggests that Hu Jintao "did not seem to make many changes" during his tenure (2001, 116). Others maintain that "Hu Jintao did his best to improve the economy of the land-locked province" (Lam 2006, 7). But most reviews of Hu's career remain almost completely silent on his tenure in Guizhou. True, the importance of Guizhou in Hu's eventual rise to the height of Chinese politics can be overstated; most scholars suggest that Hu's ascension (he was designated a core leader in 1992) was more directly attributable to his having dealt decisively with extensive demonstrations during his subsequent service as the party secretary of Tibet and his success at forging the political outcome of the Fourteenth Party Congress, the first congress held after the Tiananmen Incident (Tkacik 2002; Lam 2006).

17. Lam (2006, 7) reports that this was said of his tenure in Guizhou as well.

Nonetheless, Hu's service in this western backwater remains undervalued. While leading Guizhou, Hu hosted an impressive list of central leaders, including then General Secretary Hu Yaobang (who spent Spring Festival, the most important holiday in China, in Guiyang with Hu Jintao) and then Premier Zhao Ziyang, as well as Li Peng, the conservative Politburo Standing Committee member and their political rival—an unusual guest list for the leader of an obscure province. Hu's service in Guizhou was cited by President Jiang Zemin when justifying Hu Jintao's promotion to vice president in 1998 (Tkacik 2002). More important, Hu's tenure in Guizhou reveals the seeds of ideas that subsequently served as the core of Hu's Scientific Development Concept, part of Hu's focus on establishing a Harmonious Society (*hexie shehui*). This policy deemphasized his predecessors' singular dedication to economic growth in favor of addressing other social problems, including poverty, inequality, and illiteracy (Saich 2006). In particular, Hu consistently focused on mitigating inland-coastal provincial inequality and rural-urban inequality through strategies such as agriculture reform and better public goods provision, especially grassroots health care and basic education (Saich 2006, 2007; Li 2005). Not coincidentally, these ideas, and the policies that emerged, were also central to Hu's economic strategy in remote rural Guizhou. This approach then persisted in the province after Hu's tenure (see chap. 2) and helps to explain the impressive reduction in poverty in Guizhou despite its slow economic growth rate. Although the credit for these ideas is often ascribed elsewhere, the Scientific Development Concept that Hu implemented at the central level is a reflection of his concern for the poor both prior to his tenure in Guizhou and during his tenure there as provincial general secretary.

In chapter 1, I describe my methodology further and introduce the two provinces under consideration. I review the literature on the economic, social, and political situations in Guizhou and Yunnan, and I compare and contrast their initial conditions. In chapter 2, I examine why the governments of these two very similar provinces chose different policy approaches. I do so by applying theories of provincial decision making to provide a more extensive understanding of the political and other factors that influenced the adoption of different pathways. I also examine the special role played by Hu Jintao.

In chapters 3–6, I turn to the four areas that contribute to explaining the puzzling relationship between economic growth and poverty reduction: road building, migration, tourism, and coal mining. My focus in each chapter is on three aspects of these areas—their volume, distribution, and structure (i.e., whether poor people could access the benefits derived from them)—that explain how they affect the puzzle. The four areas together exemplify the broad models that the provincial governments followed to reduce poverty and encourage economic growth.

In the concluding chapter, I apply my results and evaluate the extent to which previous theories are useful in understanding Guizhou and Yunnan. From the divergent experiences of the two provinces emerge strategies that may be applicable in other contexts and that can enhance our understanding of the causes of and solutions to rural poverty.

Poverty in Guizhou declined without much growth because the government promoted opportunities that poor people could access. Although this approach seems stunningly simple—even obvious—it nevertheless contrasts strikingly with the recommendations of some dominant schools of academics and the approaches of key international institutions. Identifying such additional approaches to poverty reduction is vitally important because so far we have failed—despite decades of growth and centuries of effort—to reduce the poverty that plagues a large swath of humanity. In a world where some countries face poor prospects for robust economic growth or have experienced an economic expansion that has left millions in poverty, this is an urgent mission. The micro-oriented state model is not a panacea, but it can be implemented judiciously in places like Guizhou in which seemingly intractable grinding poverty is unlikely to be solved by economic growth alone. Thus, the puzzle in this region of China reveals an urgently needed pathway to poverty reduction that has thus far been understudied and underappreciated.

1

Guizhou and Yunnan in Comparison

> There are not three *li* of level ground; there are not three sunny days in a row; there are not three coins in the people's pockets.
>
> —Traditional saying about Guizhou[1]

Just as a detective scrutinizes numerous suspects implicated in a murder mystery, so we must assess the extent of involvement of various candidate factors—geographical, natural, demographic, cultural, economic, and political—in the present puzzle. For instance, if the weather was worse in Yunnan than in Guizhou, it could reduce agricultural production quite dramatically, but it might not directly affect industrial development. Similarly, if the rural (especially poor) population of Yunnan expanded faster than that of Guizhou, farmers would have more mouths to feed, which could stretch their meager funds and directly increase poverty headcounts. High population growth rates might also enhance industrial productivity by increasing the supply of surplus labor, which could reduce wages, increasing economic growth without reducing poverty. Other candidate factors may also be important: cultural factors such as Oscar Lewis's "culture of poverty," a type of malaise caused by poverty, and more nuanced interpretations of culture such as political culture and social capital (Lewis 1968). Finally, many economic and political factors should be considered (see table 2 for a list of candidate factors).

For each candidate factor, I collected available data from five qualitative and quantitative sources (see the introduction), which allowed me to cross-check the results derived from each source. After gathering these data, I applied specific decision rules to judge which factors to accept or reject as explanations for the puzzle. After collecting as much evidence as possible, I analyzed whether each factor could explain the juxtaposition of economic

1. Goodman 1986 (p. 33) provides several sources for this saying.

Table 2. Candidate factors

Geographic and natural factors	Demographic factors	Cultural factors	Government and policy factors
Mountainous terrain Natural resource endowments Arable land per capita Natural disasters (flooding/drought) Weather (rainfall, temperature)	Population, population growth Migration	Motivation Minority ethnicities Civil society	Central policy International organization support Corruption Overall spending Spending on specific government programs Education and health Central government transfers Transportation and infrastructure Local taxation
Industrial structure	**Agricultural production**	**Industrial production**	**Services and other economic factors**
Industrial structure (GDP) Industrial structure (labor)	Overall agricultural production Grain, meat, tobacco, and other agricultural production Farm implements Fertilizer use	Town and village enterprises Nonagricultural industrial production (steel, chemicals, textiles, etc.) Power generation Agricultural added-value industries Coal and other mined materials	Inflation Foreign trade Foreign capital use Tourism

Note: GDP, gross domestic product.

growth without poverty reduction in Yunnan and/or the combination of poverty reduction without economic growth in Guizhou. For instance, a new factory should increase growth, but it should also decrease poverty, especially if new jobs were available to poor people. Unless I could demonstrate the importance of a candidate factor to the puzzling disconnect between economic growth and poverty reduction, I could not accept it as an explanatory factor.

Evidence from my sources had to be weighed. If the evidence from all five sources consistently negated the importance of a particular factor, I confidently rejected that factor. If the evidence from all five sources consistently supported its importance and I could trace the causality between the factor and the changes in poverty rates, I accepted the factor. But if the evidence from my sources was contradictory, I had to weigh the persuasiveness of each piece of evidence. Adding to this complexity is that each factor has a separate set of expected linkages to the process by which it changes the growth and poverty rates. For example, the expected linkages among economic growth, poverty level, and government spending are quite different from the linkages among economic growth, poverty level, and social capital. The expectations and causal mechanisms associated with each factor had to be carefully traced.[2]

Consider a specific example. For roads to explain poverty reduction without economic growth, we expect that they would (1) increase access to markets and (2) increase market information (3) for poor people (4) to a greater extent in Guizhou than in Yunnan. In Guizhou (where explanatory factors are expected to decrease poverty without increasing growth), a road system that explains the puzzle should not generate significant economic growth, for example by enhancing productivity or adding technology. In Yunnan (where explanatory factors are expected to increase growth without decreasing poverty), the opposite should be true; a road system should stimulate economic growth without directly benefiting poor people. If the pattern of roads in Guizhou met its standard but not that for Yunnan, we could still accept roadways as explaining the Guizhou half of the puzzle. There is no real reason to expect that the same factors explain both of the patterns seen in the two provinces (although, as it turns out, they do). In addition, we expect that there is more than one explanatory factor involved in the puzzle.

This research therefore demonstrates the power of the comparative method and process tracing. For instance, when examining Yunnan alone, many of my interviewees—especially government officials, but also some academics—suggested that the rural people in Yunnan, particularly the ethnic minorities, were lazy. Without a comparison, research on the level of motivation of rural people in Yunnan might suggest that they are indeed lazy. In comparing Yunnan with Guizhou, however, I could determine whether the levels of motivation varied between the two provinces, and if so, why. This candidate factor might explain the lack of poverty reduction in Yunnan; however, unless it differed for some systematic reason in Guizhou, it could not account for the impressive reduction in poverty found there. There would also have to be some reason why motivation varied between residents of the two provinces in such a systematic way that it caused economic growth and poverty rates to move in opposing directions.

This process is not as difficult as it sounds, in part because the neighboring provinces of Guizhou and Yunnan share several economic, geographical, demographic, and political factors that we might expect to influence economic growth and poverty rates (see table 3). The two provinces were strikingly similar, particularly at the dawn on the reform era in the late 1970s, and so several important (although less interesting) variables were the same, or nearly so, for both. This in turn permitted the isolation of several other social, political, and policy variables for testing in the search.

2. For an explanation of process tracing, see Bennett and George (2005).

Table 3. Similarities between Yunnan and Guizhou

	Yunnan	Guizhou
Geography		
Total land size	394,000 km^{2}[a]	176,000 km^{2}[b]
Plains area (%)	6	7.5
Arable land, 2000 (hectares/capita)	0.15	0.13
Irrigated area, 2000 (%)	22	13
Forest area, 2000 (%)	~32.8	~30.8
Rainfall, average (mm)	600–2,300(varies)	900–1,500
Natural resource endowment		
Coal production, rank in China	9th (2.3% of China's total)	5th (5% of China's total)
Number of minerals for which the province is considered a major source	74	59
Minerals for which the province ranks in the top five for production in China	Antimony, phosphate, silver, bronze. lead (1st), zinc (1st), nickel, tin, pyrite	Antimony, phosphate, aluminum (2nd), manganese (3rd)
Tobacco production, rank in China	1st	2nd
Demographics		
Population, 2008	45.4 million[c]	40.4 million[d]
Population density, 2007 (people/km^2)	115	226
Rural population, 2007 (%)	83	86
Agricultural GDP, 2007 (%)	18	16
Minority ethnicities population, 1991, 1992 (%)	33	35
Political structure		
Structure of government	Identical	Identical
Central level policy (subsidies, preferential policies)	Similar	Similar

Sources: State Statistical Bureau (various years-b, various years-c); author's calculations.
[a] Compared to states in the United States, it would rank 4th, between California and Montana, in terms of area.
[b] Compared to states in the United States, it would rank 22nd, between Missouri and Florida, in terms of area.
[c] Population is 23% larger than California. If it were a country, it would rank 30th in the world in terms of population.
[d] Population is 8% larger than California. If it were a country, it would rank 32nd in the world in terms of population.

Geographically, although Yunnan is larger than Guizhou, both provinces are large, country-size provinces. If it were a country, Yunnan would rank as the sixtieth largest in the world; Guizhou would rank as ninetieth. Nearly three-quarters of Guizhou province is dotted with porous karst and other carbonate rocks. Rainfall does not remain on this rocky surface long, making agriculture difficult. Even in its more usable areas, Guizhou generally has very poor soil, with only approximately 3 percent arable land (Oakes 1998, 116). These factors combine to make Guizhou, as geologist George B. Cressey states in his 1955 classic text, the poorest agricultural province in

China (in Goodman 1986, 34). Yunnan is also mainly mountainous. In addition to being 44 percent karst, Yunnan features a vertical climb of almost 4 kilometers within a horizontal distance of just a few kilometers (Litzinger 2004, 494). Only approximately 7 percent of its land mass is considered arable (Swain 2002, 183). Overall, Yunnan and Guizhou primarily consist of mountains and hills, with only tiny proportions of plains (6 percent for Yunnan and 7.5 percent for Guizhou) and tiny amounts of arable land per capita (0.15 and 0.13 hectares per capita, respectively), according to official Chinese statistics. Agriculture in both provinces is thus arduous and uncertain, although conditions in Guizhou are generally more difficult.

The two provinces are in the same temperate region, according to maps of precipitation in China (Goodman 1989, map 3). Both provinces have proportionally similar water surface areas, and both receive sufficient rainfall, although rainfall in Yunnan varies regionally within the province more than rainfall in Guizhou. The notoriously common rains in Guizhou, however, have contributed to its already harsh environment for agriculture, causing soil erosion and frequent flooding (Oakes 1998, 116; Goodman 1986, 57). Yunnan boasts four of the largest rivers in Asia, and they traverse Yunnan a mere 100 kilometers apart (Swain 2002, 183). Both provinces have focused on the development of hydroelectricity; however, in the mid-1990s Yunnan ranked seventh in China in power generation, generating more than twice the power of Guizhou. This is as much blessing as it is curse: Yunnan's hydroelectric dams are particularly controversial (Mertha 2008). The irrigation rates of both provinces are also similar, although in 2000 the rate in Yunnan (22 percent) was higher than that in Guizhou (13 percent). Forests cover nearly one-third of the areas of both provinces.

Natural resources, including coal, as well as dozens of economically important metals and minerals, are abundant in both provinces. The irony of the rich mining resources juxtaposed with grinding poverty was captured by two local scholars' depiction of southwestern China as "the poverty of plenty" (Wang and Bai 1991). Guizhou ranks fifth largest in the supply of coal in China, with some 5 percent of the total national coal reserves; Yunnan is somewhat less well endowed, ranking ninth nationally. Both provinces rank in the top five provinces for precious metals, and Yunnan is the main Chinese source for lead and zinc. The two provinces have contrasting histories of mining. The natural resources in Guizhou were largely inaccessible even as late as World War II, whereas the mining industry in Yunnan has been active for centuries. During imperial times, authorities conscripted workers to excavate the Yunnan mines, in the process increasing the number of Han people living in the region. Subsequently, Europeans were attracted to Yunnan, in part due to its natural resource endowments (Swain 2002; Spencer 1940). During Mao Zedong's time, however, the central government treated the natural resources of both provinces similarly. For instance, during the late 1950s, the central government cited the backwardness of both provinces to justify continued central control over the Guizhou coal mines (Goodman 1986, 8). Although the contemporary mining industry has been an important economic activity for both provinces, the development of coal mining varied greatly in the two provinces (see chap. 6).

One geographical factor stands out as a marked difference between the two provinces—the 4,000-kilometer border that Yunnan shares with three foreign countries. This feature has given Yunnan greater potential for contact and trade than the other remote provinces. Paradoxically, the border historically has been as much a hindrance to development in Yunnan as a stimulus. Outsiders, both foreign neighbors and the Han Chinese, invaded the province during several historical periods, putting Yunnan front and center in several armed conflicts, most recently the conflict between China and Vietnam in the late 1960s. The bordering countries have also served as safe harbors for enemies of the Chinese state, serving as a base for Guomingdang (GMD) forces, as well as for Gang of Four loyalists after their fall. These external threats to Chinese security compel central leaders to pay more attention to Yunnan than they do to its neighboring provinces (see chap. 2).

In more recent history, by contrast, the economy of Yunnan has reaped a net benefit from this border. Increasingly stable relations between China and its neighbors, notable exceptions notwithstanding, have facilitated the flow of trade and investment across the Yunnan border (Swain 2002). Even so, large swaths of the Yunnan countryside remain poorly linked with the rest of the province and, thus, do not reap the economic rewards of its border relationships. There is a nefarious side, too, to the Yunnan border. For instance, illicit narcotics flowing into the region come over this border, as well as a worrying number of Myanmar Karen minorities, who periodically cross the border to escape the oppressive military regime of that country. Thus, the position of Yunnan on the border and the legacy of conflict between China and its neighbors elevated the importance of the province in national security. This, in turn, increased central governmental scrutiny and brought additional pressure on provincial leaders to comply with central policies (see chap. 2).

The Yunnan border notwithstanding, harsh geographical conditions historically have left both provinces poor and isolated. Guizhou has long possessed a well-deserved "reputation of being incredibly poor and backward. So much so that during the Great Leap Forward, the whole province was publicized as a national model of Mao's principle of the advantage of being 'poor and blank'" (Goodman 1986, 19). A diverse range of notables, including Zhou Lin, the first CCP provincial party secretary ("all the nationalities [there] lived a frightful existence"); Wang Xiaochuang, party propagandist ("the people wore rags...and their shabbiness was indescribable"); and Alexander Hosie, explorer in the 1880s ("dangerous, barely cultivated, and economically backward") agree on this point (quoted in Goodman 1986,

33–34). The dire conditions in Guizhou in the 1940s inspired historian Joseph E. Spencer to write, "Nowhere in several provinces of central and southern China has the writer seen so many abandoned farms and farmhouses, nowhere is there the same pinched, dulled, barely alive look on the faces of so many people, almost nowhere are the villages, towns, cities and the whole countryside so devoid of those cultural adornments characteristic of the rest of China" (1940, 162).

Even though today parts of Yunnan are well off, many observers also lamented its isolated and harsh geography. Even as late as the 1970s, the province remained so isolated that much of the province was largely out of reach of Beijing (Swain 2002). The imposing Yunnan mountain peaks were effective physical obstructions to making connections with its neighbors. As Dorothy Solinger notes, the province "has historically been, at best, a peripheral outpost along China's southwest border" (1977a, 5). Threats from its neighbors made the original inhabitants of Yunnan unwilling to establish effective connections. As Ingrid d'Hooghe observed, "Yunnan has long been regarded as an inaccessible, backward and remote frontier, with hardly any potential for economic development, let alone foreign trade. Although in ancient times it flourished as a part of the Southern Silk Road, for most of the time the landlocked and inaccessible province remained a forbidding place" (1994, 286).

It was only in recent years that Yunnan finally experienced relatively rapid economic growth and development. Thus, historical observations suggest that, although both provinces were badly off, the conditions in Yunnan were certainly no worse than in Guizhou. Thus, broad historical comparisons are not likely to explain the puzzle.

In addition to these geographical similarities, the two provinces are also demographically comparable. Both have massive country-size populations. Yunnan has a larger population (if Yunnan were a country, it would rank thirtieth largest by population) than Guizhou (which would rank thirty-second). Guizhou in 2007, however, had a much higher population density than Yunnan (226 people per km^2 for Guizhou vs. 115 people per km^2 for Yunnan, and 135 people per km^2 average for all of China). People of both provinces have relatively short average life expectancies. Although the life expectancy in Guizhou has consistently been somewhat higher than in Yunnan, both provinces rank near the bottom compared to other Chinese provinces and are four or five years below the national average. Approximately 85 percent of the populations of both provinces is rural, and both their agricultural sectors make up approximately one-sixth of their total economies.

The conventional wisdom is that, despite the large Guizhou minority population, Yunnan is the most ethnically diverse province in China. For instance, one knowledgeable scholar suggests that ethnic diversity in Yunnan "is unequalled in any other part of the world" (Inez de Beauclair, quoted in

Solinger 1977a, 2). Despite these impressions, the ethnic compositions of both Yunnan and Guizhou are actually similar. Approximately one-third of the populations of both provinces consists of various ethnic minorities. In the early 1990s, approximately 34.7 percent of the Guizhou population (approximately 9 million people) was officially classified as minority, the largest groups being Miao (approximately 3.6 million), Buyi (2.5 million), Dong (1.4 million), and Tujia (slightly over 1 million). Nine other ethnicities claimed more than 100,000 members in Guizhou, and fourteen other ethnic minorities claimed at least 5,000 people. The Yunnan minority population is structurally similar. In the early 1990s, 33.3 percent of the Yunnan population was classified as minority (approximately 12 million people), the largest groups being Yi (approximately 4 million), Bai (1.3 million), Hani (1.2 million), and Dai and Zhuang (approximately 1 million each). No fewer than fourteen other minority groups in Yunnan numbered 100,000 or more people, and twenty-five other minority groups consisted of at least 5,000 people. In addition, the poor in each province are more likely to hail from minority-dominated regions, although this situation is more acute in Guizhou than in Yunnan. In Guizhou, counties classified by the central government as poor consist on average of 53.6 percent ethnic minorities, compared to 28.5 percent for nonpoor counties. A full thirty-six of the forty-eight Guizhou poor counties have higher proportions of minorities than the provincial average, compared to just thirteen of the thirty-eight nonpoor counties. Among the forty-five counties officially designated as autonomous minority counties in Guizhou, thirty-three are also designated as poor. Only fifteen of the poor counties in this province are not designated with minority status. In Yunnan, the poor counties are somewhat less predominantly minority-populated, consisting on average of 46.0 percent, compared to 33.9 percent for nonpoor counties. Forty-two of the seventy-three Yunnan poor counties (57.5 percent) have higher minority populations than the provincial average.[3]

Broadly speaking, the two provinces also have similar histories. China formally brought Guizhou into China proper as a province in 1413, during the Ming dynasty. Before that, a series of independent rulers reigned over different parts of the region. Beginning from the Han dynasty, these local leaders paid tribute to the Chinese central government, but continued to rule over their regions more or less autonomously (Oakes 1998). Yunnan came under de facto Chinese control during the Mongol-led Yuan dynasty in the thirteenth century. Before that, there was little contact between the local populations and even the Han living in Yunnan, let alone the rest of China (Solinger 1977, 6). Moreover, the historical use of cowry shells as currency suggests

3. The information in this section is primarily based on data from the Yunnan Statistical Yearbook (State Statistical Bureau 1991c, 805–14) and the Guizhou Statistical Yearbook (State Statistical Bureau 1992b, 117–20).

that Yunnan had closer economic, cultural, and political affinity with Burma and Thailand than with China (Vogel and Hieronymus 1993). Before the Yuan dynasty, Chinese emperors preferred to establish tributary relations with distant local rulers and to forgo the establishment of frontier garrisons. Yunnan even became entirely independent during the fractured Song dynasty, until it was conquered by the Yuan dynasty (Swain 2002, 186).

The histories of both provinces are also marked by waves of state-sponsored migration, primarily of Han migrants who intruded on the local ethnic populations, typically taking the most fertile land and pushing the natives further into the mountains. The Ming dynasty saw the first large waves of migrants, who entered both provinces to bring these provinces further into the fold. The 2.5 million Han who immigrated to Yunnan during this period tipped the racial balance to the extent that the Han became the majority. Then, after the Japanese invaded China in the twentieth century, a large number of Han retreated from the battle zones to the relative safety of these relatively remote areas. Finally, during the Third Front program (1964–1971), well-educated, primarily Han people were transferred to these provinces to work in the industries that were shifted from the coastal to western regions (Swain 2002; Wright 2005; Naughton 1988; Spencer 1940).

The governments of both provinces are also structured identically. In fact, nearly all provinces in China are formally structured in the same way, with identical (or nearly so) levels of prefectural and county governments, and identical organs penetrating down to the towns and townships. Like all Chinese provinces, Guizhou and Yunnan have parallel party and state government organizations, as well as provincial party congresses, to perform executive, legislative, and judicial functions. Both these provinces have prefecture level governments that are "autonomous prefectures" (designated "zhou"). Formally, the two provinces have identical relationships with the central government. The two provinces are also in the same military region, headquartered in Kunming. Thus, the formal political administrative structures of these two provinces are basically the same.[4]

Moreover, the central government has treated these two provinces in broadly similar ways for decades. Provincial and other local leaders are put in place through the same *nomenklatura* system. These leaders have adopted strikingly different policies, although they are remarkably similar in other ways. For instance, the leaders appear to be equally susceptible to official corruption, with top leaders of both provinces having been punished severely for abuses of power (see chap. 2). Since at least 1949, the central government has placed the two provinces in the same category for applying central policy. During Mao's era, state investment and intervention centered

4. On the organization of local governments in China, see Chung and Lam (2009)

on the noncoastal provinces, and Beijing redistributed the resources of the wealthier coastal areas to the inland provinces such as Yunnan and Guizhou. Both these provinces were also major recipients of investment from the Third Front program that sought to shift industries inland, where they would be safer from foreign invasion (Naughton 1988). Mao's favorable treatment of the western provinces ended with the arrival of the reform era, when much of the investment made during Mao's era became a burden. Deng Xiaoping, the supreme leader, prioritized pragmatism and efficiency over egalitarianism and focused on developing the wealthier Chinese coastal provinces first. Guizhou and Yunnan, as a result, were left with their relatively high proportions of inefficiently run state-owned industries and largely traditional forms of subsistence agriculture that contributed little to GDP. During the Seventh Five-Year Plan (1986–1990), central leaders designed a division of labor among the provinces, in which the coastal provinces were to focus on export-oriented industry, the inland provinces on developing agriculture and energy, and the western provinces on animal husbandry and mineral exploration. The central government used the power generated and natural resources found in the two poorer regions largely to develop the coast. Leaders of the inland and western provinces protested that this policy discriminated against them and further exacerbated the yawning gap between rich and poor provinces (Fan 1997; Yang 1997; Goodman 1989). But these protests were largely fruitless until, more than a decade later, the administration of Jiang Zemin implemented the Western Development program in an attempt to spread the wealth of the coast to the western provinces, with mixed results (Lai 2002). Thus, despite dramatically different policies implemented during the various PRC regimes, the center consistently classified Yunnan and Guizhou as western provinces and treated them in broadly the same manner.

Moreover, although the economies of Yunnan and Guizhou became remarkably different in later years, at the dawn of the reform era the two provinces were economically similar (State Statistical Bureau various years-b, various years-c). Even though the Yunnan GDP per capita had been much higher than that of Guizhou since at least 1978, the economic structures of the two provinces in that year were nearly the same, with both having heavily agrarian economies, with large primary sectors (42 percent for Guizhou, 43 percent for Yunnan) and small service sectors (17 percent for Guizhou, 18 percent for Yunnan). In 1980, despite Guizhou having a lower GDP in agriculture, its per capita net rural income exceeded that of Yunnan (RMB 161.5 for Guizhou vs. RMB 147.7 for Yunnan). Tobacco is a primary cash crop of both provinces; Yunnan has long been the top Chinese producer, but Guizhou ranked second in the 1990s. Inflation increased rapidly in China during the 1990s, especially after 1994. The center responded by imposing austerity measures to curb inflation. During this period, the inflation rates in the two provinces were very similar. Finally, in 1986, when Chinese State Council classified all counties in China as either poor or nonpoor (the list was amended in 1994), Yunnan contained more poor counties than did Guizhou (seventy-three vs. forty-eight). Nevertheless, the two provinces had nearly the same number of poor counties proportionally—in Yunnan 73 out of 128 rural counties (57 percent) were classified as poor, whereas in Guizhou 48 out of 87 counties (55 percent) received this designation.

The commitment of the leaders of Guizhou and Yunnan to encouraging science and technology was not remarkably high, although Yunnan outpaced Guizhou in this regard. According to Fan Shenggen and Zhang Xiaobo (2004), in 1996 Guizhou had the fewest science and technology personnel in China per rural resident (27.1 personnel per 10,000 rural residents); Yunnan ranked second-to-last (35.05 per 10,000 rural laborers). Although Guizhou did better than some of the other provinces in spending on science and technology (RMB 0.27 per rural resident), Yunnan also exceeded Guizhou in this category (RMB 0.39 per rural resident).

Similarly, the education and health-care systems of both provinces are generally weak. Although Guizhou, as a Chinese province, does provide health-care services and education in rural and, especially, poor areas, there is little evidence that it does so to a greater extent than other provinces. For instance, in 1991 and 1996 Guizhou spending on education was a fraction of what it was in Yunnan, even though primary school enrollment rates in the two provinces were similar, both in poor and nonpoor counties. This is consistent with data on educational attainment taken from the Chinese Agricultural Census for 1996. According to that census, the educational attainments of Guizhou and Yunnan residents were similar, in terms of percentage of illiterate and semi-literate people (29.95 percent for Guizhou, 28.09 percent for Yunnan), primary school graduates (45.47 percent for Guizhou, 49.11 percent for Yunnan), and middle school graduates (22.23 percent for Guizhou, 20.25 percent for Yunnan). The educational performances of both provinces were both remarkably poor compared to other provinces in the region—only the province of Qinghai has a lower percentage of middle school graduates (data from Fan and Zhang 2004). The 2000 Census revealed that Guizhou and Yunnan had the fifth and sixth highest rural illiteracy rates, respectively—a similarly poor record for both. Moreover, in the rating by the *China Human Development Report* (United Nations Development Programme [UNDP] 1999) of the education systems of the two provinces, based on the adult literacy rates and combined school enrollment rates, both provinces received the same score of 0.64, low compared to other provinces.[5] Further, the rural health-care policies and spending patterns of the two provinces are similar.

5. My fieldwork revealed some signs of improvement in the Guizhou education system, thanks to aid from other provinces. I saw numerous newly constructed schools, many funded by the four wealthy coastal cities that have partnered with Guizhou to help reduce poverty. Even so, there is little evidence that the quality of rural education significantly improved in Guizhou or in Yunnan, especially in the 1990s.

Other candidate factors form patterns that do not follow expectations. In exploring each of these factors, we must pay close attention to comparing the distributions and structures of the factors, not just their volumes. My analysis of these candidate factors indicates they move in the direction opposite from the pattern we have identified and thus do not help us solve the puzzle.

First, Guizhou, compared to Yunnan, concentrated more on basic agriculture. Because agriculture is generally less productive than industrial structure but often increases the income of the rural poor, this could explain why the Guizhou economy grew relatively slowly while its poverty rates declined. But the statistical evidence based on provincial outputs as a whole is not consistent with this expectation. Although the agricultural output of Guizhou grew rapidly on a nominal basis (134 percent) between 1991 and 1996, from RMB 16.5 billion to RMB 38.8 billion, the agricultural output of Yunnan grew even faster (154 percent) during that same period, from RMB 22.3 billion to RMB 56.8 billion. Even when we divide by number of rural residents, overall production in Yunnan grew faster, increasing from RMB 679 to 1,632 per capita (142 percent) compared with the increase in Guizhou from RMB 569 to 1,268 (123 percent). Even though the Guizhou per capita total output value of agriculture grew faster than that of Yunnan in 1993 and, especially, 1994 (36.8 percent vs. 25.6 percent), growth in Guizhou did not keep pace with Yunnan. In 1991, the Guizhou per capita output value of agriculture was 84 percent of the Yunnan output value; by 1996, this had fallen to 78 percent. In terms of distribution, grain production in the Yunnan poor counties (which rose 13.9 percent, to 400 tons per 10,000 people) grew faster than grain production in both the Guizhou poor areas (which rose 12.9 percent) and the Yunnan nonpoor areas (which increased a meager 5.4 percent, to 226 tons per 10,000 people).

A second candidate factor, the use of agricultural tools, is also inconsistent with the puzzle. If Guizhou farmers had used more advanced tools, their farms could be more productive, allowing labor to shift to other poverty-reducing activities. As it happens, however, in the early 1990s Yunnan farmers were much better equipped in terms of productive agricultural assets than Guizhou farmers. In 1991, Yunnan farmers on average possessed RMB 1,828 worth of productive fixed assets, whereas Guizhou farmers had only RMB 1,060—among the lowest in China. Yunnan also exceeded Guizhou in draft animals and machinery, enjoying a 1.5:1 ratio in the use of draft animals, a 3:1 ratio in the use of transport machinery, and a stunning 12:1 ratio in the use of farm machinery. Guizhou exceeded Yunnan only in the use of relatively underdeveloped equipment, such as large and medium-size wood and iron farm tools. Far more specific farm equipment was found in Yunnan than in Guizhou, including farm machinery, which Yunnan possessed to a far greater extent than Guizhou by a 14:1 ratio. Even though this ratio diminished through the next decade, Yunnan continued to apply more agricultural machinery to agriculture than Guizhou. In 2008, Yunnan boasted double the number of large and medium-size tractors and triple the number of combines that Guizhou did. The farmers in both provinces used much less fertilizer than did farmers in other Chinese provinces. Controlling for farmland area, in 1991 Guizhou used more fertilizer than Yunnan (247 tons per 1,000 hectares vs. 226 tons per 1,000 hectares). But by 1996, fertilizer use in Yunnan had increased faster than in Guizhou (to 339 tons per 1,000 hectares vs. 332 tons per 1,000 hectares). This trend also continued throughout the next decade; by 2008, the consumption of chemical fertilizer in Yunnan was double that in Guizhou. Thus, the pattern of agricultural productivity and use of agricultural production equipment cannot explain the puzzle. Moreover, because weather patterns would affect poverty levels and economic growth only through agricultural productivity, any variations in weather patterns are also unlikely to explain the puzzle. (Recall also that the two provinces are very similar in rainfall and other environmental conditions anyway.)

Let us consider another candidate factor. Perhaps Guizhou had fewer natural disasters than Yunnan. If so, the poverty among Yunnan farmers could be caused by floods or droughts, which might not affect the industrial production of the province. If Guizhou were relatively lightly affected, this might help reduce poverty but not directly stimulate much economic growth. But in 1991–1996, natural disasters affected far more arable land in Guizhou than in Yunnan, both in terms of average area covered (1.27 million hectares vs. 1.21 million hectares) and area affected (681,000 hectares vs. 560,000 hectares). After adjusting for total cultivated area, in terms of amount of farmland affected in all Chinese provinces, Guizhou ranked eighth, whereas Yunnan ranked nineteenth. Proportionally, in 1998–2008 the losses of arable land due to weather and natural disasters for Yunnan and Guizhou were similar. Approximately one-fifth of all arable land in both provinces was covered and approximately one-tenth was affected. Yunnan did experience a severe earthquake in 1996, but unexpectedly, it affected economic growth in the area far more negatively than it did income. The three Yunnan counties most heavily affected by the quake recorded economic growth rates 20–50 percentage points lower than comparable counties. The net rural income in these counties, however, saw unexpected increases, and two of the affected counties saw double-digit increases in grain production. The propensity of natural disasters in both provinces remains high; nevertheless, the disasters did not appear in a pattern that would explain the puzzle.

Yet another possible factor is a lower rate of population growth in Guizhou, which could help reduce poverty by decreasing the number of mouths to feed. Both birthrates and natural growth rates in Guizhou, however, remained consistently higher than in Yunnan during this period. In the first half of the 1990s, the birthrate in Guizhou averaged 2.24 percent; that in Yunnan was 1.91, and both were much higher than the overall average in China of approximately 1.8 percent. During the entire period from 1991 to 2008, although the birthrate of both provinces declined, the rate in Guizhou (1.91 percent) remained higher than in Yunnan (1.83 percent), and both were much higher than the overall rate in China of 1.53 percent. Similarly, the natural population growth rate in Guizhou exceeded that in Yunnan. In 1991–1996, the rate in Guizhou was 1.43 percent, whereas in Yunnan it was 1.33 percent; both were higher than the overall rate in China of 1.14. During the period between 1991 and 2008, the natural growth rate in Guizhou was 1.16, that in Yunnan was 1.09 percent, and the overall rate in China was 0.87 percent. Thus, the pattern of population growth is also inconsistent with the puzzle.

Perhaps the Guizhou government spent more than the Yunnan government, affecting poverty rates either overall (through an indirect Keynesian "pump priming" effect), just in poor counties, or in terms of antipoverty initiatives (addressing poverty more directly). Although these have been crucial factors in explaining poverty reduction in other economies, none of these is explanatory in the present case. The Guizhou government budget, both throughout the province and in its poor counties, was dwarfed by that of Yunnan. Moreover, the total Yunnan government budget was nearly 50 percent greater than that of Guizhou in 1978, a gap that subsequently increased to more than double by 1991. Between 1991 and 1996, Yunnan spent 45–58 percent more per capita than Guizhou. In 1991, the Guizhou government spent a total of RMB 161 per capita, compared to the Yunnan expenditure of RMB 293 per capita. In 1996, that gap increased, with Guizhou spending RMB 280 per capita, compared to the Yunnan expenditure of RMB 669 per capita. Thus, during that five-year period the Guizhou government total expenditure increased 74 percent, compared to the Yunnan government spending increase of 128 percent. Guizhou, therefore, began the 1990s at a lower rate of spending and fell even further behind Yunnan. Although the gap started to close in the late 1990s, Yunnan still spent twice as much per person as did Guizhou until 1999. The gap between spending in Yunnan and Guizhou continued to close in 1999–2008, yet even as late as 2008, Yunnan spent 19 percent more than Guizhou per person—and much more on an absolute basis. The answer to the puzzle, then, is not likely to lie in the overall spending of the Guizhou government.

Instead, perhaps the Guizhou government spent more not overall but in the poor counties, where such spending would make a bigger difference. In 1996, Yunnan government spending increased to RMB 683 per capita for its nonpoor counties, whereas Guizhou government spending on its nonpoor counties was a mere 25 percent of that amount, or RMB 173 per person. And in 1996 Yunnan government spending on its poor counties doubled to RMB 377 per capita, whereas Guizhou spending on its poor counties was only 37 percent of that amount, or RMB 139. By 2000, Guizhou spending on its poor counties reached approximately RMB 253 per person, less than one-half the Yunnan expenditure of RMB 537.[6]

Despite the lower spending overall, perhaps a higher investment by Guizhou in antipoverty programs might help explain the patterns of economic growth and poverty reduction seen in the two provinces. But, in three broad categories of spending in areas that should help the poor, Yunnan government spending consistently outpaced that of Guizhou. For instance, spending on agriculture production in Yunnan outpaced that of Guizhou every year between 1978 and 1998, a pattern consistent with faster-growing agricultural sector in Yunnan. Furthermore, the Yunnan budget for this category was between 220 and 267 percent higher than that for Guizhou, and the gap in spending between the two provinces continued to increase. Guizhou government spending in this category between 1991 and 1996 rose approximately 58 percent (from RMB 19 to 27 per capita), whereas Yunnan government spending increased more than 90 percent (from RMB 42 to 80 per capita). At its peak in 1996, the expenditure to promote agriculture production in Yunnan was nearly triple per person the spending in Guizhou. This trend continued until 2001 (the last year for which comparable figures are reported).

In terms of spending on pensions and social relief, Yunnan also spent at a higher rate per capita each year from 1978 on. During 1991–1996, Guizhou government spending in this category grew steadily. In contrast, Yunnan government spending declined between 1991 and 1994 and then increased again in 1995–1996. In some years, the gap in spending between the two provinces narrowed from RMB 7.4 in 1991 (RMB 10.8 per capita for Yunnan vs. RMB 3.4 per capita for Guizhou) to RMB 4.4 in both 1993 and 1994 (in 1994, RMB 9.2 per capita for Yunnan vs. RMB 4.8 for Guizhou). By 1996, however, Yunnan government spending had accelerated to RMB 22.9 versus RMB 7.6 for Guizhou, a gap of RMB 15.3. Overall during the period, Guizhou government spending in this category increased 57 percent versus 91 percent for Yunnan (both grew more slowly than the total Chinese government expenditure). This gap did not start to narrow significantly until 2001, yet even as late as 2004, Yunnan spent in excess of 50 percent more per capita on this category than did Guizhou, although the ratio dropped to below 15 percent over the next two years. Despite this narrowing, Yunnan government spending on this category was much always higher than that of Guizhou, the opposite of what we would expect to explain the puzzle.

Finally, Yunnan government spending to support developing areas also outpaced that of Guizhou. In the early 1990s, Guizhou government spending in this area was more than that of Yunnan; nevertheless, both provinces

6. Guizhou government spending in during this period was much more equal between its poor and nonpoor counties. For instance, in 2000, on average, it spent on its nonpoor counties 17 percent, or RMB 43 per person, more than on its poor counties. To compare, the Yunnan government spent on its nonpoor counties 23 percent, or RMB 121 per person, more.

spent very little (in 1992, RMB 5 per capita for Guizhou vs. RMB 2 per capita for Yunnan). By the mid-1990s, however, the levels of spending in both provinces had increased dramatically, with Yunnan government spending increasing at a much faster rate. In 1996, the Yunnan government spent RMB 16 per person, compared to the Guizhou government spending of RMB 11.5 per person. This pattern continued into the next decade. By 2001, Yunnan was spending RMB 33 per capita on support for its developing areas compared to the Guizhou expenditure of RMB 25 per person. Thus, this pattern of spending is also inconsistent with what we would expect, except that overall spending in Yunnan may have contributed to the overall economic growth rates in the province through a Keynesian-type stimulus and by supporting urban areas.[7]

Given the high poverty rates in Guizhou, we might expect central government transfers of financial resources to the province to be at least as high as those to Yunnan, if not higher. The central government transferred money to the provinces at varying rates; if Guizhou received much more of this kind of assistance than Yunnan did, this might help explain the patterns that emerged in the two provinces. But, in fact, the central government provided much *less* aid in terms of transfers to Guizhou than it did to Yunnan (based on partial statistics). In 1997–2005, official sources reveal that Yunnan received RMB 248 billion (approximately US$30.2 billion) in net central transfers whereas Guizhou received only RMB 152 billion (US$18.5 billion). Even on a per capita basis, Yunnan received between 14 and 100 percent more in central transfers during these years. This is not really a surprise, given that the transfer system in China is known to benefit the more productive provinces far more than it does the more backward ones (Park et al. 1996).

So far, this analysis of several possible explanatory demographic, economic, and political factors has revealed several similarities and differences between the two provinces and some factors that moved in the opposite direction than expected. Thus, the puzzling pattern of economic growth and poverty reduction seen in the two provinces remains a mystery. We next move to the factors that actually explained the puzzle.

7. Only one category of spending relevant to poverty and development was greater in Guizhou than in Yunnan. Guizhou spent a little more on its food-for-work program than did Yunnan (see chap. 3).

2

Why Do Similar Areas Adopt Different Developmental Strategies?

You take your bright path. I'll traverse my narrow wooden bridge.
—Chinese saying

The top leaders of Guizhou and Yunnan set about establishing and implementing strikingly dissimilar strategies to effect economic improvements. Even the goals pursued were markedly different. Why did the leaders of two similar provinces do so? After all, these leaders faced similar challenges, operated in similar contexts, and answered to the same vigilant and opinionated bosses in the central government. So we expect them to have adopted similar policies and approaches. Were the contrasting strategies adopted due to initiatives from provincial leaders, some centrally initiated experiment, a historical or geographical factor, or a combination of these factors? My evidence suggests that, although the central government constrained and encouraged certain actions and approaches in the provinces, the experiences and backgrounds of the individual provincial leaders affected the choices of strategies. Moreover, once a particular course was set and had received central support, a form of path dependency caused the strategy to continue even after the original leaders had departed.

Scholars have studied the variety of strategies and policies that Chinese provincial and local governments have adopted. The earliest contemporary studies of subnational governments provided insights into Mao Zedong's era. Dorothy Solinger (1977b) studied the process of integrating the sometimes autonomous and restive provinces of southwestern China into the newly formed PRC. David Goodman (1986) analyzed the diverse experiences of Sichuan and Guizhou during the Great Leap Forward. Victor Falkenheim (1969) analyzed the Cultural Revolution as implemented in Fujian, Yunnan, and Guangxi. With the launch of the reform era, and especially after the more recent moves toward "soft centralization," provincial decision making has become more autonomous and influential (Mertha 2005; Naughton 1993; Li 1998). Because provincial governments now implement central policy in diverse ways, as well as design their own strategies and approaches independent of Beijing, studies focusing on central decision making no longer (if they ever did) provide a complete picture of Chinese politics. Provincial governments, although answerable to the center through the *nomenklatura* system (Chan 2004; Sheng 2005), have sufficient autonomy to be considered decision makers in their own right and thus provide a good laboratory in which to study the design, implementation, and effects of policy.

Given the great importance of the provinces, however, the number of explicitly comparative studies of Chinese provinces, although not trivial, is surprisingly small. Many studies confine their analysis to single localities (Goodman 1997; Hendrischke and Feng 1999; Fitzgerald 2002; Cheung, Chung, and Lin 1998). Other research has been more systematically comparative (Chung 1995). For instance, Chung Jae Ho (2000) has studied the variation in the implementation of rural reform in pioneering (Anhui), bandwagoning (Shandong), and resisting (Heilongjiang) provinces; Elizabeth Remick (2004) compares tax collection in Tianjin and Guangdong, both during the republican and the early reform eras; and Linda Li (1998) has studied investment policy in Shanghai and Guangdong. These studies take advantage of the strengths of the comparative method, such as controlling for several factors to isolate important causal variables.

Although these comparative studies have been crucial for understanding how development in provincial China varies, most have focused on coastal China or, sometimes, on the inland provinces; there is thus a paucity of studies on reform-era western China. The impoverished western provinces of China, with a large proportion of their populations consisting of rural poor, were largely left behind during the first years of reform. Enhancing our knowledge of the western provinces is crucial to understanding the impact of various development policies adopted at the central, provincial, and local levels. Although some studies have focused on post-1978 provincial development policies in Yunnan (e.g., Hillman 2003; Gan, Yao, and Yang 2001; Wang R. 2001; d'Hooghe 1994), and a small handful have focused on Guizhou (e.g., Oakes 2004; Wang and Zhang 2003; Wright 2003; Lv 1995), no study of which I am aware has compared the adoption of development and poverty reduction strategies by these two provinces during the reform era.

Thus, this book contributes to our understanding of the reactions of provincial governments to central reform policies in the important yet understudied region of western China. In addition, between 1985 and 1988, Hu Jintao, the current president of China and general secretary of the CCP, served as the top provincial leader of Guizhou. As I discuss in the introduction, the policies in Guizhou provide insights into this poorly understood leader. Finally, comparing these two provinces contributes to our understanding of Chinese provincial leaders in general. Huang Yasheng's (1996) commonly used, relatively parsimonious approach to studying provincial politicians cannot fully explain the patterns found in these two provinces; a refinement of his approach could help increase its accuracy. All this must be qualified by saying that even extensive interviews, fieldwork, and study of secondary sources cannot fully penetrate the opaque provincial politics in this region. Nevertheless, my study does cast new light on the variation in policy approaches adopted by the governments of provinces that did not benefit from reform to the same extent as the rest of China.

In contrasting the decisions made by provincial and local governments in China, scholars point to three groups of factors. Some scholars explain such differences by reference to the central government, arguing that central experimentation and constraints explain the variation in policy among provincial governments (e.g., Li 1998; Solinger 1996; Shirk 1992; Tsui and Wang 2004). Others argue that characteristics of the provinces themselves—factors such as initial conditions, cultures, and histories—explain the adoption of differing policy approaches. A third group of scholars contend that individual characteristics of the political leaders of these provinces are critical to understanding policy adoption and implementation (e.g., Cheung, Chung, and Lin 1998; Chung 2000; Bo 2002; Goldstein 1994; Goodman 1986; Breslin 1996; Liu 1996; Landry 2000). Here I examine each of these in turn to determine the extent to which they explain the variations in policy selection that emerged in the late 1980s and early 1990s in Yunnan and Guizhou.

Central Government Influence

Many scholars accurately describe China as decentralizing since Deng Xiaoping, its supreme leader, started reforms in 1978; however, the center still maintains a decisive hold on power in many policy areas (Tsui and Wang 2004). Chinese central leaders hope that decentralization and local innovation will increase the efficiency of development policy, yet they fear the lack of control that decentralization also brings. Thus, Chinese leadership faces what Chung Jae Ho calls a "centralizing paradox," in which the center simultaneously confronts the seemingly incompatible goals of reaping the benefits of policy decentralization and maintaining central control (Chung 2000, 11; Donaldson 2009). In managing this paradox, the center can mandate or encourage local experimentation and/or impose centrally mandated constraints, both of which can explain variation in provincial policy.[1]

1. These two categories (experimentation and constraint), although identifiably distinct in the literature, are related and can overlap. For instance, central experimentation will constrain local policymaking. In the case of Yunnan, experimentation in the province can be tied to its role in national security, which is identified as a constraint.

Although central government leaders promulgated plans and strategies that applied either to China as a whole (such as the agricultural reform policies of 1978–1984) or to particular regions (such as opening coastal areas to foreign investment first or the more recent plans to develop the western and northeastern regions), they have also initiated or encouraged provincial government experimentation. Regarding the puzzle being examined here, we could hypothesize that the central government hoped to test different approaches to development and poverty reduction in the two provinces.

Guizhou and Yunnan are not typically included in discussions of central government experiments, which are thought to have been implemented primarily in coastal provinces (Shirk 1993).[2] Although there is little to suggest that formal experimentation occurred in the two provinces, evidence gleaned from public speeches suggests that central authorities directed crucial elements of the economic policies of the provinces and sought to encourage provincial leaders to implement various strategies. In fact, central officials, during visits to the provinces, frequently offered advice to the leaders of one province that contradicted advice they proffered to the leaders of the other. For instance, as described below, in his January 1984 and February 1986 visits to Guizhou, General Secretary Hu Yaobang suggested that Guizhou officials focus on building rural roadways linking villages with the nearest marketing towns, according to one scholar I interviewed. This is in direct contrast with the advice that Transportation Minister Qian Yongchang offered Yunnan leaders during his 1986 visit; he directed the province to build cross-provincial, transnational highways to open up counties to development and to create channels for imports and exports (Yunnan Nianjian Bianjibu 1987).[3] But Qian, during a visit to Guizhou that same year, discussed more modest plans for the Guizhou highway system and underscored Hu Yaobang's advice about constructing roads linking rural areas to open up mountain areas, provide access to additional resources, and improve the economy of the province (Guizhou Nianjian Bianjibu 1988). Similarly, during a 1993 visit to Guizhou, Zhu Rongji, vice premier at the time, recommended that provincial leaders concentrate not on higher-class paved roads but on concrete roads of the kind that generally link townships to counties (Guizhou Nianjian Bianjibu 1994, 133–34).[4] The next year, during the Second Plenum of the Eighth People's Congress, when discussing Guizhou, Zhu reemphasized this focus on concrete (not paved) roads. Although he

2. White (1998) notes that in the 1980s Guizhou was marked as a base for the development of energy resources but that little came of this effort.

3. As another example, Hu suggested that Guizhou officials focus on developing small-scale mines to employ poor rural residents, and Guizhou followed this strategy. In contrast, Yunnan leaders focused on developing more automated medium-size mines that required more experienced and educated workers, as well as more capital.

4. Concrete roads are much cheaper than paved roads, allowing the road system to be laid more extensively. Guizhou, which in the mid-1990s ranked third in the density of country roads linking villages to markets, has reduced rural poverty in part by focusing on this kind of road (see chap. 3).

emphasized road construction as a way to promote industrialization in Guizhou, he also specifically linked this policy to poverty reduction and tellingly added that the country would "continue to recognize Guizhou as a priority in the country's poverty reduction program" (Guizhou Nianjian Bianjibu 1995, 402).

The roadway plans of both provinces conformed closely with these contrasting suggestions, which suggests central experimentation was indeed a factor. Yunnan officials planned the construction of an extensive highway system linking the province with the capitals of three other provinces and with the three countries that border the province. Underscoring the importance of the province to national development, Yunnan (unlike Guizhou) had been part of the centrally designated highway system plan since at least 1985 and received significant central transportation funds as a result (Yunnan Nianjian Bianjibu 1986). This highway system promoted the provincial economy, but it did remarkably little to reduce rural poverty. By contrast, the Guizhou government constructed a modest system of intraprovince highways of fewer than 1,400 kilometers and focused primarily on constructing rural roadways (see chap. 3). The Guizhou plan explicitly prioritized reducing the isolation of poor areas by linking them to markets, increasing their access to information, and thus spurring the reduction of rural poverty.

Even more striking is the contrasting advice that central officials gave the two provinces regarding the development of their tourism industries. In May 1992, Vice Premier Wu Xueqian visited Yunnan and suggested that it was time for the province to enter "a new stage of development." Yunnan policymakers should concentrate first on developing destinations that were already advanced and possessed "a certain degree of notoriety" and should attract additional foreign investment to make further strides in constructing the tourism infrastructure. By August of that year, the Chinese State Council had approved its first set of vacation spots, which also focused on a small number of Yunnan's well-known scenic areas (Yunnan Nianjian Bianjibu 1993).

This advice conflicted with the previous Yunnan tourism policy. During the late 1980s, provincial leaders had been poised to expand the number of key tourist destinations available for investment and development. While Yunnan provincial officials remained focused on developing "key point" tourist spots (specifically, Kunming, Dali, Lijiang, and Xishuangbanna), they were also preparing other locations for development. In their report for 1990, Yunnan tourism officials emphasized the breadth of the tourism resources in the province. In addition to the tourist attractions officially recognized on the national and provincial levels, these resources included 119 cultural artifact protection offices and "numerous" prefecture- and county-level natural regions. The provincial government was considering distributing development to several "dispersed regions with tourism resources." Along with Kunming, Dali, Xishuangbanna, and Lijiang, targeted areas included

Nujiang, Dehong, Baoshan, Yuxi, as well as unspecified places in southern and northeastern Yunnan (Zhongguo Lvyou Nianjian Bianjibu 1990, 364, 361–65). If these plans had come to fruition, the Yunnan tourism industry might have become distributed in ways that helped reduce rural poverty.

But simultaneously with Wu's visit, Yunnan provincial authorities suddenly reversed course in their development plans for the tourism industry. Instead of following the earlier plan, in the early 1990s provincial officials abruptly decided to concentrate investment only in the nonpoor areas that had previously been popular with tourists—policies that conformed to the advice that Vice Premier Wu had given them. Provincial leaders made a major commitment to promoting a more concentrated Yunnan tourism industry, which they had recently declared a pillar industry for Yunnan. The initiative included completing a "comprehensive plan for the tourism industry" that included devising the Ninth Five-Year Plan (1995–2000) for the province as well as a Fifteen-Year Plan for the development of the tourism industry; "increasing investment and improving infrastructure" in the older tourism areas of Kunming, Xishuangbanna, Dali, Lijiang, and the Stone Forest; expanding the participation of outside investors to expand Lijiang and accelerate the construction of a golf course in Shizonghai; purchasing eighty airplanes and quickly connecting airports in Kunming, Xishuangbanna, Dali, Lijiang, and Ruili; and strengthening the leadership over the tourism industry.

Subsequent visits by central leaders reinforced this model of concentrated development for the tourism industry. In his October 1995 speech in Yunnan, then Vice Premier Zhu Rongji suggested that Yunnan continue its development of Kunming, Lijiang, Dali, Xishuangbanna, and "even Ruili" (a nonpoor county in western Yunnan, bordering Myanmar), which Zhu added as a fifth site.[5] Each of these tourist areas, Zhu advised, should build roads, restaurants, hotels, and restrooms to attract international tourists especially.[6]

Remarkably, in April 1996, just months after his inspection tour to Yunnan, Zhu Rongji offered Guizhou officials much different advice. For Yunnan, Zhu had suggested that provincial officials focus on increasing the scale of their tourism investments in the province. In Guizhou, by contrast, Zhu suggested that provincial officials focus on small-scale development of the tourism industry (Wright 2003). Zhu reasoned,

> Tourism is one of your advantages; you have the conditions to develop this sector. Just focus on making good use of your abundant natural resources. That

5. Ruili county is in Dehong, a prefecture with five counties, all nonpoor. In 1995, the year of Zhu's visit, Dehong received 9,501 visits, just 2.3 percent of all visitors to Yunnan.

6. Ironically, Zhu specifically intended these suggestions to help reduce poverty in Yunnan, even though these places had largely emerged from poverty at least a decade previously.

> would be enough. There is no need to invest in all kinds of crazy stuff...like fancy hotels. You don't need to do that. Just make sure you build decent [toilets], and keep them clean. That and a good shower are sufficient....There's no need to thoughtlessly spend money. Focus on efficiency. As tourism develops and the transportation conditions improve, that, one day, will be true prosperity. (quoted in Wright 2003, 139)

We might take these events as clear evidence of the role of central experimentation in the development strategies of the two provinces. There is a problem with this conclusion, however—the advice dispensed by the central officials to each province in many cases came several years *after* the provinces had already begun implementing the very strategies that central officials subsequently advocated. Well before Qian's 1992 visit and Zhu's visit in 1996, Guizhou officials were already focusing resources on construction of the simple rural roads that these central officials later suggested. In the early 1990s, leaders in both Guizhou and Yunnan announced plans for their road systems. Guizhou planned to concentrate on the construction and improvement of country roads linking villages to townships to reduce the isolation of impoverished farmers. This initiative began in the mid-1980s under a plan formulated by Hu Jintao, then the Guizhou Communist Party secretary, and was intentionally designed to reduce rural poverty; this policy continued during the early 1990s. In addition to positioning these roads explicitly to reduce poverty, the Guizhou leadership also used a food-for-work policy (see chap. 3), ensuring that poor people benefited directly from the actual construction of the roads. Yunnan planned, as a part of its strategy designed to spur economic growth and development, to construct an ambitious highway system to ease the flow of imports and exports and to allow more convenient access to tourist areas. Yunnan continued to lack the relatively extensive rural road network found in Guizhou.

Likewise with policies on tourism, Guizhou from the early 1990s linked the development of that industry with poverty reduction in the rural economy. For instance, in 1992, a full three years before Zhu's visit, provincial leaders attempted to structure the tourism industry to increase the participation of poor rural residents. With the slogan "the tourism industry promotes openness to the outside; use tourism to promote poverty reduction," Guizhou became the first Chinese province to tie tourism explicitly to poverty reduction. As Guizhou Vice Governor Lou Jiwei argued later in May 1996, "The tourism industry can spur employment, solve the food shortages among the people and reduce poverty. It can also bring income to local governments, and improve the healthy, continued and stable development of local economies" (Zhongguo Lvyou Nianjian Bianjibu 1996, 186).

There was substance behind these sentiments. The provincial government leveraged the volumes of tourists visiting the popular Huangguoshu Waterfall to reduce poverty, both by increasing participation of rural residents on the site itself and by linking that site to nearby smaller-scale tourist attractions. Instead of focusing on constructing large hotels in rural areas, Guizhou expanded the housing that was already in its ethnic villages and other tourist areas to develop an alternative style of tourism, known as *nongjiale* (loosely, "joyous village life"). In this popular form of tourism found in much of China, tourists stay in rustic rural homes, eating food prepared by poor people and enjoying ethnic song, dance, and culture. Thus, in addition to earning tourist money from selling handmade clothing, jewelry, and other handicrafts, residents also directly host tourists in their own homes. Although this form of tourism may not appeal to many—or perhaps most—elite international travelers, the relatively authentic and rustic nature of *nongjiale* tourism attracts many more hardy tourists.[7] Also commonly found in Guizhou is a similar style of tourism known as *nongye guanguang lvyou* ("agricultural sightseeing and tourism"), which tends to have shorter excursions to the countryside than *nongjiale*. The June 1995 Red Bayberry Festival was explicitly designed as a tourist activity to help reduce rural poverty (Guizhou Nianjian Bianjibu 1996, 623).

Similarly, the tourism policies that Zhu Rongji suggested for Yunnan had also been implemented since at least 1992—years before Zhu's visit in 1995, although many of these changes were concurrent with Vice Premier Wu's visit in 1992. In a 1996 report by Li Lu'an, director of the Yunnan tourism bureau, laid out the accomplishments of the province in constructing its tourism industry during the previous five years, a pattern of development consistent with the strategy of concentrated development (Yunnan Nianjian Bianjibu 1996, 16–18). In his report, Li emphasized the importance of these key places to the development of the tourism industry, as well as to the overall Yunnan economy. Li detailed a set of "developmental points of emphasis," which included "three lines, four places and five regions." Although on the surface this list might seem to include a variety of tourist destinations, these lines, places, and regions actually centered primarily on the four familiar regions that had been the key Yunnan tourist sites since the early 1980s—Kunming (including the Stone Forest), Xishuangbanna, Dali, and Lijiang—as well as Ruili. Thus the "three lines" were Kunming to the Stone Forest, Kunming to Dali to Lijiang to Tengchong to Ruili, and Kunming to Xishuangbanna; the "four places" were Dali, Lijiang, Jinghong (Xishuangbanna), and Ruili; and based on these three lines and four places, the five regions are our familiar list: Kunming, Lijiang, Dali, Ruili, and Xishuangbanna. The director reemphasized the provincial commitment to the six Yunnan "vacation areas" established in early 1993, including one national-level destination around Dianchi Lake in Kunming, and five provincial-level vacation areas: Dali, Yulong Snow Mountain (in Lijiang),

7. The authenticity of the experience is relative, however. See Oakes (1998) for a nuanced discussion of the authenticity of Guizhou tourism sites.

Xishuangbanna, Yangshihai (in Yiliang County, a nonpoor county within Kunming prefecture some 55 kilometers outside the capital), and Fuxian Lake (in Chengjiang, a nonpoor county in Yuxi prefecture, one of the wealthiest tobacco-growing areas in Yunnan). In addition, during a provincial party meeting held in August 1995, before Zhu's trip, provincial leaders announced the "opening of a new page in Yunnan's tourism industry" as a "pillar industry for the province," positioning the industry as an integral part of its effort to promote economic and social development (Yunnan Nianjian Bianjibu 1996, 259).

The timing of these events suggests that central experimentation remains a possible explanation but a tenuous one. Central advice does not seem to be a factor explaining many of the provincial policies, particularly those in Guizhou. Something else must have happened.

It is possible that the Chinese central government provided different constraints and opportunities to each of the provincial governments that affected their policies. There is evidence that this happened in other instances. For example, according to a study by Linda Li (1997), Guangdong and Shanghai implemented reform and development policies under widely different contextual constraints, which to some degree determined their choices of investment policies. Similarly, Solinger (1996) argues that central policy, although increasing the policy flexibility of some localities, actually stifled Wuhan city officials' innovative development policies by constraining their range of activities. Scholars apply several indicators of central constraints. Kenneth Lieberthal and Michel Oksenberg (1990) argue that among the crucial variables that affect the extent to which Beijing tries to influence provincial policy are the economic role of the province in the Chinese economy, its role in national security, and its ability to earn foreign exchange.[8]

The success of the reform initiatives in China hinged on the development of the coastal provinces, especially those in the southeast. As was typical of central policies, the western provinces, such as Yunnan and, especially, Guizhou, received significant national investment under Mao's Third Front Program, but were categorized as third-tier provinces in the post-Mao period and given the lowest priority for development (Naughton 1988; Fan 1997). But, even though central officials did not emphasize the development of the western provinces as a group during the first decades of the reform era, the constraints placed on these provinces varied. The Yunnan government operated under tighter central constraints than did the Guizhou government, based on evidence related to transfers, subsidies, and extraction of taxes.[9] Compared to Guizhou, Yunnan transferred more finances to the

8. Other variables that these authors cite, such as physical distance and central strength in local areas, do not vary much between Yunnan and Guizhou.

9. Higher levels of remittances from a province to the center also correlate with the longer tenures of top provincial officials. This is consistent with the experience of Yunnan (Bo 2002).

center, received more transfers from the center, and benefited financially far more, especially after the implementation of the 1993 tax reform policies (Wang S. 2001; see also chap. 1). Further, the central government was much more effective at collecting value-added taxes from Yunnan than Guizhou, at least between the mid-1990s and the end of the decade (Choi 2006). This suggests that the central government constrained Yunnan more than Guizhou. Yunnan is a border province and for centuries has been more significant to Beijing national security than the isolated hinterland province of Guizhou, despite the historical restiveness of the Guizhou ethnic minorities (Oakes 1998).[10] Moreover, because of its crucial tobacco production and international trade, Yunnan has a more prominent economic role, contributing more to the national economy. According to informants knowledgeable about this era, central officials had much lower expectations of Guizhou than of Yunnan and also did not really understand the economic situation in Guizhou. For these reasons, according to my interviews, the leaders in Yunnan were under more pressure to adopt policies that conformed closely to central policy than were leaders in Guizhou.

Accordingly, the Yunnan strategies and plans were much more consistent with central policies and approaches. The Thirteenth and, especially, Fourteenth Party Congresses (held in 1987 and 1992, respectively) each laid out policies that emphasized growth and development and that sought to reward provincial leaders for their ability to grow the economy at a steady rate and promote productive industries (Rosen 1988; Saich 1992). Although top Chinese leaders debated vigorously such crucial issues as the role of the state in development,[11] the importance of limiting political reform, and the need to maintain an ideologically conservative stance, most, both reformer and conservative, agreed on the need for rapid large-scale development that would grow the economy. In 1992, during his well-known southern tour designed to reinvigorate pro-market reforms (a few years after the Tiananmen Square massacre), Deng Xiaoping promoted development as measured by GDP growth as the "absolute principle" (*ying daoli*)[12] for the country (Deng

10. The historical significance of Yunnan for Chinese security was emphasized during the military conflicts between China and Vietnam, according to an interview with one Chinese scholar.

11. The debates at that time among central officials over the use of planning versus the use of markets are largely irrelevant for Yunnan and Guizhou, both of which relied on the power of the state to alter their economies. Neither the Yunnan developmental state approach nor the Guizhou micro-oriented state approach relied primarily on market forces. Central conservatives had little problem with the reliance by Yunnan on tobacco and state-owned cigarette companies to grow the economy. Tobacco today remains among the last agricultural products to be channeled through state monopolies. Other central concerns, such as political stability and population control, were carefully—although often unsuccessfully—emphasized by leaders of both provinces.

12. *Ying daoli,* often translated as "absolute principle" (e.g., Fan 2006, 709), has also been translated as "unimpeachable law" (Lam 2006, 43), "hard truth" (e.g., Chen 2007, 18), and "only truth" (Lin 1995, 14).

1993). In this spirit, in 1993 the CCP embraced the doctrine of "efficiency first, and equity second" (Guo 2008, 28). Based on this strong endorsement of what is known in China as "GDPism," Chinese officials at all levels undertook the aggressive pursuit of economic development as measured by GDP growth, largely disregarding the festering social and environmental problems that ensued (Zheng 2007, 3). The Yunnan developmental state strategy, emphasizing GDP growth, was overall much closer to this central government "absolute principle" of development. By contrast, the relatively minor central constraints on Guizhou allowed its leaders to implement a different approach. Thus, central constraints seems to be a factor that is consistent with the evidence from the two provinces.

Initial Provincial Conditions

In addition to experimentation by and constraints imposed by the center, characteristics specific to Yunnan and Guizhou might also affect the decision-making processes. First, differing initial conditions in each province might influence the priorities of provincial leaders. The provinces might have started with industries or sectors that are relatively well developed or with inefficient state-owned industries. Differences in initial conditions such as GDP, industrial structure, poverty rates, and natural resource endowments thus could cause variations in provincial strategies. Second, provinces have different cultures and histories, which might affect leaders' choices. Some scholars argue that certain groups have beliefs or values that affect factors that influence economic changes, such as the tendency to migrate. In addition, historical policy decisions can constrain or enable subsequent decisions by making certain choices more or less costly.[13]

As we have seen in chapter 1, Yunnan and Guizhou were remarkably similar economically, politically, and geographically at the outset of the reform era. It is true that the histories and cultures of Guizhou and Yunnan do vary but not in ways that affect policymaking for migration or other issues (see chap. 4). The two provinces, however, do vary dramatically with regard to the amount of financial resources available to them. Although both provinces boast significant tobacco production, leaders in Yunnan went to great pains to develop the industry. In doing so, the Yunnan government secured a large stable revenue source, which in turn allowed its budget to expand. The province ranked first in China for government revenue as a function of GDP between 1992 and 2000. Moreover, the Yunnan budget was

13. These variables provide an environmental or background condition, operating as the context in which either provincial elites or central officials make policy choices. Although policy decisions are certainly influenced by historical or cultural peculiarities or by initial conditions in the province, why policy is shaped in a certain direction remains an open question.

consistently much greater than the Guizhou budget. The lack of resources restricts the range of options available to provinces, as Li (1997, 780) notes about Guizhou specifically. This factor can also motivate provincial leaders to resist central policies and take their own path. So, lack of resources in Guizhou may have encouraged its leaders to pursue policies that were more appropriate for reducing poverty and not the more costly policies aimed at scaling up industry and developing the economy. Thus, the financial situations of Yunnan and Guizhou also contributed to their differences in policy by constraining their choices between more and less costly options.

Provincial Leadership

Finally, some argue that the unique characteristics of top provincial leaders (typically the provincial party secretary, governor, vice secretaries, and vice governors) can influence provincial policy, creating variation from province to province (Bo 2002; Zeng 1991; Chung 2000; Huang 1996). Within this general category, one possible explanatory factor is a leader's career prospects, a primary method used by the center to maintain a measure of control over the provinces (Chung 2000).[14] Top provincial leaders serve at the pleasure of the central government and thus should be responsive to central dictates in any case, but some officials know that they have a better chance of promoting their careers than others do and are especially compliant with central demands. Because the available data rarely allow us to evaluate someone's actual career prospects per se, scholars usually adopt an imperfect proxy—the next position actually obtained by the leader.

A second possible factor affecting provincial decision making is the top leader's origin (Zeng 1991). Huang formulates a fourfold classification system for origin: (1) concurrent centralists, provincial officials who simultaneously hold central positions; (2) centralists, officials who previously occupied central positions; (3) outsiders, officials transferred from other provinces; and (4) localists, officials who spend their entire careers in the provinces where they are currently appointed (Huang 1996; Sheng and Huang 2006; Choi 2006). Huang envisions this classification as forming a spectrum with regard to the center, with those closer to the concurrent centralist end of the spectrum being more likely to comply with central directives. Officials' "home" provinces are usually determined by where they have spent most of their careers, and officials who were born or educated in the locality in which they serve may also be considered localists. Localists are assumed to care more about and have more local ties with their own provinces, and thus

14. Thus, this factor is directly related to central constraints, a previous factor. In fact, many factors overlap.

to be more likely to deviate from central dictates to promote local interests than those on the other end of the spectrum.

A third possible factor in this category is the clientelistic relationships between central and provincial leaders. Some provincial leaders belong to specific political factions and tend to implement policies that their patrons desire. Scholars who study these relationships examine such indicators as working in the same party or state organization and graduating from the same university as a senior politician. For instance, membership in the China Youth League and graduation from Tsinghua University are considered to be signs of membership in Hu Jintao's faction, whereas experience in the Shanghai government is seen as evidence of membership in Jiang Zemin's clique (Li C. 2001; Chung 2000).[15]

A final possible factor in this category that might explain the variations in decision making is a leader's individual characteristics, such as personality, ideology, or level of corruption (Chung 2000; Remick 2004; Lieberthal and Oksenberg 1990). Provincial leaders sometimes have strong idiosyncratic ideological beliefs (apart from their personal background and membership in a faction), including beliefs about "the proper role of the local state in the economy" (Remick 2004, 260). In addition, top officials can be vigorous or sluggish, innovative or conservative, proactive or passive. As Chung argues, "In the final analysis, [local variation in implementation] may all come down to the issue of leadership" (Chung 2000, 10). To the extent that provincial leaders are given sufficient latitude, their own ideas and values may come to the fore.

In sum, these personal characteristics of the provincial leaders—career prospects, origin, clientelist relationships, and other individual characteristics—might explain the variation in provincial policy.[16]

Let us consider first the Guizhou leaders. Like most Chinese provinces, for Guizhou 1993 was a year of transition in which eight of its twelve leaders were replaced.[17] Before that year, between 1983 and 1993, Guizhou had been led by a series of three provincial party secretaries who each served between two and six years. The first of these, Zhu Houze (1983–1985), was a local, having been raised in Zhijin, a poor county in Bijie prefecture.[18] Zhu

15. Li Cheng and Lye Liang Fook (2005) caution that not all officials with tenures in the Youth League can be considered supporters of Hu, but they also note that there are only a few exceptions.

16. Unless otherwise cited, the information here is taken primarily from provincial yearbooks (Guizhou Nianjian Bianjibu various years; Yunnan Nianjian Bianjibu various years), and bibliographical reference books about China's political leaders (e.g., Bartke 1991; Editorial Board of *Who's Who in China* 1989, 1994; Zhang Guoliang 2003).

17. This was part of a wider sweep of the Chinese leadership that occurred that year. Intended to renew and rejuvenate the leadership, this sweep replaced 40 percent of all provincial leaders throughout China (Bo 2002).

18. Like Hu Jintao, Zhu was also a protégé of Hu Yaobang (Lam 2006). Zhu was apparently the first local to serve as the top leader in Guizhou since 1965.

had extensive experience in the cigarette industry, having served as the general manager of the Guiyang Cigarette Company. His tenure as party secretary ended with his promotion to minister of the Propaganda Department of the Central Committee of the CCP. The two other provincial party secretaries were outsiders. Hu Jintao (1985–1988) was transferred from the central government, where he had served as first secretary of the China Youth League. As mentioned earlier, after serving more than three years in the province, Hu was ultimately promoted to the Standing Committee of the Politburo during the Fourteenth Party Congress in 1992 and now serves as the top leader of China. Liu Zhengwei (1988–1993) transferred laterally from Henan province (he served as vice secretary in Guizhou for one year before becoming secretary). After his term as Guizhou secretary ended (at age sixty-three, a couple of years before normal retirement age), he became deputy secretary of the CCP State Organs Work Committee, possibly a symbolic post he held just before retirement. While serving in Guizhou, these top leaders were supported by three vice secretaries (not including Governor Wang Chaowen, who concurrently served as vice secretary), all of whom were local and two of whom were from one of the poorest Guizhou rural counties. Each of them retired after their service as vice secretary ended.

Serving concurrently with these party secretaries was Governor Wang Chaowen, a localist who had worked his way up from his birthplace, Huangping, a poor county in southeastern Guizhou. Wang served in this position for more than ten years—among the longest tenures for any governor in the reform era—until his retirement. Although seven of the nine vice governors of Guizhou serving between 1983 and 1993 had been born outside the province, all had strong ties to the province, with eight serving in Guizhou for more than a decade and the ninth serving for eight years. Five of these had been transferred to the province in the 1960s to promote Mao's Third Front Program and had subsequently obtained extensive experience working in industries such as electronics, power, steel, metallurgy, and mining. After leaving their position as vice governor, most of them retired, either outright or by serving in the Guizhou People's Congress or elsewhere (one became president of Guizhou University).[19]

In 1993, this pattern changed markedly when Liu Fangren was transferred laterally from Jiangxi province to Guizhou as CCP secretary (1993–2000). Probably the most despised top official in Guizhou from the reform era, Liu's tenure ended in disgrace—he retired briefly before being jailed for life for corruption in 2003 (along with former Vice Governor Liu Changgui), for crimes committed during his tenure in Guizhou. Three governors served under Liu. Two of these, Chen Shineng (1993–1996) and Wu Yixia

19. Bo (2002) notes that it is fairly common for leaders to serve in their own provinces as vice secretaries or vice governors and then to be transferred to other provinces if they are assigned to top provincial positions.

(1996–1998), came directly from the central government, and the third, Qian Yunlv (1998–2000) had been transferred from Hubei and had ties to the Youth League (Li 2005). Governor Chen Shineng, a centralist and a classmate of Hu Jintao, was assigned from, and subsequently returned to, leadership positions in the Ministry of Light Industry. His successor, Wu Yixia, was a popular and proactive governor, whose experience as an engineer and in the Ministry of Agriculture informed the antipoverty policies he designed for Guizhou. Unfortunately, Wu died in office in 1998, and many of these policies reportedly died with him. The third post-1993 governor, Qian Yunlv, transferred from Hubei, served briefly as acting governor before succeeding Liu Fangren as party secretary. Although the top two officials in post-1993 Guizhou came from outside the province and had little experience in Guizhou, most of Guizhou vice secretaries serving between 1993 and 2000 and most of the vice governors were from Guizhou, had studied there, or had worked their way up from Guizhou local governments (or a combination of these). Thus for Guizhou during this period, the presence of locals serving below the top two positions is significant.

Based on this evidence, we should not be surprised that Guizhou policy was heavily influenced by local elites whose concern for reducing poverty probably stemmed from their having been raised in poor areas. As we have seen, before 1993 Guizhou policy was influenced heavily by leaders who had either risen through the ranks of local Guizhou politics or who had strong ideas about economic policy. The former include Governor Wang Chaowen and Party Secretary Zhu Houze, both of whom were localists with ties to the provincial Youth League and (in the latter case) to then General Secretary Hu Yaobang. This also put them in contact with Hu Jintao, the young rising political leader who led that organization at the central level.

Raised in Taizhou City in Jiangsu province on the northern banks of the Yangtze River, Hu Jintao himself grew up in a family that, although not poor, was not especially wealthy.[20] While in Gansu, Hu came to the attention of Song Ping, an economist and Tsinghua University graduate, then the Gansu party secretary.[21] Song Ping cared deeply about the poverty that was endemic throughout Gansu, and this concern apparently brought this issue to the forefront of Hu's concerns as well (Wen and Ren 2002). Zhu and Hu, faced with limited resources and central level support, placed a high priority on reducing rural poverty. The third pre-1993 party secretary, Liu Zhengwei, was not considered to be particularly active. Given this,

20. Many sources (even official ones) list Hu Jintao as being a native of Jixi, Anhui province. Although Hu's ancestral home was in Anhui, he actually spent most of his pre-university days in his birthplace of Taizhou Municipality in Jiangsu province (see, for instance, Ma 2006). Contrary to Hu's official biography, some scholars even suggest that Shanghai was Hu's actual birthplace (Tkacik 2002).

21. This was also the point at which the rising star of Hu Jintao caught the attention of Deng Xiaoping, then the top Chinese leader (Zheng 1999, 11).

Governor Wang is considered to have been politically dominant, especially after Hu Jintao left this position in 1988.

The Guizhou government adopted poverty reduction policies that did not operate primarily through economic growth, the accepted central strategy, but via micro-oriented policies that reduced poverty but did not stimulate the overall economy very much. One of Hu Jintao's biographies (one of the few that focus on the Guizhou era) argues that while in Guizhou, the leader emphasized poverty reduction measures even to the point of sacrificing rapid economic expansion (Wen and Ren 2002).[22] Hu sent provincial officials to poor counties to investigate the local economies and make suggestions, and he was applauded for having personally visited during his tenure each of the eighty-seven counties in Guizhou and for making special visits to the remotest parts of the province early in his tenure there. Moreover, Hu implemented experiments in Bijie prefecture in northwestern Guizhou (which contained the hometown of the previous party secretary, Zhu Houze), then considered the poorest prefecture in China. The threefold approach adopted for Bijie emphasized neither heady GDP growth nor no-holds-barred economic development but, instead, the combination of poverty reduction, environmental sustainability, and family planning (Zhao 2003). Although only modestly successful in Bijie, these approaches echo Hu's ideas that were subsequently encapsulated in his Scientific Development Concept (see the introduction).

Supporting these two party secretaries were Governor Wang Chaowen, long-standing localist, and a set of locally oriented vice secretaries and vice governors, many of whom hailed from or had worked in the poorest areas of Guizhou and none of whom apparently had prospects for advancement (nearly all of them subsequently retired from their positions after reaching retirement age). The resulting strategy focused on promoting opportunities, especially supporting small-scale township and village enterprise (TVE) coal mines, constructing modest roadway systems linking villages to townships and counties, encouraging migration, and later establishing a grassroots style of tourism. Provincial policymakers distributed and structured these elements to maximize benefits for poor people. In this way, these leaders laid the groundwork for the subsequent remarkable reduction of rural poverty in Guizhou despite its having one of the slowest economic growth rates in China.

By contrast, after 1993 central officials assigned to Guizhou a series of party secretaries and governors transferred from outside the province, either from the central government or from other provinces; this was the usual practice in the 1990s (Bo 2002). The vice secretaries and vice governors who served under these leaders, however, were mainly locals who had either

22. This conflicts with Li's tentative conclusion (noted in the introduction) that, during his tenure in Guizhou, Hu Jintao "did not seem to make many changes" (Li C. 2001, 116).

worked their way up from local government service or had lived in the province since the 1960s. Remaining in charge of important portfolios, these second-tier officials ensured the continuation of the Guizhou micro-oriented policy approach established before 1993. Meanwhile, the Guizhou micro-oriented approach had achieved at least some central support, as evidenced by the endorsements of central leaders (the most influential of these, then Vice Premier Zhu Rongji, made his support explicit in 1994). The combined support from both above and below the top provincial leaders helped keep the original strategies intact, despite the top officials' being outsiders and other constraints, such as the corruption of Party Secretary Liu Fangren. The governors, appointed by the center, who served concurrently with Liu, moreover, had experience in areas (light industry and agriculture) that were relevant to the micro-oriented approach. The fact that Secretary Liu was succeeded by acting Governor Qian Yunlv, a politician with ties to the Youth League, and was supported by lower-level officials with ties to Tsinghua University or the Youth League, is further evidence of the attempt to continue policies that Hu Jintao had years before helped set in place as Guizhou party secretary.

Yunnan, by contrast, had top leaders with extraordinarily long tenures who survived the national wave of retirements of top provincial leaders in 1993 (Bo 1996).[23] The two top positions in Yunnan during 1985–1995 (and beyond) were especially stable, each being held by just one powerful local leader from a nonpoor area of the province. Party Secretary Pu Chaozhu (1985–1995) was a localist who had risen from the local government of his birthplace, Yuxi, the largest tobacco-growing region and one of the wealthiest areas in Yunnan. Among the ninety-five provincial party secretaries to serve during the reform era, Pu's nearly decade-long tenure was the fifth longest. Serving an even longer tenure (twelve years), Governor He Zhiqiang (1985–1998) was the longest-serving Chinese provincial leader from the post-Mao era.[24] Governor He was a member of the Naxi minority and a native of Lijiang, which subsequently became one of the most popular and well-developed tourist sites in the province. Both of these long-standing top leaders reached the apex of their careers in Yunnan and retired from politics after their long stints there. The pair were also two of the four members of the self-named *Diannan Bang* ("southern Yunnan clique") of local leaders who stayed in power long past 1993 (when, as we have noted, approximately 20 percent of provincial officials, including most of the Guizhou leadership,

23. According to Bo, officials who successfully grow the economies of their provinces are most likely to be retained (although not promoted). Bo also notes that central authorities tend to retain minority provincial leaders longer than others, in part because they are "scarce resources" (Bo 1996, 149). This explains the lengthy tenures of Governor He Zhiqiang in Yunnan and Governor Wang Chaowen in Guizhou, but it does not explain not the nearly decade-long tenure of Secretary Pu Chaozhu in Yunnan, who is a member of the Han majority.

24. The ranking data were provided by Philip Hsu of National Taiwan University.

were retired).[25] This group focused on developing the sectors that were crucial to rapid economic growth in Yunnan—tobacco, highways, mining, and tourism. The development of each of these areas was large in scale and primarily benefited the Yunnan counties that were already nonpoor. Not coincidentally, these policies also directly served the economic interests of the areas that the four members of the *Diannan Bang* called home.

After Secretary Pu and Governor He at last retired, the next two Yunnan party secretaries served approximately three years each. Gao Yan (1995–1997) was transferred from his post as governor of Jilin province to become the Yunnan party secretary just after Pu Chaozhu retired. After his service in Yunnan, Gao (the protégé of former Premier Li Peng) was promoted to the position of president (equivalent of minister) of Power Generation, but in 2002 he fled to Australia to escape punishment for corrupt activities (Oakes 2004; Eckholm 2002).[26] The next party secretary, Linghu An (1997–2001),was assigned from his position as vice minister of the Ministry of Labor. Linghu's career prospects were reportedly dimmed by the arrest for corruption of Governor Li Jiating, who served during 1998–2001, concurrently with Linghu's term in office and after He Zhiqiang retired. For his part, Li Jiating, a Tsinghua University graduate, was born in Shiping, a tobacco-producing county in Yuxi prefecture, but had served for three decades in Heilongjiang province as vice governor and later as vice secretary of Harbin Municipality. Thus, just one of the party secretaries and governors who had served after Pu and He retired in the mid- to late 1990s can be considered local and that one, Li Jiating, although born in Yunnan, had spent most of his life and career in a province in the opposite corner of China. Moreover, although many of the vice governors serving under Pu and He over the course of the 1980s and the mid-1990s had extensive ties to Yunnan politics, only two of the subsequent eight vice secretaries were local. This lack of localist ties in Yunnan also helps explain Yunnan top officials' continuing compliance with central development strategies.

Weighing the Factors

Three primary conclusions emerge from the analysis so far. First, the pattern found in the two provinces is consistent with the literature on central-provincial relations. Given the strategic location of Yunnan and its position in the Chinese national economy, we expect Yunnan officials to have been

25. The other two members of this group were Li Jiating, the disgraced former party secretary, who was also born in a tobacco-growing region, and Yin Jun, the head of the Yunnan People's Congress and a native of the nonpoor tourist area of Dali.

26. Gao was under suspicion for corruption related to the Three Gorges Dam project. Oakes (2004, 481) also notes that Gao was being investigated for suspect activities that had occurred during his tenure in Yunnan.

much more responsive to central priorities than Guizhou officials, and indeed this turned out to be the case. The center directed much more investment to Yunnan, supported the development of its tobacco and tourism industries, guided the construction of its extensive roadway system, and generally nurtured its policies to promote rapid economic growth.

Central-provincial relations worked quite differently in Guizhou. The propensity of Guizhou to deviate from central policy when local needs demanded started early. For instance, the province was considered a pioneer in the policy to return agriculture to household responsibility after the dismantling of most communes in the early 1980s—policies crucial to the impressive rate of poverty reduction in China in 1978–1984. Although Anhui province is often cited as a pioneer in agricultural reform in the early 1980s (Chung 2000), Guizhou-based scholars argue that their province was equally pioneering, if not more so. Several Western scholars substantiate this claim. According to Lynn White (1998), Guizhou had returned a higher proportion of its land to farmers than Anhui did. Moreover, during the fervor of the Cultural Revolution, Guizhou officials reportedly bravely expanded private plots and established production quotas for households rather than for production brigades. Similarly, during the later stages of the Great Leap period, Guizhou leaders allowed households to set quotas for sideline production (Goodman 1986, 132).

Just as they had done during the pre-reform period, Guizhou leaders during the reform carefully justified their actions by couching them in terms of central policy or by citing central directives that appeared to support the unconventional strategy that they were implementing. Central authorities were consistent in their overt support of, and even demand for, the development in Yunnan of tourism, the highway system, and especially tobacco, whereas the center seemed to tolerate that the policy in Guizhou was less in compliance with central dictates. By 1993, Beijing had apparently accepted and even supported some form of Guizhou exceptionalism, with central leaders such as Vice Premier Zhu Rongji overtly allowing and supporting provincial leaders' attempts to reduce poverty, even at the expense of economic growth. Nevertheless, because the center relied on development, including rapid industrialization and economic growth, as a primary mechanism to reduce rural poverty, the policy in Guizhou deviated markedly from the central policy, as well as from the path that most other provincial governments, including Yunnan, traversed.

Although central-provincial relations appear to fit Guizhou and Yunnan better than Huang's version of elite analysis, there is nevertheless an important element of elite motivation to this story. Huang's approach overlooks two important elements: (1) the type of officials that were politically influential (Huang's theory assumes that having a formal title automatically translated to influence) and (2) the characteristics of the specific locations from which these elites originated (Huang does not look at the origin of officials on a level lower than the province). Regarding actual political influence, although it is true that the CCP secretaries in Guizhou for most of the years between 1978 and 1993 were outsiders or centralists, the longstanding localist provincial governor, Wang Chaowen, was especially influential, compared to his counterparts in other provinces. By the time that Secretary Liu Zhengwei took up his position, Wang had already served as governor for several years. Thus, according to local scholars, Wang was already positioned with a well-established local network and strong policy positions to be more influential than his relatively hands-off outsider superior. Localists were also influential during the post-1993 period. The vice secretaries and vice governors of post-1993 Guizhou were mainly localists and were also surprisingly influential compared to their outsider superiors; with some support from key central leaders, they were able to continue the previous policy direction. The Guizhou top leadership was not only dominated by localists but also by officials with ties to the CCP Youth League or Tsinghua University (which are taken to be signs of ties to Hu Jintao, who had supported these policies during his tenure as provincial party secretary) virtually without interruption from 1984 to the middle of the 2000s. This supports the notion that the promotion of the micro-oriented antipoverty policies remained consistent through this period.

The second element, a leader's specific point of origin (not just which province the leader was from) is also crucial. Guizhou localists had significant local ties to the poor counties of the province and were inclined to reduce endemic poverty there even at the expense of economic growth. Moreover, even though some of the top Guizhou officials were not local, they, particularly Hu Jintao, appear to have been motivated by specific ideas about how rural poverty should be addressed and by a nuanced multidimensional view of how to measure economic success that transcended simple measures such as GDP. As a result of their direct personal experiences in poor areas and the comparatively hands-off attitude of the central government, Guizhou officials were able to implement policies that opened up new opportunities for poor people. By contrast, top Yunnan officials, although hailing from rural counties, were born and had served for years in some of the wealthiest areas of Yunnan, including the tobacco-rich farming areas of Yuxi and the most attractive areas for promoting tourism. The Yunnan localist leaders were more interested in implementing growth-oriented policies that promoted industries that benefitted their home areas.

A similar pattern appears with the direct antipoverty efforts by the two provinces, adopted in both cases in 1993. The Seven-Year Priority Poverty Alleviation Programs of both Yunnan and Guizhou, although sharing the same goals as the central policy, varied from the central antipoverty initiative of that era. Although most of the wording of all three plan documents is precisely the same, there are revealing differences. For instance, the Guizhou plan omits several planks of the central plan, including the requirement to reduce poverty through integrating "trade, industry and agriculture" and through developing enterprises. The Guizhou policy also added several telling elements that are absent from the central plan (and from the Yunnan plan); for instance, it directs that all projects must employ at least 70 percent of the required labor from impoverished households and emphasizes subsistence projects. The Yunnan policy, unlike the central government plan (and the Guizhou plan), specifically emphasizes long-term development in its antipoverty plan; for instance, according to the plan, "the choice of specific poverty reduction programs should not only satisfy the immediate demand of food and housing for the poor, but also consider long-term and sustainable development. The arrangement of particular anti-poverty programs shall be determined based on a combination of short-term and long-term views, and focus on profit." In another section, the Yunnan plan calls for "developing social-economic service institutions, gradually standardizing and professionalizing scattered family businesses, expanding the scale of production and improving quality, thus increasing competitiveness." In addition, missing from the Yunnan plan (but included in both the central and Guizhou plans) is a policy to use funding from the food-for-work program for rural transportation projects, the requirement to employ poor people in assistance projects, initiatives to build water conservation projects, and the provision of employment services and technical training. Thus, the Guizhou antipoverty policy, much like its overall economic strategy, deviates from central policy in ways that are more consistent with the effort to reduce poverty through opportunities that are sufficiently small in scale to allow poor people to participate. By contrast, Yunnan differs in emphasizing larger-scale development and in omitting several elements of the central plan that do not conform to the Yunnan developmental state strategy.

What about the initial conditions of the provinces that scholars posit, along with central versus provincial leaders, as being important to understanding provincial variation? Even though Guizhou and Yunnan had similar initial conditions, this factor cannot be completely rejected. For instance, it appears that the recent history of Guizhou and the smaller groupings in which its minorities lived (see chap. 4) contributed to the success of the province in poverty reduction, facilitating provincial leaders' ability to encourage migration. Nevertheless, compared to the other possible explanatory factors discussed here, this factor contributes much less to our understanding of Guizhou economic policies during this period. (Moreover, as we see in chap. 4, minorities from both provinces do in fact migrate, and rural residents from minority regions in Yunnan also migrate at higher rates than those from the rest of the province.)

Thus, each of these major factors—central constraints and opportunities, characteristics of provincial officials, and (to a lesser extent) initial conditions—contributes to our understanding of the differences between the two provinces. These factors are not in conflict. China watchers can and should use all these factors in concert to understand provincial policymakers. In the case of Guizhou, however, both initial conditions and lack of central constraints were factors that permitted Guizhou leaders to create and implement its unorthodox economic strategy.

The second primary conclusion we can draw from this analysis relates to the theory of provincial elite motivation. As noted earlier, this fourfold categorization of provincial elites predicts outcomes that are the opposite of what we have found, reflecting weaknesses in this conceptualization. Furthermore, the analysis of provincial elites in China, as conducted by Huang and others, has focused on elite origins in the aggregate and is based on inadequate assumptions about power. First, the provincial elite analysis assumes that localists will vehemently support provincial interests and resist any central dictates that oppose such interests. In Guizhou and Yunnan, however, localists of very different ideologies, characters, and origins contested and helped define exactly what was in the provincial interest. In Guizhou, localist leaders defined provincial interests primarily as reducing rural poverty; in Yunnan, by contrast, localist leaders interpreted provincial interests in a manner more consistent with the dictates of the central government (which, in any case, was paying closer attention to Yunnan). Second, elite analysis assumes that centralists will implement policies in close alignment with the central leaders. If this were true, among all the provincial leaders discussed here, none should have been more sensitive to central demands than Hu Jintao, the rising centralist who (even at the time) had great prospects for advancement. Despite this, Hu proved to be an innovative leader, implementing strategies that were in many ways inconsistent with central dictates.

Although the outcomes here are inconsistent with the predictions of elite analysis, this does not mean that we should reject this approach completely. After all, elite analysis does quite well on other issues, such as predicting inflation and the collection of central taxes, in which provincial interests are clearer, and it does so based on data that are readily available. But for the analysis of particular provinces, a more nuanced and less aggregated analysis based on all available data is justified. This is especially true regarding issues in which what constitutes provincial interest is far from clear-cut and is subject to political contestation and interpretation.

The third primary conclusion we can draw from this analysis is that Guizhou appears to be pivotal to our understanding of Hu Jintao, the current top Chinese top leader, and of the origins of his thinking. As a prominent member of the fourth generation of Chinese leaders, Hu Jintao broke several times from the policies of his predecessor, Jiang Zemin. One area of disagreement between the two leaders is encapsulated in Hu Jintao's Scientific Development Concept (part of his vision for a Harmonious Society). Despite being contested (Zheng 2007), this approach was institutionalized in 2006 as "*the* policy orientation of the Party" (Zheng, Wang, and Tok 2006, 2).

Through these policies, Hu has sought to temper some of the GDP-first policies of his predecessor in favor of improving the livelihoods of Chinese rural residents, reducing income inequality, investing in grassroots education and health care, and focusing on the environment. The social problems that emerged during Jiang's tenure had, to some, called into the question the very legitimacy of the CCP, a political party that was supposed to bring prosperity to the people. Hu's policy shift was designed to reestablish that legitimacy (Saich 2007; Guo 2008; Fan 2006). In this spirit, the central government introduced criteria for evaluating local officials that reflected the new weight placed on social indicators other than GDP (Lam 2006).

Scholars have presented several possibilities for the origin of Hu Jintao's ideas. David Shambaugh (2008) suggests that theorists associated with the Central Party School, which Hu Jintao led for nearly a decade (1993–2002), were responsible for developing and even originating the Scientific Development Concept. It was at this same school that the theory was first launched in 2005 in an important speech for provincial party leaders (Chen 2007). Zheng Yongnian (2007) traces the seeds of these ideas to the 1980s, to the humanitarian socialism of General Secretary Hu Yaobang, Hu Jintao's mentor and political patron. While others may have made important contributions to this idea, both before and after this period, evidence suggests that Hu Jintao himself personally contributed the initial ideas behind the Scientific Development Concept and also implemented policies consistent with them during his poorly understood and infrequently studied tenure in Guizhou.

Because this policy echoes the approach that Hu and his colleagues adopted to address economic challenges of Guizhou in the mid-1980s, it is not surprising that, of the five "major changes" that are associated with the Scientific Development Concept, three directly reflect the spirit of the micro-oriented state.[27] The first, which discusses changes in the concept of development, criticizes the overreliance on GDP, which tends to promote the pursuit of production and efficiency at the expense of social equity. The second seeks to temper the exclusive reliance on injecting capital resources to promote GDP, in part by seeking alternative paths to prosperity. The third, which focuses on the measurement of performance, criticizes the tendency of local authorities to construct "image projects" or "achievement projects" that have little impact on social problems. The construction of these wasteful projects contributes in the short term to increasing the GDP, but does little good for the broader provincial economy (Zhao 2006). As a part of this overall framework, many of the specific approaches to economic management that Hu advocated in Guizhou are also evident on the central level. The shift toward a serious emphasis on rural road construction, emphasized

27. The other two major changes are change to the economic structure and change to the functions of government. See Wei Liqun (2005) for a more detailed description of the Scientific Development Concept.

in the Eleventh Five-Year Plan and the 2007 "No. 1 Document," is a case in point.[28] Although Hu Jintao was not the only influential leader setting the course taken by Guizhou (Secretary Zhu Houze and the long-serving Governor Wang Chaowen were also highly influential), his approach to developing the economy is nevertheless telling.

Given this understanding of the causes of the differing policy approaches that leaders of these two provinces adopted, in chapters 3–6 I turn to the specifics of those approaches. Surprisingly, both the Yunnan developmental state approach and the Guizhou micro-oriented state approach were expressed through similar policy areas. Starting in the late 1980s and early 1990s, the leaders of the two provinces adopted markedly different approaches to the construction of roads, migration of poor rural residents, development of tourism, and development of the coal industry. Chapters 3–6 focus on each of these policy areas in turn.

28. Signs of the shift in Chinese road construction plans were apparent in 2002 (Lin 2007).

3

Roads

Building Connections to Markets

> If you hope to become wealthy, first build a road.
>
> —Chinese saying

In an administrative village in northwestern Guizhou, a large crowd of farmers, carrying heavy loads of fresh-cut vegetables on their back, had gathered. An informal weighing station had been set up, and the villagers waited patiently as men in a large green truck weighed and purchased their produce. This truck turned out to be a green China Post truck, like those common in cities throughout China. These middlemen had somehow gotten hold of the truck, which they used to transport their purchases in bulk to larger markets in Bijie and Guiyang, where greater demand and higher prices awaited. The farmers, for their part, were also satisfied with the arrangement because the prices offered by these intermediaries were significantly higher than those offered at the local market. Much of this activity had been sparked by the recently constructed roadways that connected the nearby villages to the town. Because the town was also connected by road to the prefecture capital of Bijie and larger cities beyond, this relatively modest road system provided numerous new opportunities for the villagers in the entire area. The roads not only improved the access of middlemen but also reduced travel time between the villages and marketing towns where villagers could buy and sell goods, obtain better marketing information, and even hear of work opportunities outside the area.

What are the economic effects of road construction? Empirical research on the impact of roads suggest that, although the linkage between increased road infrastructure and economic growth is robust, its connection to poverty reduction is more complicated. By reducing travel time and costs and by facilitating the transportation of goods and people, roads can stimulate the production of cash crops, encouraging economic diversification, improving incomes, and enhancing quality of life. Roads allow farmers to bring land that was formally inaccessible into cultivation. Roads also can make it easier for public officials to enter villages to deliver health care, basic education, and extension services, among other government programs. New industries and services can become viable due to the reduced costs of travel (Howe 1984). Research by the Asian Development Bank on the relationship between roads and positive economic development throughout the world concludes that roads stimulate economic growth, with every 10 percent increase in infrastructure boosting GDP by an average of 0.4 percent (Jalilian and Weiss 2004). Studies estimate that the typical economic returns for roads are approximately 80 percent and reach as high as 200 percent in extreme cases (Estache 2004). Thus, a consensus among academics and policy makers has emerged that appropriate, well-designed, and well-positioned roads promote economic growth by connecting people to markets, reducing the costs of transportation and inputs for farmers and the costs of food for urbanites (Fan and Chan-Kang 2008).

The evidence concerning the connection between roads and poverty reduction is more mixed (Howe 1984). Many argue that roads reduce poverty directly by lowering the costs of agricultural inputs, enhancing agricultural productivity, and increasing nonagricultural employment opportunities. Advocates also point to the benefits of roads for the poor in terms of opening up new markets for agricultural goods, enhancing information about market demand, and mitigating the effects of natural disasters and economic shocks.[1] Skeptics, in contrast, argue that roads have little relevance for the poor, that purported benefits of roads are exaggerated, and that road construction is often a conduit for corruption (Estache 2004; Bryceson, Bradbury, and Bradbury 2008). Hossein Jalilan and John Weiss's (2004) cross-national research concludes that the linkage between roads and poverty reduction is clearer for the better off among the poor (those earning an income of $1–2 per day, compared to those with incomes of less than $1 per day) and that this factor is significant only when combined with differences in education levels.[2] To bring countries to average levels of poverty, Jalilan and Weiss's model suggests that infrastructure improvements must be large.[3] Moreover, although some case studies found a direct link between road construction and poverty reduction, other case studies in Indonesia (Kwon 2000; Balisacan, Pernia, and Asra 2002) and the Philippines (Balisacan and Pernia 2002) demonstrated that increasing road stocks did benefit the poor

1. For instance, research in eighty-five districts in India concluded that government investment in roads increased crop outputs, rural nonfarm employment, and agricultural wages, all helping to increase the income of the poor (Khandker, Lavy, and Filmer 1994).

2. For instance, when schooling increases by 25 percent, the poverty elasticity over the $1 headcount increases to -0.38.

3. According to the study, to reduce the poverty headcount rate to the sample average (of the total sample) at current schooling levels, Bangladesh would need to enlarge its infrastructure stocks by 13 percent and India by a stunning 35 percent.

but that the mechanism was indirect—through economic growth.[4] Despite this skepticism, most experts recognize that rural infrastructure such as roads typically reduces poverty, especially when the roads are dispersed widely enough to serve areas with low population densities (Estache 2004). Therefore, the link between roadways and poverty reduction often depends on the available opportunities, as well as on the particular structure of the road and whether it provides access to the poor.

Resolving this debate requires an examination of the effects of different kinds of roads. Not just the simple presence of roads but also their volume, distribution, and structure contribute to poverty reduction. After all, road types are numerous, with myriad functions and contrasting effects on growth and poverty. For example, highways can allow the efficient transport of imports and exports, better linkages for investment and aid, reliable and convenient conveyance of people to and from neighboring provinces, and more comfortable ferrying of visitors to popular tourist spots. In this way, highways enhance productivity, potentially contributing a great deal to promoting economic growth. But unless a poor person lives adjacent to a highway or convenient feeder road, he or she will not benefit directly from highway construction (Jalilian and Weiss 2004; Estache 2004; Fan and Chan-Kang 2008). Thus highways by themselves are rarely sufficient to reduce poverty among dispersed, often isolated rural populations, and they are too expensive to build in far-flung areas.

Moreover, highways in poor areas will be clogged with tractors, horse-drawn carts, and peddlers attempting to sell products to passing motorists or to middlemen, unless countermeasures are taken. Therefore, designers of highways are often compelled, in the interests of efficient transportation, to construct fences and impose tolls to prevent such intrusions on traffic flows, further blocking poor people from benefiting directly. Further, highways are expensive to build and maintain, especially in mountainous areas, and constructing highways often diverts funds from other projects that would benefit poor people more. Also, highways can reduce the demand for labor by substituting capital, as the trucking industry and other services replace less efficient but more labor-intensive practices. Highways in some contexts will not help stimulate agriculture much because some of the produce is consumed locally and transportation costs represent a small proportion of the overall costs of production (Howe 1984). Worse, if highways are used to bring in imports, such as cheaper food, that effectively compete with cottage industries that support poor people, such roads can increase poverty. In China, for instance, Melinda Herrold-Menzies (2005) describes the sharp declines in prices for agricultural produce that occurred as Weining county, Guizhou, became linked with Chinese highway and railroad systems,

4. Kwon's (2000) report shows that, for provinces in Indonesia with good roads, growth is better for the poor (i.e., the elasticities of growth with respect to poverty increase).

hurting local farmers. Thus, roads can undermine the local economies on which poor people depend for their livelihoods while creating opportunities and spurring growth in other areas and for other people.

By contrast, a country road linking poor villages to nearby market towns can make a significant difference in the lives and livelihoods of poor rural residents at a fraction of the cost of a highway. Rural roads are especially effective in China because they meet many of the conditions that facilitate the link between roads and poverty reduction. For instance, in other countries, due to inequitable land distribution, building even modest roads has not benefitted the poorest and has even exacerbated the gap between rich and poor. China, however, has distributed its land among the rural population. Farmers do not own the land but, rather, receive long-term land use rights. The buying and selling of rural land is prohibited (renting to other farmers is allowed). Due to this favorable distribution of land, building rural roads in China can benefit both the rich and poor more equally and affect rural land prices less than in other countries.

Furthermore, in other countries outside labor is used to construct roads, reducing the benefits for the poor. In China, however, locals build most rural roads, often via the food-for-work program. In other countries, these roads have not made a significant difference due to the lack of incentives and complementary government programs (Howe 1984; Fan and Chan-Kang 2004). In contrast, the privatization of much of the transportation in rural China, combined with the marketization of the prices of agricultural products, provides incentives for the use of roads. Further, the relatively well-developed system in China of extension and other government services supports farmers, helping ensure that roads translate into increased farmer income.

Country roads vary a great deal in quality, width, and materials—from concrete roads to dirt roads. My fieldwork made it clear that even dirt roads vary a great deal in terms of overall quality, durability after heavy rains, and accessibility by various sorts of vehicles. Although such variation can make some difference in the effectiveness and efficiency of the road, the existence of such linkages, especially dependably navigable ones, can significantly improve the lives and incomes of ordinary people.

Towns in China have long been the locus of markets (Skinner 1964). For the rural poor, a modest paved road, or even a dirt road, that leads to a market town or county center makes a greater difference than a highway by increasing access to markets and information. Reducing time to markets also enhances farmers' incentives to produce marketable products and, over time, can increase confidence in the value of investing in or borrowing money for expensive productive assets such as fruit trees. Linkages with county towns increase the exchange of market information as farmers learn what products and handicrafts are in demand and can shift their production practices accordingly. Country roads can also reduce the price of agricultural inputs, such as seeds, fertilizers, and tools, and increase farm productivity. Navigable roads expand the range of middlemen who drive into rural areas to buy surplus agriculture directly from the farmers and sell it in farther-flung markets. New roads also spur migration to job-rich urban areas, often far from home villages, by increasing information about the job market and facilitating the movement of people (Howe 1984; Fan and Chan-Kang 2008). For instance, Jocelyn Songco's (2002) research on Vietnam indicates that improving low-grade roads can help improve mobility, reduce prices of goods, and mitigate health hazards. In all these ways, improving village roadway networks can have a profound effect on poverty.

On the other side, skeptics counter that the benefits of rural roadways are exaggerated. For instance, Bart Minten and Steven Kyle (1999), in a study of Congo, find that dirt roads double transportation costs compared to paved roads. Hilton Root, C. S. Shaijumon, and Ramya Ghosh (2004) note that allowing communities to decide by themselves about infrastructure improvement projects tends to spur the development of access roads, creating an undersupply of growth-enhancing, higher-grade roads.

Nevertheless, even if dirt roads are more expensive to use than they may appear, they are typically much cheaper to construct and, thus, are more easily spread across wide areas. Overall then, although highways can spur the growth of the economy as a whole, in many cases rural roadways contribute more to rural incomes and livelihoods.

Most research on roadways to date, however, does not separate roads by type, which might explain the mixed results in studies of the relationship between roads and poverty reduction (Fan and Chan-Kang 2008). And, until recently, quantitative studies weighing the costs and benefits of different types of roads have underestimated the value of rural roadways. In part this is because the quantitative data available, especially the more commonly available GDP statistics, did not capture some of the social benefits of roads, including better access to schools and the facilitation of household production. These quantitative studies often assume that the primary goal of transportation projects should be improving economic efficiency. The resulting policy recommendations tended to channel investment to wealthier areas where the willingness to pay for transportation and other goods is greater, to the detriment of alternative goals such as equity (van de Walle 2002). Although more innovative methods implemented during the past decade have allowed researchers to take such goals into account, disappointingly few policy-relevant academic articles have addressed the issues of distribution, affordability, and regulation of roads (Estache 2004, 18). More recently, however, theorists have recognized the increasing importance of rural roads for poverty reduction. Such recognition culminated in a World Bank report, signed by then president James Wolfensohn, which notes a shift "more toward funding rural roads, feeder roads, and urban transport so that the poor can reach jobs and markets more easily, collect water and fuel more quickly, and get to schools and health clinics more efficiently" (Wolfensohn 2000, 35).[5] The evidence I present here supports the argument that different kinds of roads affect growth and poverty differently.

To understand the role of roadway construction in China, we must first understand its road classification system. The Chinese government classifies roads into categories based on function, expected use, and number of vehicles per day.[6]

- *Expressways* have auto-only lanes, with controlled access for high-speed travel.
- *Class 1 highways* also have auto-only lanes, with partially controlled access, that link important political and economic centers and key industrial and mining areas.
- *Class 2 highways* are main highways that link political and economic centers, large industrial mining centers, or busy areas on the outskirts of cities.
- *Class 3 highways* are ordinary main roads that link county seats and cities that are prefecture level and above.
- *Class 4 highways* are secondary roads that link county seats with townships.
- *Nongraded roads* are nonpaved township roads of improved earth.

These are the six grades of roadway that statistical bureaus commonly record in the national and provincial statistical yearbooks. Also important are:

- *Village-to-market roads,* which are usually navigable dirt roads below nongraded roads that link villages with townships, towns, and counties.

Although these roads have only recently been recorded in the official statistics and are rarely considered in analyses of roadways in China, they add significantly to the volume of road stock in each locality. For instance, although Hebei in the early 1990s had 47,000 kilometers of these village-to-market roads, official statistics for Hebei recorded only a total of 41,000 kilometers of roads from the six official categories (Benziger 1993, 4). The lack of accurate data on the volume of village-to-market roads impedes the calculation of road densities and exacerbates the difficulty of analyzing the effect of roads on poverty reduction. Both provinces started including this type of road in their statistical yearbooks, adding them to the "non-rated road"

5. The World Bank *World Development Report 2009,* in contrast, does not make this kind of distinction, praising the importance of high-quality roads for reducing "distance," one of the three key factors that it highlights.

6. The information in this section is drawn primarily from Benziger (1993); Fan and Chan-Kang (2008).

category. Yunnan did this starting in 2001, while Guizhou included them in 2005 (State Statistical Bureau various years-b, various years-c).

In most areas, the lack of a road does not mean that farmers cannot get to the market town. If no road exists between villages or between villages and county towns, the farmers themselves will beat a path. These simple paths, sometimes difficult for visitors to traverse without getting lost, are helpful, but they are not nearly as important for poverty reduction as even the most rustic dirt road—as long as that road is navigable by car. Interviews conducted during my fieldwork revealed that farmers in some areas of Guizhou and Yunnan were so isolated that they had to walk for hours just to get to their fields and traversed far longer distances to get to the nearest market town. Such isolation generally precluded selling agricultural surpluses due to the difficulty of transporting commercially viable volumes of agricultural goods across vast distances. In addition, some areas, for technical reasons, have little hope of obtaining even dirt roads. For instance, in some mountainous areas, where agricultural conditions are already the most difficult, road construction of any sort is unfeasible. These areas often face severe hardships, prompting some experts to argue that relocating the residents of such places provides the only hope of effective poverty reduction (Unger 2002).

Over the course of the reform period, the Chinese government focused on roadway construction as an integral part of its national growth strategy and dramatically increased the total road length in the country. In the first few years of the reform period, the government contribution to capital construction for roadways was similar in scale to that of the pre-reform era. By 1984, the central government had more than doubled its spending in real terms, from RMB 481 million to RMB 1.25 billion. Chinese government spending also increased sharply after 1992, from less than RMB 3 billion to more than RMB 5 billion. In support of government efforts to grow the economy and manage transportation bottlenecks, the majority of this spending was on constructing higher-grade highways (Benziger 1993). By the 1990s, the construction of highways became a high central government priority, with massive investment in the expansion of roads, especially in the coastal provinces. With these waves of investment, by 2002 the length of Class 1 highways in China had quadrupled, whereas the length of lower-grade roads had increased only 3 percent. Annually between 1980 and 2002, the length of Class 1 highways increased by 28.5 percent, Class 2 by 14 percent, Class 3 by 5.1 percent, and Class 4 by 3.5 percent; the length of nongraded roads decreased by 1.3 percent because some were improved to higher-class roads (Fan and Chan-Kang 2004, 32).[7]

7. Subsequently, starting with the 2005 Development Plan for Highways and Waterways in the Eleventh Five-Year Plan, the Hu Jintao administration shifted the focus from highways to smaller-scale rural roads. This change was impeded, however, by the reliance by the

In addition to this imbalance in road types, the distribution of roadways in China is also inequitable. From the mid-1980s to the turn of the century, the government focused the majority of its road construction in the faster-growing coastal provinces. This was a reflection of the central government's prioritizing development in that region and of the fact that coastal governments had greater resources with which to construct roads. Overall, the funding of roads was primarily borne by local governments, which were responsible for approximately 85 percent of the capital expenditures for highways between 1998 and 2001, compared to the central government share of approximately 8.3 percent and the share funded by foreign capital of approximately 3.8 percent (Fan and Chan-Kang 2004, 36).[8] The rapidly lengthening highways in coastal China, combined with its geographical advantages and more liberal economy policies, explains much of the economic differences among the regions in China, both in terms of agriculture production and of economic growth overall (Felloni et al. 2001; Demurger 2001).

Road building in the inland and western provinces has until recently lagged behind the coastal region. Despite the shift in central government attention during the late 1990s toward developing the long-neglected inland and western areas, the Chinese coastal areas still received the majority of central funding for roads. Even though the central financing for roads there decreased, it still averaged 50 percent in 1998–2001, compared to the inland provinces, which averaged 26.8 percent, and the western provinces, which averaged 23.1 percent (Fan and Chan-Kang 2004, 21).

Despite the unequal distribution of road construction, studies in China nevertheless have linked road system improvements to poverty reduction. For instance, Fabrizio Felloni and colleagues (2001) show that higher road densities in China improved agricultural production as well as the productivity of land and labor. Fan Shenggen, Zhang Linxiu, and Zhang Xiaobo (2002) conclude that central government spending on road construction had a large and important impact on economic growth and poverty reduction; every yuan invested in roads increased rural GDP by RMB 8.83, and every RMB 10,000 invested in roadways lifted 3.2 poor people out of poverty. Although not as effective for reducing poverty as investing in agricultural research and education, these authors find that spending on road construction was more effective than other infrastructure investments, such as electricity and rural telephony. Jyotsna Jalan and Martin Ravallion (2002) discover that road density was a key factor in the escape by Chinese households from regional "poverty traps," areas in China that had difficulty in emerging

---

center on provincial implementation and on the clear preference of the provinces for highways (Lin 2007).

8. Moreover, reliance on local extra-budgetary revenues for road construction exacerbated this unequal situation. Wealthy provinces had more extra-budgetary revenues, which came from fees and levies, usually from businesses (Wong 2002, iv, 10–12).

from poverty on their own. Sylvie Demurger (2001) concludes that the relationship between infrastructure endowment and economic growth in China is concave[9] and that improvements in provinces with poor infrastructure benefited growth more than adding infrastructure in provinces with already well-developed infrastructure. Although these studies—like those conducted outside China—do link increasing road endowments with positive economic results, they also typically treat all roads as equal, failing to differentiate the types of roads.

Filling this gap, research by Fan Shenggen and Connie Chan-Kang (2004) not only links road construction with economic growth and poverty reduction but also concludes that different types of roads have had different economic effects in China.[10] For instance, although each kilometer of high-quality roadway generates on average RMB 1.7 million in total GDP (compared to RMB 1.1 million for each kilometer of low-quality roadway), high-quality roads have no significant effect on agricultural GDP; in contrast, each kilometer of low-quality roadway generates an average of RMB 290,000 of GDP in the agricultural sector. Similarly, although investment in high-grade roads makes no significant difference in agricultural productivity, each yuan invested in lower-grade roads generates RMB 7.66 in agricultural productivity. In addition, high-quality roads generate less rural nonfarm GDP than do low-quality roads (RMB 730,000 per kilometer vs. RMB 1 million per kilometer). Given their lower construction costs, low-quality roads have a higher return on investment than higher-quality roads in terms of GDP overall in both the urban and rural nonfarm sectors.[11] In terms of poverty, the length of low-quality roads again makes a greater difference (each kilometer reduces poverty counts by twenty-two people) than the length of high-quality roads (each kilometer reduces poverty counts by nine people). Low-quality roads also bring a greater return on investment for poverty reduction. For instance, for every 1 million yuan invested in low-quality roads, 177 rural residents emerge from poverty; the same amount invested in higher-quality roads brings but 13 rural residents out of poverty. This difference is most true in southwestern China. Whereas 1 million yuan invested in high-grades road there reduces rural poverty by nearly 65 rural residents, the same amount invested in low-grade roads reduces rural poverty by a remarkable 1,239, four times more than in the northwest region,

9. This conflicts with the conclusion in Fan, Zhang, and Zhang (2002) that the relationship between road spending and poverty reduction is linear in China.

10. Fan and Chan-Kang define *high-quality roads* as expressways and Class 1 and 2 highways and *low-quality roads* as Class 3 roads and below. Although they do consider substandard roads, their data may not have captured all village-to-market roads.

11. There is a difference between Fan and Chan-Kang's (2004) conclusions and mine regarding the impact of rural roadways on GDP growth. This is probably because their rural roadway classification includes not just town and village roads but also all other roads, Class 3 (such as those that link counties and prefectures) and below.

the next highest region in China. Thus, these researchers conclude that for China lower-quality roads of Class 3 and below are far superior to high-quality ones at directly reducing poverty.

Yunnan and Guizhou Roadways

As noted earlier, for the pattern of road construction to help explain the pattern of economic growth and poverty reduction found in Yunnan and Guizhou, the volume, distribution, and structure of the construction should be markedly different in the two provinces. We should expect to find that Yunnan engaged in building highways connecting its cities with its neighbors and that such roads not only primarily serviced nonpoor areas but also were structured so that poor people were not able to access them. Convincing evidence that such highways spurred economic growth in the province would include indications of increased trade or tourism. We should also expect evidence that the production and export of cash crops increased during this time and that these cash crops were primarily produced in the nonpoor regions of the province. In Guizhou, we would expect to find road construction of a different sort. We would expect to find that Guizhou leaders added primarily to the stock of provincial rural roads, especially increasing the numbers of the lowest classes of road that primarily link villages to market towns or counties. Moreover, we would expect that any more advanced roads constructed in the province served poor areas to a greater extent than in Yunnan. We would also expect more modest increases in Guizhou trade flows and in the production of cash crops that are exported to other provinces.

Overall, Yunnan has more total road length than Guizhou. At the beginning of the 1990s, road length in Yunnan at all levels totaled 58,123 kilometers, compared to 31,588 kilometers in Guizhou. Far more relevant for our understanding of the effect of roads on economic development and poverty reduction, however, is road density, a factor in which Guizhou exceeds Yunnan. In 1991, overall road density in Guizhou was 17.9 km per 100 km^2, exceeding the 14.75 km per 100 km^2 in Yunnan. By 1996, Yunnan ranked the third longest in total roadway length of any province in China (70,279 kilometers), whereas Guizhou ranked twentieth, even though its total roadway density still exceeded that of Yunnan (18.58 km per 100 km^2 vs. 17.84 km per 100 km^2). Moreover, even though Yunnan province constructed new roadways at a brisker pace than Guizhou, the road density in Yunnan did not catch up with or exceed that in Guizhou until after 1998.

More important than road length in explaining the particular patterns of economic growth and poverty reduction in the two provinces is the fact that the roads in Yunnan and Guizhou were of different types. The Yunnan government focused on developing its highway system. In an effort to increase its exports of cash crops and industrial products and to spur its tourism industry, the provincial government focused primarily on constructing expressways and Class 1 and 2 highways linking the province with its neighbors—three provinces and three foreign countries. The Guizhou leadership, following a plan that had originated under then provincial Party Secretary Hu Jintao (see chap. 2), focused instead on building Class 4 highways linking the county seats with townships and on building nongraded roads and village-to-market roads linking townships with villages. As a result, the road systems in the two provinces were structured quite differently. Even though the construction of all types of roads in Yunnan exceeded that in Guizhou for most of the 1990s, the structure of the Guizhou roadways helped link a higher proportion of its poor people to nearby markets, thereby providing them access to information on demand for agricultural products, as well as job opportunities within and outside the province.

Starting in 1992, Yunnan implemented its ambitious plan, which focused on building a set of six highways radiating out from the central axis of Kunming, the provincial capital (see table 4). Three of these linked Kunming with three major border crossings: two with neighboring Myanmar and Laos, and the third with Vietnam. Three additional roads linked Kunming with three provincial capitals: one to Nanning (Guangxi province), one to Chengdu (Sichuan province), and one to Guiyang (Guizhou province). The six spurs, consisting primarily of Class 1 and 2 highways, totaled 3,458 kilometers (Yunnan Nianjian Bianjibu various years). The Guizhou provincial leaders that same year announced plans for three main roadways: one east-west highway linking Hunan with Yunnan and two north-south roads linking Guiyang with Guangxi and Chongqing. These three roads totaled of 1,378 kilometers. The volume of funds used to finance roadway investments also contrasted between the two provinces. In 1991, Guizhou government announced that its fixed capital investments in roadways was RMB 79.1 million; this climbed to RMB 1.1 billion in 1996. Yunnan, in contrast, spent RMB 971 million in 1992, RMB 1.75 billion in 1993, and RMB 1.56 billion in 1994 on roadways. Whereas Yunnan spent nearly RMB 1 billion in 1992, Guizhou did not reach that level until 1996. Overall, during the Eighth Five-Year Plan (1991–1995), the Yunnan budget allocated more than RMB 7 billion to roadway construction. Even with its more modest ambitions, Guizhou needed an estimated RMB 12 billion for its entire plan, but the province could provide only a fraction of that (Gong 1996). In part for this reason, the Guizhou eastern spur was not completed until 2004, fourteen years after it was planned.

The distribution of lower-grade roads, found almost exclusively in rural areas, is difficult to determine systematically. Transportation maps, however, allow us to pinpoint the areas that higher-level highways serve. In Yunnan, despite the predominance of poor counties in the province, the highway system disproportionately serves the nonpoor counties. The six Yunnan

Table 4. Highway plans for Yunnan and Guizhou, 1992

Yunnan 1992 highway plans	Distance (km)
Kunming to Myanmar border	925
Kunming to Guizhou border	221
Kunming to Sichuan border	471
Kunming to Guangxi border	480
Kunming to Laos border	864
Kunming to Vietnam border	497
Total:	3,458
Guizhou 1992 highway plans	**Distance (km)**
Hunan border to Yunnan border	735
Guiyang to Guangxi border	321
Guiyang to Chongqing border	322
Total:	1,378

Sources: Author's calculations; Guizhou Nianjian Bianjibu (1993); Yunnan Nianjian Bianjibu (1993).

highways pass through 50 of its 127 counties but only 16 of these are poor. In contrast, the three Guizhou main highways connect 35 of its 86 counties, of which 17 are poor. Moreover, in the 1990s the Guizhou government planned fewer higher-grade highways that denied access to rural residents through the use of fences and tolls.[12] Not only did the Guizhou leaders focus the limited transportation funding on areas where it could benefit poor people, the highways they did construct were better distributed than those in Yunnan.

The Yunnan highway system was part of the successful provincial strategy to promote economic growth through increased tourism, trade, and tobacco production. The most popular Yunnan tourist sites are Stone Forest and Xishuangbanna (Shilin county), Dali, Lijiang, and Kunming (see chap. 5). In addition to investing hundreds of millions of yuan in constructing airports in each of these areas (except the Stone Forest, which is a mere 100 kilometers outside the capital),[13] the provincial government ensured that its new highway system also connected each of these spots with a high-quality roadway. These investments successfully promoted the tourism industry of the province. Due in large part to the construction of this highway system, the

12. By the late 1990s and early twenty-first century, however, Guizhou did have at least three roads (from Guizhou to Bijie, to Duyun, and to Zunyi) that excluded all but high-speed vehicular traffic.

13. Yunnan spent RMB 910 million on airports during the Eighth Five-Year Plan alone. Airport construction is a costly capital investment that might not save significant amounts of time in a province such as Yunnan. The economic impact is thus unclear.

Yunnan tourism industry grew from a minor part of the provincial economy to become a pillar industry, driving the development of the service sector and accounting for 5 percent of the total GDP of Yunnan. Nevertheless, the ability of the Yunnan tourism industry to reduce rural poverty was surprisingly limited (see chap. 5). The structure and distribution of tourism ensured that roads connecting cities to the tourist sites primarily benefited the nonpoor areas.

Similarly, the Yunnan highway investments also successfully spurred the exports of the province to its foreign neighbors. In 1981, Yunnan exports were valued at just over US$100 million and grew steadily at an average of 10 percent per year throughout that decade. In the early 1990s, soon after Yunnan leaders began the drive to connect the province with its neighbors, the exports of the province began to grow even more rapidly. In 1991 and 1992, Guizhou exports per capita were approximately one-half those of Yunnan, but this gap widened because the Guizhou trade grew much more slowly. Yunnan exports doubled between 1993 and 1995, whereas Guizhou exports increased only 70 percent during this period. Because Yunnan is a border province, we would expect the total exports for Yunnan to exceed those of Guizhou. The Yunnan road building projects bolstered this geographical advantage, contributing to the expansion of the Yunnan GDP. The more modest Guizhou highway system contributed less to trade, and the Guizhou economy overall also benefited less.

But, there is little evidence that the increase in Yunnan exports benefited its poor people to the extent that economists expect.[14] In addition to the fact that the Yunnan highway system crosses proportionally few of its poor counties, the main trade items are produced primarily by nonpoor people in Yunnan. The sectors benefiting from trade included cash crops (primarily tobacco), heavy industry (primarily chemicals), mining (primarily nonferrous metals), and machines and equipment; for instance, the exports of nonferrous metals from Yunnan more than doubled to US$144.7 million, chemicals doubled to US$138.25 million, and the export of machines and equipment tripled to US$96.3 million. The participation of the poor in these industries was generally limited. By contrast, the main exports from Guizhou in 1996 included not only manufacturing equipment (US$78 million) and chemical products (US$77 million) but also industries in which poor people have traditionally found employment, such as agricultural products, primarily tobacco (US$16 million), beans (US$9.13 million), rice wine (US$6.87 million), and blended fabrics (US$16.7 million). These data suggest that Yunnan industrial development primarily and disproportionately benefited its nonpoor and that the pattern in Guizhou was strikingly different.

14. Economists often posit trade as a favored mechanism for poverty reduction. See, for example, Dollar and Kraay (2001); Bannister and Thugge (2001).

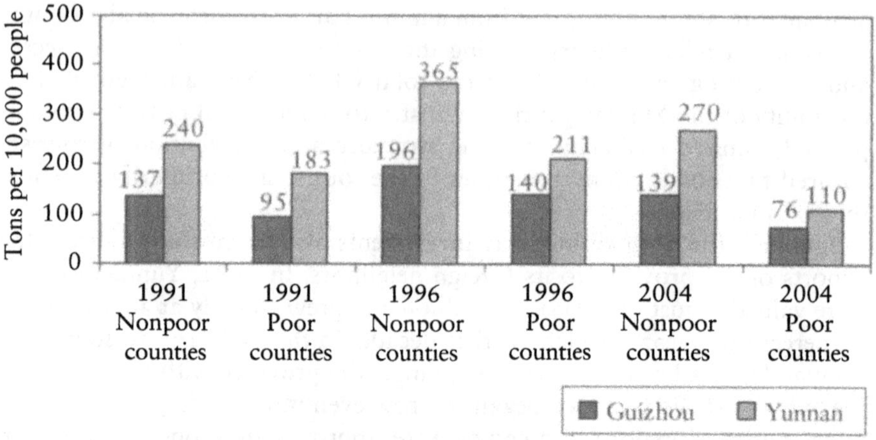

Fig. 2 Tobacco production per capita—poor and nonpoor counties in Yunnan and Guizhou, 1991, 1996, 2004.
Source: State Statistical Bureau (1992b, 1997b, 2005b; 1992c, 1997c, 2005c).

For tobacco, the story is similar. As mentioned previously, both provinces are major producers of tobacco, with Yunnan ranking first and Guizhou second in China. Although the total production of tobacco in Guizhou was consistently lower than in Yunnan, production in both provinces moved in parallel during most of the post-1978 period. Yunnan tobacco exports tripled overall from US$62.9 million in 1991 to more than a quarter of a billion dollars (US$258.9 million) in 1996, including a quintupling of exports of flue-cured tobacco (from 3,190 to 16,539 tons) and a tripling of exports of rolled cigarettes (from 4.2 billion to 13.3 billion cigarettes). Increasing exports of this cash crop might be expected to benefit poor farmers at least as much as wealthy ones, especially given the ranking of Yunnan as the top Chinese producer. But, as it happened, the development of highways helped primarily the nonpoor tobacco producers in Yunnan. This was in part because such farmers were largely in the best position to benefit from them (see fig. 2).

In contrast with the Yunnan highway plan, the Guizhou government focused primarily on constructing rural roadways, a plan that explicitly prioritized rural poverty reduction. Starting in the mid-1980s, a key element of the Directives Concerning the Work of Strengthening Poor Areas was the construction of town and village roads that would connect remote areas to the nearest market towns and quicken response times in case of natural disasters. Guizhou officials were helped by the central government *Yigong-Daizhen* (food-for-work program). This program, which started in 1984, reduces poverty directly by providing poor recipients with jobs and incomes (often in-kind). In addition, it indirectly reduces poverty by enhancing the skills of participants and constructing basic grassroots infrastructure. Under this program, rural residents in poor areas take part in government-organized infrastructure projects, including terracing land, digging wells for drinking water, improving irrigation, and building rural roads. These projects generally take place during the off-season, and thus farmers get a chance to supplement their income without the work interfering with their agricultural production. In exchange for their labor, farmers receive payments in-kind, including food, and after 1991, "industrial product coupons," which could be exchanged for farm tools, daily consumer goods, and other items. Studies of the food-for-work program show that it has had an important impact on the incomes and welfare of poor farmers (Zhu and Jiang 1995, 1996). The difference in spending on food-for-work programs by Guizhou and Yunnan is relatively modest. For instance, in 1996, the Guizhou budget allocated approximately RMB 9.6 per person to this program, ranking eighth among the Chinese provinces; the Yunnan budget allocated approximately RMB 8.5 per capita, ranking ninth (Ministry of Finance 1997). What is remarkable is that Guizhou spent more on this program than did Yunnan, although in almost every other category Yunnan spent much more.

Guizhou was also able to integrate its food-for-work program with other aspects of its strategy more successfully than did many other provinces. With an army of poor rural residents at its disposal, Guizhou leaders promoted the development of the rural roadway system of the province, combating poverty both directly, by putting poor people to work, and indirectly, by linking isolated villages to marketing towns. This strategy continued throughout the early to mid-1990s, when Guizhou policymakers reaffirmed the importance of rural road systems as a part of its poverty reduction policies. As two Guizhou-based scholars summarize this part of the strategy: "In 1991, a key provincial infrastructure project was to construct, expand, deepen and repave public roadways, particularly emphasizing the proactive application of the food-for-work program to build mountain roads, link administrative villages with navigable roads, and to support the construction of township and village roadways" (Wang and Zhang 2003, 403; my translation).

The 1994 Guizhou plan for poverty reduction explicitly linked the use of rural roadways with its antipoverty plan, by constructing "local roadways for poor towns and townships, as well as most market places and commercial areas" (Guizhou Nianjian Bianjibu 1995, 36). Overall, between 1989 and 1999, Guizhou invested more than RMB 4 billion to build 8,919 kilometers of roads linking counties and townships, thereby connecting for the first time 315 townships with their county cities (Ran and Lie 2000). Funded in part through the application of the food-for-work program as early as the mid-1980s (Zhu and Jiang 1995), the provincial and local Guizhou governments expanded and improved the rural infrastructure. In 1996, the Guizhou road density of its nonrated road (the kind connecting villages with towns) ranked third among the Chinese provinces. In 2000, the Guizhou road density for this kind of road still ranked third among the

Chinese provinces, and by 2005, it ranked second. By contrast, despite its well-developed highway system, Yunnan had a relatively underdeveloped country road system, in 1996 ranking twelfth in China for length and sixteenth for total density; in 2000, these ranks rose modestly to eleventh and fourteenth, respectively. Although the Yunnan government more recently has focused on constructing these kinds of village-to-township roads, the density of this category of roads in Guizhou consistently exceeded that in Yunnan—by around a 6:1 ratio in 1996 and 2000, and a 3:1 ratio in 2005 (Zhongguo Jiaotong Nianjian Bianjibu, various years; State Statistical Bureau, various years-b, various years-c).[15]

In addition to these township-based roadways, statistics culled from various official sources indicate that the total length of Guizhou village-to-market roads (not normally published in official statistical yearbooks) increased from 15,282 kilometers in 1985 to 22,534 kilometers in 1997. By the mid-1990s, the density of such roads in Guizhou (12.78 km per 100 km^2) exceeded that in Yunnan (7.58 km per 100 km^2) by about 40 percent. Moreover, whereas statistics for Guizhou suggest that more than 2,000 kilometers of village-to-market roads were built in 1993–1996, the length of such roads in Yunnan declined from 31,299 kilometers in 1991 to 29,876 kilometers in 1996. Although it might seem counterintuitive, during my fieldwork I found that country roads I traveled in Guizhou were of much higher quality than those in Yunnan. More packed, less muddy during rain, and wider, often with concrete borders on each side, Guizhou country roads were more navigable, probably reducing costs and facilitating the transportation of farm goods to market. Overall, a key element of Guizhou development was the construction of low-level roadways, which are vital for the village-level economy, although having limited impact on economic growth in the province (Yunnan Nianjian Bianjibu, various years; Guizhou Nianjian Bianjibu, various years).

The question of whether roadways spur economic growth or poverty reduction is linked not just to the *volume* of roadways, as implied in many quantitative studies that test correlations between road length and economic changes (see, among others, Jalilian and Weiss 2004; Fan and Chan-Kang 2008). As many social scientists and global leaders, such as James Wolfensohn, argue, the *distribution* and especially the *structure* of roadways matter just as much and probably more. Whether roads help poor people depends vitally on access by the poor to the roads.[16]

15. The statistics for nonrated roadways in Guizhou and Yunnan between 2001 and 2004 are not comparable. Yunnan began calculating its roadways using a different system, which Guizhou did not adopt until 2005.

16. Important additional factors, as van de Walle (2002) argues, include the economic potential of different areas and the effect of geography on costs. In Guizhou and Yunnan,

The distribution and structure of the roadways in both provinces, and the economic effects of such roads, are generally consistent with our expectations. The primary strategy of the Yunnan leaders in their road construction policy was to focus resources on building highways, which successfully stimulated the exports of the province and supported the development of the tourism industry. The Guizhou government, on the other hand, concentrated on rural roadways, becoming in the process a leading province in the density of such roadways. In implementing their policies, both provinces planned proactively. In addition, although these decisions affected the resulting patterns of provincial development, both policies primarily fall into the category of market facilitation because the intentions of each roadway policy was to expand market opportunities and access (although for different segments of the population and economy). Although the two provinces adopted a similar role for the state, they nevertheless did so while following different strategies. Yunnan leaders adopted a strategy that most clearly emulates the developmental state, promoting large-scale construction intended to maximize economic growth largely through industry. Guizhou leaders, in contrast, focused on small-scale activities and poverty reduction, which is more consistent with a micro-oriented state.

---

geography is a factor in understanding the impact of roads on poverty and development, but this factor interacted with roads in similar ways in both provinces.

4

Migration

Go East, Young Man (and Woman)

> Move a tree and it dies. Move a man and he thrives.
>
> —Chinese proverb

The livelihood of the Zhaos, a Miao family living in impoverished Leishan county (the name means "Thunder Mountain") in Guizhou was greatly enhanced by the work of their indomitable daughter. At a relatively young age, this remarkable young woman made the arduous trek to Guangdong province, one of the wealthiest areas in China, to seek work. There, she was quite fortunate; she found work in a small shop, helping with sales and stocking inventory. Her hard work earned her several hundred yuan per month, most of which she sent back home to support her parents and younger brother. In spite of her good fortune, however, this young woman faced many difficulties in Guangdong. For instance, she felt compelled to hide her minority status for fear that prejudiced employers might not hire her. Despite such hardships, she worked hard, and her wages helped to defray the costs of sending her younger brother to school.

Migration in China has helped to reduce poverty for millions of families like the Zhaos. At the same time, however, the effects of migration on economic growth and poverty reduction are not straightforward. Rural-to-urban migration contributed to both poverty reduction without growth in Guizhou and growth without poverty reduction in Yunnan. Understanding the role of migration in the puzzle requires that we first examine the development of migration in these two provinces and in China as a whole, and the complex ways it has influenced the lives of the rural poor.

Starting in the early 1980s, Deng Xiaoping's reforms sparked fresh waves of migration in China, flows that had previously been dammed by the strict controls over population movement established in the early years of the PRC.[1]

1. The 1949 revolution and the subsequent establishment of the communist regime did not end migration so much as suppress uncontrolled population movements. The government initiated much of the migration that occurred during that period.

Directly after the reform, starting in 1978, the majority of rural-to-urban migrants were former urban residents who had been compelled to move to the countryside. This group included previously purged political leaders; radical students who had been sent down to the countryside to bring revolution to the peasants; and others who had traveled, voluntarily or otherwise, to the countryside during the pre-reform era (Wu and Zhou 1996, 25). Migration for economic purposes was effectively prohibited during the early years of the reform period, although many thousands of people still migrated to cities in search of work between 1978 and 1985 (Wang 2002). After the government relaxed migration restrictions around 1984, the flows of rural residents migrating to cities, primarily of those seeking economic opportunities in the rapidly industrializing Chinese urban areas, increased rapidly (Du, Park, and Wang 2004, 1).[2] Despite the rough life and discrimination that economic migrants experienced in cities, the opportunities for many young people working in construction or labor-intensive manufacturing were often far superior to staying in the country and supporting an overcrowded family by farming tiny plots of land.

Other patterns of population movements were also seen during this era, such as international, rural-to-rural, urban-to-urban, and (rarely) urban-to-rural migration, but rural-to-urban migration dominated the mid-1980s onward as tens of millions of primarily young rural laborers brought inexpensive labor to cities of all sizes, further stimulating industrialization and construction in the Chinese coastal cities.[3] Simultaneously, such flows reduced poverty in the countryside, both by reducing the number of mouths to feed and by the migrants' contributing small but significant remittances back to their families. Many migrant families saved a portion of these remittances, accumulating the capital needed to start small businesses once the migrants, endowed with new experience and skills, returned to the countryside.

Social scientists studying migration expect migration to be spurred by regional differences in wages and income. In his classic conception, W. A. Lewis

2. Before 1985, the majority of rural-to-urban migrants were students who had been sent out to "promote revolution" among the rural population and were returning to the urban areas from which they had originated. In contrast, after 1985 one survey revealed that more than one-third of all migrants listed finding employment as the primary motivation for moving (Wu and Zhou 1996).

3. Migrants are notoriously difficult to count. Fearing legal consequences, many migrants avoid officials of every kind, including census takers, especially before reforms legalized their activities. Moreover, a large percentage of migrants migrate temporarily, returning home often, making it more difficult to determine an individual's actual residence. To make matters worse, scholars studying the complex issues of migration in China face numerous methodological challenges, exacerbated by inconsistent definitions and analytical frameworks (Rozelle et al. 1999). As a result, estimates of the total number of rural-to-urban migrants, by experts and officials alike, vary widely. Nevertheless, most experts agree that the number of migrants leaving the countryside for the city grew from a trickle between 1978 and 1985 to tens of millions by the 1990s.

(1954) argues that surplus labor in agriculture will transfer to industry due to differences in income and that migration will cease only when urban and rural wages are equivalent. Michael Todaro (1969) amends this conception by arguing that migration occurs because of perceived, rather than actual, differences in income.[4] Both Lewis and Todaro expect migration to reduce economic inequality and poverty. These expectations are tempered by barriers to migration, such as legal restrictions on population movements, available information about opportunities in other regions, and costs of migration. Such barriers can be mitigated through social networks—connections with friends and relatives who migrate first, arranging jobs and housing for those who come later, thus reducing the costs and risks of migration. Governments can also lower these barriers by facilitating the labor market (providing training, information, and help finding a job), thus spurring movements of labor to areas with higher incomes, reducing poverty and spurring economic growth in the process.

These expectations are largely consistent with the patterns of migration seen in China during the post-1978 reform era. Nevertheless, as Ma Zhongdong (1999) argues, the initial wave of migration from rural to urban areas diverged from the expectations of these mainstream economic theories in at least one aspect—the poorest rural residents from the poorest Chinese provinces did not migrate first. Rather, the first wave of migrants to take advantage of rapid industrialization in the Chinese coastal cities came from the relatively less-well-developed areas of the rapidly growing Chinese coastal areas. Poor rural residents from the relatively underdeveloped inland and western regions of China faced additional barriers, including a lack of information about job opportunities and prohibitively expensive transportation costs.[5] As Ma (1999) calculates, the propensity to migrate was highest among those in the wealthiest provinces and municipalities on the coast and was relatively high in the less-developed but still relatively wealthy coastal provinces of Liaoning, Shandong, and Fujian.

Migration, combined with agricultural reforms and other factors, improved the livelihoods of coastal Chinese workers to such an extent that, by the early 1990s, the most severe forms of poverty were primarily concentrated in the more remote regions, away from the urban and industrial centers. Although the isolation of the regions with endemic poverty made

4. Variations on this "relative income" theme that have been applied to China include imbalances in the ratio of the amount of land to the amount of labor and capital (Wu and Zhou 1996). Others argue that relative distances are important (Lin, Wang, and Zhao 2004).

5. Other studies suggest that the ease of transportation, measured by the availability of a bus route through the home village, makes little difference in migration rates. This is because transportation contributes little to the total costs of moving and because convenient transportation also enhances the likelihood that local industries can succeed and thus absorb local surplus labor (Rozelle et al. 1999). Perhaps, then, disaggregating the various types of transportation systems, such as buses, is crucial to understanding migration patterns. We might also speculate about the effects that different types of bus systems have on the local economy.

finding jobs in those areas difficult, easing restrictions on migration encouraged many rural residents in western China to bear the risks and expenses of rural-to-urban migration. In the late 1980s and early 1990s, vast numbers of migrants from inland and western China joined the flows of migrants and sought economic opportunities not only in cities in their own provinces but also in those of other provinces. As Scott Rozelle and his coauthors (1999) argue, migrants of both genders increasingly came from remote areas between 1988 and 1995. By 1993, the percentage of laborers working in nonagricultural sectors in western China grew faster than in the rest of China—by 9 percent annually in southwestern China, compared to 6.6 percent in eastern China and 5.3 percent in the central provinces (Du, Park, and Wang 2004, 5). At the turn of the twenty-first century, the rate of migration from southwestern China (9.3 percent) had exceeded the national average (8.5 percent). From this region, 5 percent of the population moved out of their native provinces and primarily to the coastal areas, compared to the national interprovincial migration rate at the time of 3.42 percent.[6] Thus as the legal restrictions relaxed and information and transportation infrastructure improved, the patterns of migration in China appeared to resemble patterns of migration that economic models anticipate—relatively poor laborers migrating from areas in which their labor was plentiful to areas in which it was more valuable (Lin, Wang, and Zhao 2004).

In addition to these factors, the establishment of social networks among migrants reduced the costs and risks of migration throughout China—particularly in western China. Typically, braver and more educated members of a village were the first to migrate. If these pioneers succeeded in finding jobs, they generally introduced other members of the same village to their workplaces, arranging jobs for them, for instance, before returning to their home villages for holiday festivals.[7] One survey of migrants revealed that more than three-quarters of new migrants first found employment through people from their home province and often migrated together with small groups of friends and relatives from home (Zhou 1997).[8] In contrast, if no one leaves the home village in the first place, a vicious cycle ensues—lacking

6. Not all poor regions experienced similar migration rates. For instance, in northwest China in 2000, the migration rate as a whole was 5.72 percent, of which only 1.74 percent emigrated outside the province.

7. A survey of migrants conducted in the mid-1990s in four Chinese cities discovered that nearly three-quarters had returned home the previous year for the Spring Festival holiday (Knight, Song, and Jia 1999).

8. The Chinese government has also recognized the virtues of chain migration, particularly regarding the positive cultural changes. Central government documents laud the ability of migration to spark further migration and create more modern attitudes, not only in the migrants but also in their home villages. In this, one document is not atypical in arguing that "a great many laborers from China's west have already become missionaries that preach the eastern way of life and production as well as culture and skills to the western regions" (State Council LGPAD 2003).

connections, rural laborers are unwilling to move. Rozelle and colleagues (1999) show that migration networks are highly significant—the most highly correlated factor they examine—in creating opportunities for further migration. For instance, villages with no out-migration in 1988 had only a 6 percent chance of experiencing out-migration by 1995, whereas areas with established networks at least doubled their number of migrants by 1995. Lawrence Ma and Xiang Biao's (1998) study of migrants in urban areas shows that migrants band together in identifiable enclaves with those from their home provinces, for both social and practical reasons. As the authors suggest, "It is rare to find any peasant in the city who is not living or working with a few *laoxiang* [people from one's hometown]" (Ma and Xiang 1998, 560).

Social networks are especially important given the reluctance of rural migrants, particularly temporary and female ones, to use institutionalized channels to obtain job market information (Fan 2002; Zhang 2006). Many were also reticent to use employment agencies because the credibility of such agencies was often dubious and ads spread throughout the countryside were mistrusted. Ultimately, social networks were typically the most trustworthy and reliable sources of job opportunities for rural migrants.

The Chinese central and local governments gradually relaxed restrictions on migration and played an increasingly proactive role in promoting migration. However, even as the government lifted these restrictions, other policies and social pressures had already emerged, deterring migration. These included job discrimination, lack of safe working conditions, and the harsh form of justice that local law enforcement sometimes arbitrarily meted out to migrants. This occurs despite the reputation that migrants developed for working hard without complaint.[9] This reflects an ambivalence held by the local governments in provinces that have become the common destinations for migrants about the costs and benefits of high volumes of migrant inflows. This ambivalence is rooted in fears about job competition between rural migrants and urban residents, as well as about heightened crime (Zhao 2000). Officials from the home provinces, meanwhile, have become concerned about the tendency of residents with the most human capital to be the first to migrate away from the province. Although central government authorities were not blind to the benefits of economic growth and poverty reduction brought about by migration, they also feared the inherent instability caused by millions of often unregistered migrants outside the purview of municipal officials, who had few mechanisms for enforcing laws, such as

9. For instance, a survey of employers in four Chinese cities revealed that the majority (60 percent) were satisfied with their migrant workers, whom they had hired for their ability to endure hardship without complaint, in addition to their willingness to accept lower wages and to perform tasks that urban workers were unwilling to do (Knight, Song, and Jia 1999).

those related to family planning (Knight, Song, and Jia 1999). Efforts made on behalf of local government officials at the provincial level and below to control migration varied a great deal from place to place and over time.

We would expect rural-to-urban migration in China to reduce poverty. But, because the poorest rural residents often lack the wherewithal to migrate, these flows might not contribute directly to poverty reduction. In fact, some evidence suggests that the most skilled and best-educated laborers leave the villages disproportionately in search of work. One survey revealed that residents of villages with annual incomes under RMB 3,000 per capita were less likely to migrate than were residents of middle-income villages (Li 1994, in Rozelle 1999). Moreover, those who migrated tended to be endowed with the most human capital and were among the youngest and best educated in their villages (Rozelle et al. 1999, 388–90; Yang and Guo 1999).[10]

In spite of this, economic deprivation is a primary factor in the propensity to migrate, and migration is a major channel toward poverty reduction. Research based on national and provincial samples confirms that, although many of the early migrants hailed from relatively wealthy provinces, migrants tended to come from poor and remote, although relatively urbanized, villages (Ma 1999). More recent evidence suggests that, although the poorest among the poor might not have the resources to migrate, migration as a whole reduces poverty. Du Yang, Albert Park, and Wang Sangui (2004) for instance, find an inverted-U relationship between average income and propensity to migrate; that is, those who are neither the poorest nor the wealthiest tend to migrate to cities. The peak of this inverted U is at income levels near the poverty line for China (RMB 640 per capita in 1997—approximately US$78). Moreover, a survey of all poor counties in China reveals that migrant families had on average less land and larger families than did nonmigrant families and that they tended to live in hilly and mountainous areas, farther away from market towns than nonmigrant families (Du, Park, and Wang 2004). Another survey confirms that poor villages ranked as "the biggest beneficiaries of emerging migration markets" (Rozelle et al. 1999, 388). Overall, the poorer the region, the greater were the benefits of migration (Ma 1999). Moreover, a survey in Hubei province concludes that less well-off households experienced a higher rate of income growth due to migration, suggesting that migration may help reduce income inequality (Zhu and Luo 2008).

In leaving home, rural migrants contribute to poverty reduction by reducing the number of people for whom the family must regularly provide. Moreover, belying the stereotype of the shiftless and wasteful migrant worker, the typical migrant focuses on work; infrequently spends time or

10. Compared to non-migrants, migrants also tend to be single, male, and younger (Yang and Guo 1999; Hare 1999; Rozelle et al. 1999).

excessive money on food and alcohol; and relies on inexpensive leisure activities for entertainment, such as visiting local scenic sites or watching television (Lan 1997). The vast majority of migrants work diligently and spend frugally, mailing the bulk of their earnings to their home villages to provide for basic family needs, the education of siblings, the improvement of housing, and other necessities.[11] Qian Wenbao (1996) shows that such remittances are of a scale that makes a major difference in the household economy, although these effects are felt primarily on household income. By comparing the net incomes of migrants with those of average rural families at the origin, Ma (1999) also shows that remittances are especially beneficial in poorer noncoastal provinces, where the income ratio is 5:1 in favor of families with migrants. J. Edward Taylor, Scott Rozelle, and Alan de Brauw (2003) also find that remittances bolster rural incomes by 16–43 percent. A study of six provinces in 2000 concludes that, on average, migrants remit one-third of their total income, and families with migrants have incomes per capita on average 77 percent higher than those of families without migrants. Migrant remittances as a proportion of total income are greater the poorer the family. Whereas migrant income constituted approximately 43 percent of the income of the wealthiest 50 percent of rural households, it represented 62 percent of the total income of the poorest 10 percent of households in the sample. Migration diversifies household incomes, reducing the dependency of rural households on income from agriculture. Whereas two-thirds of the income in households without migrants consists of agriculture-based income, that figure drops to 46.2 percent in households with migrants (Du, Park, and Wang 2004, 13–14). Among residents of the poor counties in China, controlling for resource endowments, households with migrants tend to have per capita incomes 12 percent higher than those households without migrants. Zhu Nong and Luo Xubei (2008), simulating the impact of the absence of migration on income, predict that without migration Hubei households with migrants would see their income per capita drop by 17.1 percent. A similar simulation conducted on three Guizhou villages revealed that, without remittance income, poverty incidence would increase by 13 percent (Xing et al. 2008). Overall, then, remittances make an important contribution to reducing poverty rates in these areas (Du, Park, and Wang 2005).[12]

11. One survey of migrants in four Chinese cities discovered that in 1995, less than one-third of migrants remitted no money and that the majority of these nonremitters were female migrants who intended to remain in the city. Average remittances exceeded RMB 1,200 per year, more than one-fifth of migrants' total income (Knight, Song, and Jia 1999). Sociologist Li Qiang's (2001) survey of Sichuan migrants found that 70 percent of all migrants remitted some money back home.

12. Using a poverty line of RMB 635 in annual income, Du, Park, and Wang (2005) find that poverty rates after remittances declined from 67.1 to 49.2 percent in 2000.

In addition to reducing rural poverty, migration helps spur urban development and economic growth. Migrants contribute to the growth of the areas to which they migrate by providing low-wage services that urban workers, endowed until the mid-1990s with cradle-to-grave job protection and urban residence permits that guaranteed them a degree of social protection, remain unwilling to perform (Knight, Song, and Jia 1999).

In contrast with its impact on urban areas, migration contributes only modestly to the income growth of rural areas of origin. Because migrants are almost exclusively the youngest, best-educated, and most vigorous people in their village (Rozelle et al. 1999; Yang and Guo 1999; Hare 1999), migration often removes the most productive workers from the village. In two villages with significant remittances that Qian surveyed, migration actually reduced agricultural production because of the loss of labor. He concludes, "the impact of out-migration on local economic development in these two villages turned out to be more negative, although some of the remittances were invested in some small household businesses" (Qian 1996, 138). Similarly, Taylor, Rozelle, and de Brauw (2003) argue that reducing the village labor force reduces incomes from crops, although it does not reduce the overall yields. This is because some of the remittances, which partially make up for lost labor, are used to purchase agricultural inputs, making agriculture more productive but more costly.

Over the long term, however, migration can help develop rural areas, primarily through remittances that are used to start businesses when the migrant returns home.[13] The extent to which this occurs is debatable. The survey conducted by Taylor Rozelle, and de Brauw reveals only weak evidence that households reinvest remittances in "self-employed activities," and it also finds that these investments rarely returned immediate profits (2003, 94). Another survey of five villages revealed that, although remittances in four villages increased household income, in only two of these villages did migration spur new businesses (Qian 1996). The absence of a link between remittances and productive investment appears to be particularly true in poor areas. As de Brauw and Rozelle (2008) demonstrate in their study, because of the especially low returns to capital in impoverished villages, this relationship is even weaker in poorer villages than in nonpoor ones. Overall, this suggests that migration provides urban China with far more economic

13. Knight, Song, and Jia (1999) suggest that a majority (57 percent) of migrants surveyed planned to return home and that less than 10 percent planned to farm when they returned. Only approximately 14 percent planned to settle permanently in the city, although this proportion might have increased due to subsequent reforms that allow some migrants in some cities to obtain urban residence permits. The majority of migration is temporary for three reasons: (1) as migrants age, their ability to earn money through their physical assets declines; (2) forming and settling down with a family increasingly becomes a goal; and (3) the skills and knowledge obtained in urban areas can be productively applied in rural areas (Ma 1999, 785).

growth that it does rural China (especially in poor areas), although poor rural areas do benefit through reduced poverty.

Migration in Guizhou and Yunnan

Although Guizhou and Yunnan shared many attributes throughout the 1980s that might lead us to expect that the patterns of migration in the two provinces would be similar, the actual migration rates in the two provinces were dramatically different; Guizhou had significantly higher rates of migration than Yunnan during the 1990s (Fan 2005).[14] During the mid- to late 1980s, the migration rates in both provinces (as in most western provinces, save Sichuan) were low; legal restrictions, lack of information, distance, and insufficiently developed migrant networks deterred many potential migrants. Starting in the late 1980s and increasingly in the early 1990s, Guizhou saw an upsurge in migration, reaching a pace that by 1996 exceeded the average rates in China as a whole and in southwestern China and dwarfed the more modest increases in Yunnan migration (see fig. 3 later in this chapter). Moreover, Guizhou migrants remitted money back home, although usually in quantities insufficient to invest in productive businesses.

Despite the fact that the migration of this inexpensive labor did stimulate economic growth, a large number of Guizhou laborers migrated to work outside the province, so migration contributed most to the GDP of other provinces. Many Guizhou migrants who left the province settled in neighboring Sichuan and Yunnan; the majority of them, however, settled in the wealthy coastal provinces. In 2000, for instance, more than three-quarters of cross-provincial Guizhou migrants (1.2 million people) settled in Chinese coastal provinces, including Guangdong (37 percent of all cross-province Guizhou migrants), Zhejiang (19 percent), Fujian (9 percent), and Jiangsu (7 percent). Significant numbers also settled in neighboring Yunnan (12 percent) and Sichuan (4 percent) (State Council Population Census Office 2002). Thus, in Guizhou, migration contributed to the pattern that emerged in the 1990s: poverty reduction without economic growth.

In contrast, the Yunnan migration rates, both internal and cross-province, were among the lowest in China. Because the majority—about three-quarters for much of the mid-1990s—of the relatively few rural Yunnan migrants stayed within the province, their labor contributed to both economic growth and poverty reduction in the province. Of its migrants who did settle outside Yunnan, a majority (62 percent, or 215,000 people) settled in coastal

14. In this discussion, *Guizhou migrants* and *Yunnan migrants* are natives of Guizhou and Yunnan, respectively, who have left their home village for work or training. I deal here with two kinds of migration: internal and cross-province. *Internal migrants* travel to urban centers that are in their native province; *cross-province migrants* travel to other provinces.

provinces, including Guangdong (19 percent), Zhejiang (14 percent), and Jiangsu (10 percent). Others (in larger numbers than Guizhou migrants) settled in inland provinces such as Sichuan (16 percent), Guangxi (4 percent), and Guizhou (4 percent). The relatively low Yunnan migration rates meant that Yunnan did not benefit from the reduction in poverty associated with migration.

The differences between the two provinces were stark enough to lead one economist to cite Guizhou and Yunnan as examples to emulate and to avoid, respectively, in stimulating migration.

> Where there is labor migration, there is also a rapid increase in wealth. At least such places collect start-up capital together with remittances from migration and the return of funds.... For example, Guizhou and Hunan, the great provinces for labor migration, earned a great amount of capital through migration over the past several years, and not only helped individuals become rich, but also helped the regions develop.... Yunnan has a lot of natural resources, but people from Yunnan are too lazy to go out for work. Therefore, their economy is clearly worse than other places. (Lu 2004, my translation)

According to three national sources of migration data for Guizhou and Yunnan (the 1990 and 2000 censuses and the 1995 1% population sample survey, a survey of 1 percent of the population taken between the formal population censuses), as well as the annual yearbooks (Guizhou Nianjian Bianjibu, various years; Yunnan Nianjian Bianjibu, various years; State Statistical Bureau various years-b, various years-c; Chinese Academy of Social Sciences, various years), between the mid-1980s and 1990 the migration rates among rural residents of Guizhou and Yunnan were lower than both the national and regional average.[15] According to the 1990 census, Guizhou and Yunnan residents were among the least likely to migrate in China. Some 777,500 Guizhou residents (approximately 2.4 percent of the whole population; Guizhou ranked twenty-fourth in China) and 1 million Yunnan residents (approximately 2.7 percent; Yunnan ranked nineteenth) had settled somewhere other than their hometowns by 1990, out of

15. Unfortunately, Chinese statistical sources on migration are difficult to use. First, the data underestimate the incidence of migration. Many migrants, especially in the early years, moved illegally and, despite the improving legal infrastructure in China, still experienced social discrimination. For this reason, poor rural migrants avoided social scientists and census takers, increasing the difficulty of making accurate estimates of the size and flow of migration. Second, the 1990 census, the 2000 census, and the 1995 1% survey calculate migration rates in different ways. The 1990 census considers as migrants all those who were away from where they had lived for the previous five years (which includes in-province migration), whereas the 2000 census considers as migrants all who were living in a province other than the one in which they were officially registered. The 1995 1% survey may be less accurate than either census in terms of its sampling. With these caveats in mind, a general pattern nevertheless emerges from these primary sources, as well as from my secondary sources.

34 million Chinese who had by then migrated. Overall, the patterns we see in Guizhou and Yunnan during this period were consistent with the pattern in China as a whole, in that migrants then primarily hailed from the coastal provinces. Rural residents in Guizhou and Yunnan, however, migrated even less frequently than those in other southwestern provinces.[16] Despite the similarity between the volume of migrants in Yunnan and Guizhou, one enduring element of the difference in migration between the two provinces became evident during this period—Guizhou migrants tended to travel to other provinces more frequently than Yunnan migrants did. According to the 1990 census, 40 percent of Guizhou migrants (the ninth highest percentage in China) traveled to other provinces. To compare, of the more than 1 million Yunnan migrants, only 27 percent (the nineteenth highest) migrated outside the province.[17] The differences between Guizhou and Yunnan widened between 1990 and 1995. According to the 1995 1% population sample survey, Guizhou migration slightly exceeded Yunnan migration in proportion to its population. According to this survey, approximately 2.7 percent of the total agricultural population of Guizhou (compared to 2.5 percent of Yunnan) had migrated by 1995. The total migration rates in both provinces increased in 1990–1995, but the proportion of Guizhou cross-province migrants grew, whereas the proportion of Yunnan cross-province migrants remained about the same as in 1990. Overall, two-thirds more Guizhou rural residents left the province than did Yunnan residents, despite the fact that, in 1995, the rural population of Yunnan exceeded that of Guizhou by more than 13 percent.[18]

These trends in Guizhou and Yunnan continued in 1995–1998, according to Chinese provincial data (see figs. 3 and 4). According to this source (which calculates migration rates differently than the other official sources), 1.4 percent of Guizhou residents migrated either internally or cross-province in 1995, far above the 0.16 percent of Yunnan residents who migrated but still below the 2.4 percent average of all Chinese provinces (Chinese Academy of Social Sciences, various years). The rates of migration for the two provinces grew steadily, with the Guizhou rate exceeding the national

16. For instance, during this period Sichuan ranked as the largest source of migrants in terms of total population (although the province ranked eleventh in terms of proportion of its population that had migrated, either internally or cross-province).

17. The Guizhou figures represent nearly 1 percent of the total Guizhou population; Guizhou ranks seventeenth among the thirty provinces counted. The Yunnan figures represent approximately 0.75 percent of the total Yunnan population, with Yunnan ranking twenty-fifth.

18. According to the 1995 1% survey, approximately one-half of Guizhou migrants departed the province to seek work (compared to 40 percent in 1990), whereas only 30 percent of Yunnan migrants left the province (basically the same proportion as in 1990). In all, according to this survey, approximately 1.3 percent of the Guizhou rural population had left the province by 1995, about double the proportion of the Yunnan rural population (approximately 0.7 percent of the rural population of Yunnan had left the province).

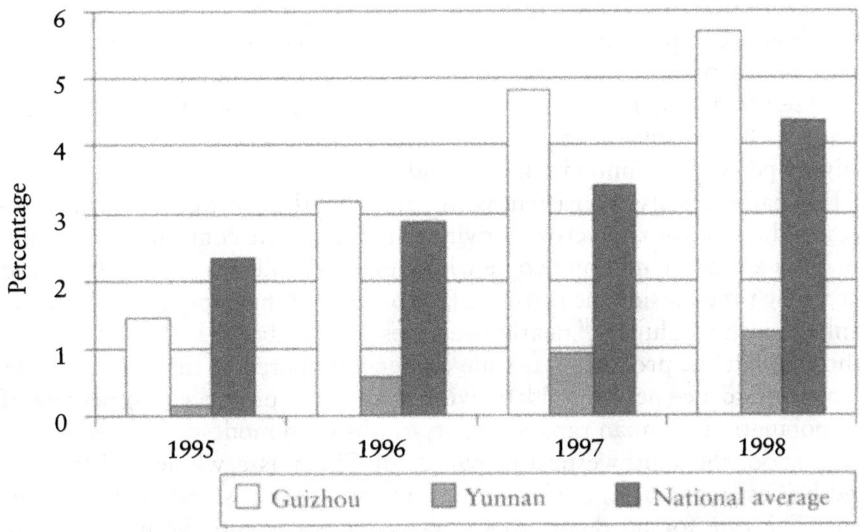

Fig. 3 Combined internal and cross-province migration rates for Yunnan and Guizhou, 1995–1998 (%).
Source: Chinese Academy of Social Sciences, 1996–1999.

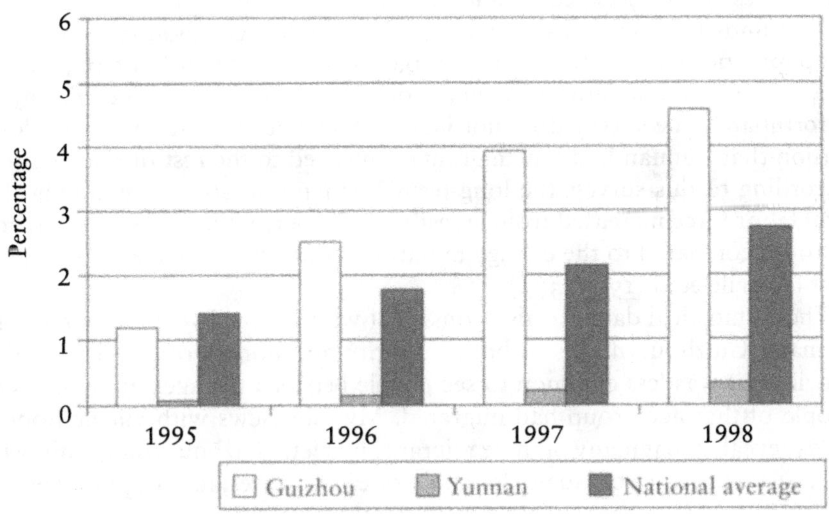

Fig. 4 Cross-province migration rates for Yunnan and Guizhou, 1995–1998 (%).
Source: Chinese Academy of Social Sciences (1996–1999).

average by 1996. By 1998, 5.7 percent of Guizhou rural residents lived away from home, compared to 1.2 percent of Yunnan rural residents and the average of 4.4 percent for China as a whole (Guizhou ranked tenth among Chinese provinces; Yunnan ranked twenty-fourth). Moreover, whereas the majority (80 percent) of the Guizhou migrants traveled to other provinces, only 30 percent of Yunnan migrants did.

This pattern is also consistent with data from the 2000 census, which indicates that the Guizhou cross-province migration rate continued to accelerate.[19] By 2000, 1.6 million people with Guizhou residence permits had lived for a long time outside the province (4.9 percent of the population; Guizhou ranked ninth in China),[20] nearly five times the number (312,800) of people who had left the province a decade earlier. Compared to this, the 343,542 Yunnan residence permit holders living outside the province (0.9 percent of the population; Yunnan ranked twenty-sixth) seem modest.

By 2000, the southwestern provinces of China as a whole had the second highest regional rate of migration in the country, standing at 9.3 percent. The rate for northeastern China was 9.4 percent; the national rate was 8.5 percent. Moreover, the southwestern region had the highest rate of cross-province migration, at 5 percent; the national rate was 3.4 percent (Du, Park, and Wang 2004).

Research by Western social scientists confirms this pattern. Estimating cross-province migration rates between 1990 and 2000 by calculating the differences between expected and reported populations, D. Gale Johnson (2003) finds that, whereas 2.27 million people left Guizhou (7 percent of the population) during the decade, 730,000 people entered Yunnan (adding 2 percent to its population). A survey of six provinces (Rozelle et al. 1999; unfortunately the survey does not include Guizhou) also supports the conclusion that Yunnan had few migrants compared to the rest of the country. According to this survey, the long-term Yunnan migration rate among the total labor force increased from an estimated 0 percent in 1988 to 4 percent in 1995, compared to the change in national rate from 5 percent to 12 percent (Rozelle et al. 1999, 372).

These statistical data are also consistent with my fieldwork observations. In many Guizhou villages in both minority and nonminority areas of the province, it was less common to see people between the ages of 16 and 35; people of that age group had migrated. My interviews with village households revealed that many of these migrants had left Guizhou, going mainly to the coastal province of Guangdong to work in factories, in shopping centers,

19. According to Du, Park, and Wang (2004, 7), the 2000 census data are more accurate for measuring migration because the census asked not only where respondents currently lived but also the location on their residence permits. Nevertheless, the 2000 census measures only migrants who had left the province and thus cannot be used as a source for internal migration.

20. Compare this figure with the average of 3.4 percent for China as a whole and the average of 5 percent for southwestern China (Du, Park, and Wang 2004).

or on construction sites. Most of the families had received remittances from these migrants, although in many cases the remittances were not large—typically a few hundred yuan per month. Interviews with Guizhou migrants who had returned home for festivals supported the conclusion that fewer Guizhou people migrate than Sichuan people but more than Yunnan people. For instance, my migrant interviewees, working in Sichuan, Guangzhou, or other provinces, almost invariably reported that Sichuan migrants were very common and were far more common than Guizhou migrants; Yunnan migrants were rare indeed.

These data show the contrasting migration trends in the two provinces. Guizhou residents participated in the second wave of migration that began in the late 1980s and early 1990s. Unlike migrants from inland provinces (such as Sichuan, Anhui, and Hunan), who participated most in migration from the 1980s, Guizhou migration started in earnest in the early 1990s. From the start, a majority of the Guizhou migrants left the province. Although Guizhou did not catch up with the scale of migration of more prominent provinces, its rural residents took advantage of the networks of earlier migrants and were well represented in the coastal, especially southeastern, cities where well-paying jobs could be found. On the other hand, Yunnan had very low rates of migration, and the majority of its migrants remained in the province.

But an examination of the migration rates in the two provinces tells only part of the story. It is also important to examine whether the migrants came from poor or nonpoor rural areas in the two provinces because migrants from poor areas make a more direct effect on rural poverty. Unfortunately, it is difficult to find systematic evidence about this. A survey of rural residents (Du, Park, and Wang 2004) in each of the poor counties in China reveals that, compared to Yunnan, Guizhou had a higher proportion of rural households with at least one migrant laborer. In poor counties in Guizhou, on average, one in five households had at least one migrant, and remittance income from those migrants probably supported these households.[21] Moreover, the Guizhou percentage was at least 8.5 percentage points higher than the Yunnan rate during the period of the survey (1997–2001). Moreover, the Guizhou proportion exceeded that of the entire southwestern region of China in 1998, 2000, and 2001; this is especially impressive given the status of Sichuan as an exporter of labor. Official sources also indicate that Guizhou households had more migrant workers than Yunnan households. In 2005, for instance, Guizhou had 0.58 migrants per household, dwarfing the percentage in Yunnan of 0.19, a gap that only increased

21. The 1990 census includes migration statistics from poor areas of each of the two provinces. The rates are almost identical—41 percent of Yunnan migrants and 40 percent of Guizhou migrants came from poor counties (Chinese Academy of Social Sciences, 1992). By the 2000 census, the rate in Yunnan had declined to 36 percent (Yunnan Provincial Population Census Office, 2002). Unfortunately, I found no equivalent county-level 2000 census data for Guizhou.

the next year (State Statistical Bureau various years-b, various years-c). The statistics are clear; overall Guizhou workers had a greater propensity to migrate than did those in Yunnan.

Much more evidence is available concerning the impact of remittances on poor areas in Guizhou. Data collected by the provincial labor employment office include only the funds that cross-province migrants mailed back home and do not include money that migrants brought back with them during holidays or money that they mailed within the province. As these statistics make clear, the remittances were collectively large and important, increasing in size starting in the early 1990s. The volume of remittances increased by several orders of magnitude between the early 1990s, when remittances totaled more than half a billion yuan, and the mid-1990s, when remittances reached a high of RMB 3.5 billion. Given that the Guizhou budget expenditure in 1995 totaled RMB 8.5 billion, migrant remittances made a major difference to the local economy. For instance, the Guizhou provincial labor employment office concluded that remittances sent back by migrant laborers exceeded the entire government revenue of twenty-two of the eighty-seven counties in Guizhou and that, in some cases, they were more than three times larger (Wang and Zhang 2003, 548).

Despite these promising numbers, my interviews with migrants living in Guiyang suggested that many of them, due to inexperience, have less well-paying jobs. For instance, at many construction sites in Guiyang, the management positions are mainly filled by people from the east coast while the foremen are typically from provinces with longer histories of migration, such as Sichuan. The Guizhou internal migrants toil in lower-skilled and lower-wage jobs. Similarly, interviews with migrants who had temporarily returned home for cultural festivals revealed that Guizhou migrants tend to work in lower-level jobs in the construction, manufacturing, and service industries. For that reason, the amounts of money sent home by the numerous Guizhou migrant workers are typically not more than a few hundred yuan each month and are usually insufficient to start a rural business.

My fieldwork in Guizhou and Yunnan uncovered only two examples of remittance income being used for productive investment. The first was at the tourist site in Langde, Guizhou (see chap. 5), where a plaque in front of a large, clean, wooden building housing public toilets indicated that the funds for construction had come from philanthropic migrants from that village. The other example was in a small Miao village in Guizhou where remittance money had sponsored a general store with an impressive ornate latticework window. When asked about the remittances and investment, informants typically reported that they had not heard of any successful investment using migrant remittances and that remittances were usually not sufficient to invest outside the farm and family. Although the Chinese literature (e.g., Wang and Zhang 2003) cites examples in which remittances fund successful industries (e.g., a bamboo furniture factory in Chishui county and a small rural factory manufacturing industrial bags in Zheng'an county), I found that in the majority of cases remittances from migrants were too modest to invest in productive enterprises.

Although remittances are infrequently used for productive assets, they do improve living standards. I found, throughout both Guizhou and Yunnan, that many families receiving migrant remittances lived at a higher standard of living than those with neither migrant-related income nor alternative nonfarm income. For example, many areas in rural Guizhou appeared to be experiencing a housing boom, with rural residents adding or improving their houses and even whole sections of villages moving several hundred meters down the road to construct new houses. A new wooden house can cost several thousand yuan, and the farmers constructing houses reported that the income from remittances, although rarely covering the entire costs, contributed to and made possible this new construction. Other uses of migrant income included educating younger siblings or cousins or purchasing farm animals. Both uses can make an impact on the prospects of a family over the short or long term. Nevertheless, due to the lack of increased productivity, they often have more modest, short-term effect on GDP.

Migrants often acquire skills and training that they would otherwise not be able to develop. In a township in central Weining county (Guizhou), one young woman left home to study hair care in Guiyang and then returned home to run a beauty parlor part-time from her mother's guesthouse. Although in this case the investment capital for the business came from her mother's business, by migrating the young woman was able to obtain the human capital needed to transfer her out of farming and into a service industry. Two other migrants, one from Guizhou and one from Yunnan, had opportunities to work in the tourism industry outside their home areas as ethnic minority entertainers. One, a Lisu woman from Fugong county, Nujiang prefecture (Yunnan), had worked in Fujian province until the SARS epidemic forced her out of the industry. After returning to her home county, she opened a successful car wash with her cousin. The other, a Dong minority woman, sang traditional songs for tourists at Huangguoshu Waterfall (Guizhou) and returned home years later to open a restaurant (one that rated a mention in a Lonely Planet guidebook; Mayhew, Miller, and English 2002) across the road from the Congjiang county bus terminal. Therefore, migration can provide new skills and experience that prove to be productive and profitable after these migrants return home.

Yunnan has unusually few migrants, both internal and cross-province. One possible explanation for this, that the prosperity of Yunnan makes migration unnecessary, is not convincing. The GDP of Yunnan is high, but its poverty rate is also high. Few of the poor people from Yunnan moved to wealthier areas, whether within the province or outside of it.

Why then did Yunnan have fewer cross-province migrants? When interviewed, older members of villages complained that many migrants who had left home had not succeeded in earning sufficient money to send more than a trickle of remittances back, in part because finding useful work was difficult. Younger residents in the age group likely to migrate cited two reasons for not migrating: a lack of education (i.e., they had not completed junior high school) and a lack of information (i.e., they had no friends or relatives outside the province who could help them find work). Chinese experts in Guizhou and Yunnan commonly cite the cultural differences between the two provinces to explain the relative lack of migration in Yunnan. The theoretical literature on migration cites an additional factor, geographical isolation/physical distance. Thus, we have five possible barriers to migration: lack of job opportunities, lack of education, lack of social networks, culture, and geographical isolation/physical distance.[22] One last barrier has received less discussion—government policy. I discuss each of these in turn.

The lack of job opportunities, a barrier that many older rural residents interviewees in Yunnan mentioned, is not commonly cited as a barrier to migration in Du, Park, and Wang's (2004) survey of poor counties throughout China. Many reports indicate that, despite poverty and underemployment in western China, numerous jobs go unfilled in the coastal provinces. Perhaps potential migrants miss these opportunities due to lack of information. Alternatively, the jobs that remain unfilled might be ones that require experience and skills that new migrants lack. Furthermore, some migrants I interviewed suggested that jobs that were available paid only slightly more than they could earn back home. Job posters hung throughout most villages in both provinces, but these were widely distrusted. Better social networks would probably increase the information about appropriate job opportunities in distant areas, just as they do for many rural migrants in other provinces.

The second barrier cited is education. When young people cite a lack of education as a barrier to migration, they typically mean the lack of a middle school education. This belief is reinforced by propaganda signs painted on public buildings throughout the countryside of both provinces that urge local residents to complete a middle school education before they migrate.[23] Moreover, most rural residents seem aware of the demonstrated link be-

22. Two of these (lack of education and lack of social networks) are consistent with Du, Park, and Wang's 2004 survey of male migrants conducted in six provinces. Although the most common barrier mentioned in that survey was labor demand (i.e., that labor was needed on the farm), few people cited this is as a factor during my research in Guizhou and Yunnan. This is not surprising; in both provinces, large families farm small plots of land. The next two most common barriers mentioned in the survey, however—education (25.3 percent) and information/social contacts (18.3 percent)—were commonly cited in my research. Women typically cited children (46.3 percent), farm labor demand (21 percent), and education (12.7 percent) as barriers to migration.

23. Examples of such signs, commonly seen in both Guizhou and Yunnan, include "Without graduating middle school, you will not be qualified to work outside" (*Chuzhong wei biye, Dagong bu hege*), painted on a public building in a township in Congjiang county, and "If you cannot finish middle school, you won't be able to go outside to work," (*Du bu wan chuzhong, Bu neng qu dagong*), painted on a public building near Langde town, Leishan county.

tween the number of years of education and the subsequent wages earned in coastal cities.[24]

Nevertheless, it appears that migrants in poor counties across China do not wait to complete nine years of education before migrating. Du, Park, and Wang (2005), for instance, find that the member of the average migrant household with the most education had been in school only 8.35 years and that in 1997 only 18.2 percent of migrant men had as many as 10 years of formal education. Taylor, Rozelle, and de Brauw (2003) reveal that the average migrant had 8.2 years of education. Thus, it appears that many migrants left home without having graduated from middle school (i.e., without nine years of formal education). Likewise, young Guizhou migrants rarely wait until they graduate from middle school before they travel to coastal areas in search of work. Offering even less support for this explanation, rural education in Yunnan is in some ways superior to that in Guizhou, as measured by spending per capita and schools per number of rural residents, and the two provinces were comparable in primary school enrollment in 1991 and 1996 (United Nations Development Programme 1999). Although by 2008 Guizhou boasted a higher proportion of junior high school graduates and above than Yunnan (44.6 percent vs. 39.5 percent), the two provinces ranked in the bottom four Chinese provinces in this category. Both provinces thus have a terrible track record for educating their people. Given this, the explanation that Yunnan residents migrate less due to a lack of education is not very persuasive, even though some Yunnan residents perceive education to be a factor.

The lack of social networks is also considered a barrier to migration. Recall that established social networks allow chain migration. As in other parts of China, Guizhou rural residents initially migrated to escape poverty and seek opportunities in coastal areas. In some cases, recruiters came directly into the towns, aided by the road networks. In other cases, more daring rural residents, individually or in groups, ventured to cities within or outside Guizhou in search of opportunities. A portion of these succeeded in finding positions and sent home relatively modest (but vital) amounts of money. These initial migrants facilitated the migration of others in their home areas, arranging jobs with their employers and persuading friends, either in letters or during holiday visits. In this way, the social networks sustained a virtuous cycle of migration.

But when social networks are lacking, this becomes a barrier to migration. Lacking contacts in richer areas, the residents of Yunnan rarely migrated. And most Yunnan rural residents, lacking friends and relatives who had successfully migrated to work in coastal cities, found it difficult to migrate.

24. According to the 2004 survey, in 1997 each additional year of education made migration 1.018 times more likely; moreover, by 2001 the effect of a year of education increased to 1.032 times more likely. In addition, each extra year of education increased wage income for migrants by 5.1 percent (Du, Park, and Wang 2004, 10–11, 14).

Differences in culture are also advanced as barriers to migration. Chinese academics offer several cultural explanations,[25] focusing on the history and living patterns of minorities in Guizhou and Yunnan. One common explanation is that ethnic minorities tend not to migrate, and because Yunnan has more ethnic minorities than Guizhou, Yunnan has less migration. This idea, however, rests on two assumptions that are inconsistent with the available data. First, although it is commonly assumed that Yunnan has proportionally higher ethnic minority populations, as we have seen, both provinces have nearly identical proportions of ethnic minorities (see chap. 1). Second, the sparsely available statistical information suggests that ethnic minorities do migrate and that their tendency to do so varies. For instance, an analysis of the 1990 census reveals that rural residents from minority counties[26] in Yunnan migrate at somewhat higher rates than those from nonminority counties and that the opposite is true in Guizhou (State Statistical Bureau various years-b, various years-c). Moreover, my fieldwork revealed that many minority groups in both Guizhou and Yunnan migrate, including the Dong and Miao in Guizhou and the Lisu in Yunnan. Culture does play a part in their migration but in a way quite different from what proponents of this explanation expect. For some migrants, their ethnic minority status provided an advantage in that it allows them to join entertainment troupes that perform minority songs and dances. In Guizhou and Yunnan, several of my female interviewees had previously done this kind of work. Other migrants joining the unskilled labor pool in the cities concealed the fact that they were ethnic minorities due to stereotypes that ethnic minorities are lazy or alcohol abusers.[27] Minority migrants feared that, if potential employers realized they were not of the Han majority, they would hire someone else. Therefore, ethnic minority status does not appear to be a major barrier to migration; it does, however, appear to play a part in strategies of migration.

A second cultural factor that Chinese scholars use to explain differing rates of migration is history. Guizhou, a relatively new province, is itself considered to be a migrant province. Many ethnic groups were pushed into the remote reaches of Guizhou by war, and members of the Han majority settled in Guizhou after 1250 A.D. through government resettlement programs (Oakes 1998, 89). Due to the patterns of migration and war, minorities in Guizhou also live in relatively smaller groups. By contrast, some

25. Many, like Lu Deming (2004), also invoke laziness to explain poverty. I saw little evidence, however, that Yunnan rural residents are any more or less motivated than Guizhou residents. Moreover, using laziness to explain the pattern of poverty reduction and economic growth would require explaining why Guizhou rural residents are more motivated than those in Yunnan (as the Guizhou lower poverty rates might suggest) while Guizhou urban residents were less so (as the much lower Guizhou GDP might indicate).

26. The Chinese government classifies sixty-four counties in Yunnan as minority counties; forty-nine counties in Guizhou as minority counties.

27. In 1882, a British diplomat dismissed Guizhou locals, saying that "a lazier set of people it would be difficult to find anywhere" (quoted in Oakes 1998, 99).

Yunnan minority groups can measure their histories in the province in millennia and live in larger, more concentrated groups. As a result, according to this explanation, Yunnan minorities are more tied to the land than Guizhou minorities and are thus less willing to migrate. This explanation is also inconsistent with the data; as already mentioned, minorities from both provinces migrate and rural residents from Yunnan minority regions migrate at higher rates than those from the rest of the province (State Statistical Bureau various years-b, various years-c). After all, centuries are long—I found no convincing evidence that millennia are needed for an ethnic group to become deeply rooted in a locale.

Geographical isolation is one of the barriers most often cited to explain migration rates, and it is among the most persuasive. Research by Justin Y. Lin, Wang Gewei, and Zhao Yaohui (2004) indicates that migration flows are affected by distance but that the importance of distance declines over time as transportation becomes more accessible and as migrants establish networks that ameliorate the psychic costs of migration. As we have seen in chapter 3, the country roads, prevalent in Guizhou but relatively lacking in Yunnan, enhance access to information critical to spurring migration. Although the extensive Yunnan highway network makes the province as a whole seem less remote and decreases overall travel time and expense, the density and distribution of such roads do not appear to make as much difference to Yunnan rural residents. More important to increased migration are the Guizhou country roads that link Guizhou villages to nearby towns and townships. Rural migrants tend to sacrifice travel time to reduce travel costs and, therefore, stick to the less expensive, nontoll roads.[28] Although the Guizhou highway system is not as well developed as the Yunnan system, in most of the towns and townships I visited in Guizhou there were plenty of long-distance buses traveling often daily across provinces to such destinations as Zhuhai (Guangxi province), Guangzhou (Guangdong province), and even Ningbo (Zhejiang province). In contrast, few towns or townships in Yunnan have bus stations, and the main transportation linkages connect to nearby towns or the county seat. Although Yunnan itself is far less remote than Guizhou, its poor people often live in isolated areas, which probably reduces their ability to migrate.[29] Because villages in Guizhou have relatively better connections to county towns, they are also more likely to have

28. Lin, Wang, and Zhou (2004) are puzzled that distance is becoming less of a factor in migration decisions in recent years even though railway tickets are becoming more expensive. Many migrants from southwestern China, however, do not travel by railroad but by long-distance bus.

29. Rozelle and colleagues (1999), however, find scant evidence that more bus stations correlate with increased migration and conclude that bus stations increase not only migration but also locally based nonfarm opportunities that can also absorb surplus labor, thus reducing the need to migrate. As my fieldwork reveals, villages have various kinds of bus systems. Some feature short-distance buses that move between villages and towns, which could enable local trade; others center on longer-distance buses, which might facilitate migration. Although one

access to information on possible employment opportunities. The barrier of geographical isolation can thus be reduced with the appropriate transportation system.

The direct influence of Guizhou and Yunnan government policy on the disparate patterns of migration in the two provinces is our final potential explanation. Although this barrier was rarely suggested in my interviews or the secondary literature, we should consider it because migration appears to be part of provincial strategy. The Guizhou government strategy toward its surplus labor incorporated attempts to export its labor to urban, mining, and industrial centers both internally and cross-province, especially to the coastal cities. The Guizhou 1986 Directives on Strengthening Work in Poor Areas, the first formal Guizhou antipoverty policy of the reform era, suggests that some central and provincial policies have to be relaxed to deal with poverty, among them the policies proscribing population movements. This policy directs labor departments at all levels of government to organize rural laborers in the poor areas of Guizhou to migrate for work. It further requires departments overseeing labor-intensive industries, such as mining and forestry, to reserve quotas for migrant workers to serve as contract or shift workers (Guizhou Nianjian Bianjibu 1987, 71). By 1993, the province, reporting on successful aspects of its antipoverty programs, noted that five counties in three prefectures had organized the migration of more than 50,000 rural laborers, who remitted on average approximately RMB 800 per person each year (Guizhou Nianjian Bianjibu 1994, 277). As a part of the effort to spur migration, the Guizhou government provided training and placement services for migrants, and many local governments provided specific programs to help migrants. For instance, Zunyi prefecture in northern Guizhou assigned a point person at the prefecture and county levels who is responsible for helping migrants, and every town and township has migration service offices. The Zunyi prefecture government emphasized training (with the motto: "First train, then send out") at the vocational schools and established offices in the Guangdong Pearl River Delta area to solve specific problems for migrants, collect information about employment, and provide feedback to the government (Wang and Zhang 2003, 549–50). The Chinese 8-7 Plan,[30] a national poverty reduction program, paired Guizhou province with four wealthy coastal cities (Shenzhen, Qingdao, Ningbo, and Dalian) that are popular destinations for migrating workers; this helped to promote migration. The municipal governments in these cities not only established training centers but also provided employment for migrants on their arrival. Some of these initiatives occurred several years after the large

effect of both bus systems should be to reduce poverty, the effects of the different bus systems on poverty reduction and economic growth should be studied separately.

30. The policy was named the 8-7 Plan because it was intended to bring 80 million people out of poverty over a seven-year period.

increase in migration had occurred (the Zunyi program, for instance, started in 1998). Still, according to a 1996 survey of migrant workers in Shenzhen, although a majority (54.5 percent) had been introduced to their jobs by friends and relatives, more than one-fifth (21.5 percent) had received government assistance in finding a job (Shi 2005). Although the proactive Guizhou government policies encouraging migration were probably of secondary importance, such policies contributed to the larger phenomenon. Moreover, migration spurred by government initiatives multiplied as the dynamics of chain migration took effect. Thus, each of these efforts helped make rural migration easier, and although proactive, the actions of the Guizhou government still fall into the category of market facilitation.

By contrast, throughout the 1990s the Yunnan antipoverty policies did not mention migration. For instance, recall that both provinces promulgated antipoverty policies that followed the central government Seven-Year Priority Poverty Alleviation Program (see chap. 2). In Yunnan, however, the provincial version of the policy omitted the central policy provision to provide employment services and technical training to expand the rational and orderly export of labor from poor areas.(As we have seen, the Guizhou version of the policy included this provision, and provincial officials proactively encouraged migration.) Instead, Yunnan tried to solve its surplus rural labor problem not by exporting it but by attempting to increase employment opportunities through developing new local businesses and enterprises. For instance, as early as 1986, as part of its developmental strategy, the Yunnan government provided RMB 70 million in low-interest loans annually to its twenty-six nationally designated poor counties to establish productive industries that could absorb excess workers (Guo, Yuan, and Zhao 1990).

Overall, however, the rapidly increasing growth in Yunnan attracted relatively few internal migrants, although it did encourage many migrants from other provinces to travel to Yunnan. According to my secondary sources, migrants came to Yunnan far more frequently than they did to Guizhou. According to Liang Zai and Michael White's (1997) historical study of migration in the PRC, between 1985 and 1988 a migrant was 29 percent more likely to go to Yunnan than to Guizhou. In addition, Zhu Nong and Sandra Poncet (2003), whose research focuses on migration flows in 1985–1990 and 1990–1995, list the pairs of provinces involved in the thirty largest rural-to-urban migration flows in these periods, one of which is Yunnan and Sichuan. Although in both periods, Yunnan is a destination for migrants originating in Sichuan, but in neither period is Yunnan a province of origin for migrants to Sichuan. The 1990 census also suggests that migrants were 50 percent more likely to go to Yunnan than to Guizhou; and the 2000 census suggests that three times as many migrants went to Yunnan as Guizhou. Compared to other provinces in China, Yunnan has never been a major draw, attracting not more than 3 percent of cross-provincial Chinese migrants (Guizhou never exceeds 2 percent); nevertheless, in 2000, Yunnan was the eighth most popular destination for migrants.

In sum, as Rozelle and colleagues (1999) argue, rural residents tend to migrate when they (1) lack good locally based economic alternatives and (2) are connected sufficiently to have access to information. Guizhou government policies contributed to these two factors, whereas Yunnan government policies did not.

Whereas Guizhou became a moderate sender of cross-province migrants, Yunnan sent few migrants and became a major recipient of migrants, primarily from Sichuan province. The attempts of the Yunnan leadership to develop the provincial economy proactively, primarily through altering the market, succeeded in increasing growth rate but did little to encourage internal migration flows from the poor areas to the booming regions of the province. As a result, outsiders more often took advantage of the employment opportunities generated by those flows, contributing to the Yunnan GDP growth rate but not to poverty reduction.

Starting in the late 1980s, Guizhou's policies to train and send migrants out for work interacted with the province's poverty to motivate migration. As the rural infrastructure (such as country roads) improved in the province, an increasing number of rural residents were able to migrate in search of opportunities. Although Guizhou residents were not among the first wave of Chinese rural residents to leave their farms in the reform era and did not migrate in great numbers, compared to Anhui, Sichuan, and Hunan, migration was nevertheless significant, and by the mid-1990s, it exceeded the national average. Further, chain migration through social networks proved instrumental in creating a virtuous cycle. As more migrants left their home areas and successfully found employment, others joined them. Despite stereotypes to the contrary, migrants, when successful in finding jobs, generally worked hard and gained experience, spending little on themselves and sending money back home to their families. For Guizhou, the combined remittances reduced poverty in the migrants' home villages because the recipients typically spent the money on purchasing clothing, food, and housing and on educating younger relatives. The impact of such migration on economic growth, however, has been limited; the remittances were generally too small to start industries of any scale, limiting the opportunity of rural residents to contribute to economic growth by increasing their productivity. Furthermore, the labor of Guizhou cross-province migrants contributed to the economies of the host provinces, not to Guizhou. Starting in the mid-1980s, the Guizhou government policies facilitated these trends.

Yunnan, by contrast, became trapped in a vicious cycle. Although the province as a whole is less isolated than Guizhou, many Yunnan residents lacked the country roads they needed to reach the highways that the Yunnan leaders had constructed. As a result, potential Yunnan migrants had less access to reliable information about employment opportunities and less affordable ways of traveling to such opportunities. Potential migrants were further dissuaded from migrating because they lacked connections outside the province. Yunnan laborers who did migrate from rural to urban areas stayed within the province, their labor and wages contributing both to poverty reduction and to economic growth. Moreover, people migrated to Yunnan from other provinces; whereas their labor contributed to the economic growth of Yunnan, their remittances reduced poverty only in their home provinces, not in Yunnan. The relative lack of Yunnan cross-province migration precluded the development of the pattern seen in Guizhou—poverty reduction with little impact on growth. Moreover, the Yunnan government expended little effort to encourage migration.

Thus, migration contributes to the overall patterns seen in both Yunnan and Guizhou. For Guizhou, migration helped reduce poverty, even though the modest remittances contributed little to economic growth. The mobile Guizhou labor force contributed primarily to GDP growth in other provinces. For Yunnan, migration was a missed opportunity. Few rural residents migrated, limiting potential remittance income. Had the Yunnan government adopted policies promoting vocational training and other forms of job support and promoting the construction of rural roadways, the inability or unwillingness of potential migrants to accept the risks inherent in migration might have been overcome. By encouraging migration, the Yunnan government might also have reduced poverty within the province.

5

Tourism

Joyous Village Life

> Tourism is like a fire: you can cook your meal with it, or it can burn your house down.
>
> —Asian proverb

My traveling companion and I finally arrived after our full-day hike through the heart of Thunder Mountain, a poor rural county in southeastern Guizhou. Turning the bend, we spotted the traditional wooden houses with ornate window frames of Upper Langde, the Miao village that was our destination. The sun was beginning to set over the black tile roofs and the smoking chimneys as we entered the central square, active with Chinese and foreign tourists bargaining with villagers who were selling embroidered clothing, Miao-style combs, and bamboo pipe instruments. Pursuing the sound of wind instruments and firecrackers, we caught up with a dozen or so elderly men of the village who, playing their bamboo pipes in unison, were just completing the rituals of an annual festival. Rhythmically marching through the serpentine cobblestone paths, the band was in the midst of visiting each house of the village. As they entered each house, they walked in slow circles around the main room, playing their music constantly. When they finished, each musician received gifts from the host family: one long red strip of cloth, along with a sip of rice wine consumed mid-march to the crackle of firecrackers. By the end of the evening, ornaments nearly covered the men's jet-black clothing. We joined this merry band (growing merrier with each house visited) along with a small group of tourists who, judging by the red strips attached to their clothing, had slipped into the chaotic caravan hours earlier. We participated long enough to collect a modest number of red strips; then the party suddenly broke up and the band dispersed, their circuit complete. We hastened to pick up the key to our dormitory-style accommodations from the man minding a small shop off the central square, and we went to find the family who had invited us to a home-cooked meal, which they prepared and served for a small fee.

The hot pot in the center of the family's living room simmered as we, eating together with our hosts, piled green vegetables and meat into the cauldron with our chopsticks. We waited a few minutes for the boiling water to cook our food, which we retrieved with our chopsticks and dipped it into a red hot sauce before gratefully consuming it. After a long and lively discussion, during which we were graced by the presence of the village head, we wandered back to our dormitory. The next morning, freeloading off a visiting tour group of Chinese employees from the Chinese Civil Aviation Administration, we viewed a somewhat Hollywood-ized version of a Miao traditional dance.

Upon leaving mid-morning, we reflected on the tourism model of Langde. Compared to many other Chinese tourism sites, Langde had little "development." Instead of formal hotels and restaurants—the villagers' houses had been adapted to meet those needs—the most prominent developed facilities for tourism were a few toilets and a road connecting the village to the county town. In tourist spots we had visited in other provinces in southwestern China, outside investors had constructed hotels, restaurants, and even souvenir shops, taking most of the profits in return. In villages such as Langde, by contrast, except for the fees paid by tour groups (which the village and the tour operators shared), the money tourists spent on meals, lodging, and handicrafts went directly into the pockets of the villagers, supplementing what the villagers earned from farming. Although this additional income from tourism was not on the same scale as the amounts spent in other tourist spots (we spent a fraction of what a night in a simple guesthouse in other areas would cost), tourism in such areas has demonstrably helped reduce poverty.

In fact, tourism, a US$4.4 trillion worldwide industry responsible for 12 percent of the world's employment, is often touted for its potential contributions to poverty reduction in places such as Langde.[1] This is largely because tourism is not only the world's largest industry; it also represents the most labor-intensive sector outside of agriculture, one that is potentially accessible to low-income people, who can both directly participate in tourism and indirectly benefit from tourism revenue. Popular tourist destinations were once located exclusively in wealthy nations, but developing countries have become increasingly popular tourist destinations and are, in this way,

1. In 2001, an international conference of delegates from forty-nine poor countries concluded that "for a large majority of LDCs [less-developed countries], tourism development can be an avenue to increase participation in the global economy, alleviate poverty, and achieve socio-economic progress" (United Nations World Tourism Organization [UNWTO] 2002, 19). The tagline of the United Nations World Tourism Organization (UNWTO) report on tourism and poverty alleviation reads, "Sustainable Tourism can be one of the few development opportunities for the poor. Let us use it wisely and soon!" (2002, 1). The conference also noted that the specific conditions of each potential tourism site must be assessed lest money be wasted on fruitless development.

benefiting from their natural and cultural attractions.[2] Some critics, however, counter that the benefits of tourism for poor people are exaggerated and even largely illusory because many tourist destinations in both rich and poor countries are often located in enclaves far from poor people or are structured in ways that exclude poor people from participation (e.g., Varley 1978). But, as we have seen, there are tourist destinations such as Langde that are organized and sponsored by poor people, who host guests directly by serving as hoteliers, restaurateurs, entertainers, service staff, and caretakers. The various forms and structures that tourist sites adopt can thus influence the direction of economic development and poverty reduction.

The role that the tourism industry plays in Yunnan and Guizhou can help explain the economic patterns we see in these provinces and shed light on the more general debate about the conditions under which various development activities such as tourism contribute to reducing poverty. Here, I first discuss the causal connection among tourism, economic growth, and poverty reduction and briefly introduce the development of tourism in China. I then explore the volume, distribution, and structure of tourism in Guizhou and Yunnan.

Outside China, we can find many examples of the potential benefits of tourism for poverty reduction. Under ideal conditions, tourism provides local people with the opportunity to sell their goods and services directly to foreign and domestic tourists, diversifies the economy, draws on the cultural and natural heritage of the country or region as a resource, and, given its high employment rate of women, promotes gender income equality. On the role of tourism in poverty reduction, the United Nations World Tourism Organization (UNWTO 2002, 10) argues that some of the key characteristics of developing nations, such as their culture, scenery, and wildlife, are precisely the factors that attract foreign tourists. When these natural endowments are successfully marketed to tourists, poor rural residents can engage in tourism-related, potentially income-enhancing economic activities. In hotels, local residents serve as porters, waiters, and housekeepers. In scenic spots, the rural poor sell handicrafts, fruits, or eggs to tourists or act as tour guides to featured attractions. In ad hoc groups or through long-term arrangements with hotels, restaurants, and scenic sites, ethnic minorities perform their traditional songs and dances at prices negotiated on the spot or for tips or formal wages. In addition, rural labor is often employed for the construction of tourism infrastructure. Overall, tourist sites can be structured to magnify their poverty reduction effect by (1) facilitating access to the tourism market for the local community, (2) enhancing linkages with the local economy, and (3) building and complementing local livelihood

2. According to UNWTO statistics, the share of the industry in developing countries increased from 20.8 percent in 1973 to 42 percent in 2000. Tourism has become a principal export of 83 percent of developing countries and the leading export of 33 percent.

strategies through the employment and development of small businesses (UNWTO 2002, 12).

In spite of the potential benefits of the tourism industry, even when tourist sites are located in poor regions, the connection between tourism and poverty reduction is conditional. Whereas the dominant view is that tourism is a labor-intensive, cost-effective way to develop an economy and reduce poverty, dissenters have presented contradicting evidence that tourism is, instead, a capital-intensive industry, especially compared to agriculture (Sinclair 1991; Tisdell 1998). Moreover, the employment-generating effects of tourism are said to be still weaker than other industries, including agriculture, manufacturing, and many other service industries (Varley 1978). As Clement Tisdell cautions, "Tourism is not a Cinderella industry for developing all backward regions" (1998, 16).

The connection between tourism and poverty reduction depends fundamentally on whether the tourism industry is designed to include or exclude the participation of the poor. Although the development of the tourism industry can be a boon to the service sector, developers can create enclaves that intentionally exclude poor people, reducing the benefits of tourism for them. Constructing high fences, requiring expensive admission tickets or licenses, and strictly enforcing regulations can prevent poor people from interacting with (or, some might say, "harassing") the tourists. The handicraft industry can be organized as a production line, producing "authentic traditional handicrafts" that are neither authentic nor traditionally made and that are sold to unsuspecting or indifferent tourists, thus reducing the compensation poor people receive for their traditional production, alienating them from the production process, and even eliminating the need for them entirely (Tisdell 2001; Mowforth and Munt 2003).

For example, the popular tourist resorts of the Maldives, a nation of coral islands off the coast of India, keep tourists on the resort islands, isolated from the indigenous population. The national economy is highly dependent on the income from tourism. In 1998, tourism accounted for more than 57.7 percent of its GDP, the world's highest proportion (UNWTO 2002, 30). Because of the tourism industry distribution and structure, however, the vast majority of Maldivian residents benefit only modestly from the industry. During their development, tourist facilities in the Maldives were not spread throughout the islands but were concentrated on or near the island containing the capital city. Each resort is self-contained, with independent power generators, water supplies, and harbors with motorboats to speed tourists to and from the airport. Moreover, much of the food and other necessities sold are imported, which, although supporting tourism with appropriate-quality and more efficiently sourced materials, further reduces any possibility of direct benefits for the local rural population. Because more than 80 percent of the money from the tourism industry is accrued in the resort and few linkages connect tourism with other local industries, even indirect employment is rarely generated through tourism. As Rajasundram Sathiendrakumar and Tisdell conclude, "the economy of the tourist resorts is largely separated from the general Maldivian economy, a separation also present in the sociocultural system. Therefore, tourist resorts form enclaves and give rise to economic and social duality" (2001, 263). Other examples of other popular tourist destinations in which tourism enhances economic growth while doing little to reduce poverty are Cancun, Mexico (Cooper 2003); the Caribbean (Hills and Lundgren 1977); Fiji (Britton 1980); and Hawaii (Patterson 1992).

We can identify three broadly defined, ideal types of tourism development by the effects of tourism on local economic growth and poverty reduction.

- *Exclusive resort.* This style of tourism development typically spurs economic growth without making a significant difference on poverty.
- *Tourism as development.* This style balances economic growth and poverty reduction, depending on the extent to which the local community has access to the industry through employment, the sale of goods, and encouraging small businesses.
- *Grassroots tourism.* This style enhances poverty reduction; however, because investment tends to be modest, it contributes less to economic growth.

These three types of tourism development do not, of course, exist as pure forms. Market conditions, management decisions, natural disasters, and other factors influence all these forms and can impede the ability of the tourism industry to spur growth or reduce poverty.

The Growth of the Tourism Industry in China

Tourism in China has grown rapidly since the country reopened to the outside world in 1978, increasing from a tiny US$262.9 million industry in 1978 to a US$16.2 billion sector in 2000; China ranked seventh in the world for tourist receipts in 1999 and ranked fifth in 2009 (Lew et al. 2003, 7, 16; UNWTO 2010). In the early years, officials in the nascent Chinese tourism apparatus focused almost exclusively on attracting foreign tourists. In the beginning, foreign tourists arrived in modest numbers. The volume of visitors subsequently swelled, so that by 1999 China ranked as the fifth most popular destination for international tourists (Zhang 2003, 18). Because primary goal of the government in promoting tourism was initially to obtain foreign currency, combined with a desire to use the limited Chinese tourism infrastructure efficiently, policymakers focused mainly on attracting foreign tourists. At first the government limited international tourism to a small number of sites, and gradually opened access to more and more sites over subsequent years.

International tourists visited China in great numbers each year; in addition, domestic tourists became an increasingly important part of the tourism market from the mid-1980s. According to one survey, in the first half of that decade, fewer than one-quarter of the residents of the main cities in China participated in leisure-based travel (and even fewer from smaller cities), with these activities usually linked with business trips or visiting friends (Xiao 2003, 264). The primary opportunity for longer-distance leisure travel originated with structured tours sponsored by work-units; later, rising incomes sparked domestic demand. By the mid-1980s, this demand, combined with the demonstrated benefits of tourism for the economy as a whole, spurred the central government to encourage independent domestic tourism (Xu 1999, 73–75). By the 1990s, with the implementation of the five-day workweek and urban workers' having increasing amounts of disposable income (and thus the time and resources required to take privately organized trips), leisure travel had increased rapidly (Xiao 2003, 266). In 1999, Chinese natives participated in more than 700 million trips within China (compared to approximately 72 million visitors from overseas, including those from Hong Kong, Macau, and Taiwan). Their expenditures accounted for more than 70 percent of total Chinese revenues from tourism.

The effects of tourism growth, both domestic and international, on poverty and inequality in China have been mixed. The potential of the tourism market in nature reserves and minority regions in inland rural China raised expectations that tourism would narrow the income inequality that emerged in the mid-1980s between coastal and inland, as well as between rural and urban, areas. Unfortunately, the pattern of tourism was unequal and contributed further to the inequality in these areas. International tourism in China centered in coastal, primarily urban locations. Between 1986 and 1998, the twelve Chinese coastal provinces received at least 78.6 percent of the total foreign visitors and at least 84 percent of the total tourist receipts. Domestic tourism, although its effect on inequality is more ambiguous, probably exacerbated this problem.[3] In sum, despite the booming tourism industry in China, the sector appeared to reinforce rather than ameliorate inequality between coastal and inland regions (Wen and Tisdell 2001, 105–7).

Although tourism did not apparently narrow the gap between rich and poor, did the industry help alleviate rural poverty at the tourist sites that

3. Most of the domestic tourists, some 94 percent according to an official 1999 survey, traveled relatively short distances and stayed fewer than three days, including in their itinerary only one or two cities (Xiao 2003, 272). This contradicts Wen and Tisdell's (2001) conclusion that domestic tourists tend to have fewer time constraints and thus are willing to travel further. They support this statement by showing that domestic tourism is less regionally concentrated than international tourism in China. This conclusion, however, could be an artifact of the statistics' capturing the local market—Chinese visitors visiting a tourist area for a day trip. Because the Chinese population is dispersed throughout the country, even if people travel only within their own province we would also expect domestic tourism to appear dispersed throughout the country.

were developed? In many places, such as Yellow Mountain (Anhui) and the Yangshuo area (Guangxi), where tourism is based in the countryside and the participation of local residents is widespread, tourism probably contributed to poverty reduction. Other destinations, such as the Great Wall (Beijing) and the Terracotta Army (Xi'an), also feature tourism based in the countryside. Many other sites, however, are structured such that the direct participation by the surrounding rural residents is more limited. Even in remote nature reserves, which are often surrounded by poor areas and where tourism could potentially reduce rural poverty, fewer than one-fifth of the local families benefited from tourism, according to one survey, and only one in ten nature reserves brought benefits to more than half of families living nearby (UNESCO 1998, in Xu and Kruse 2003). Many other tourist destinations, such as those located in cities, such as West Lake (Hangzhou) and the Sen Yatsen Mausoleum (Nanjing), although contributing to urban development and overall economic growth, likely had little effect on rural poverty. Moreover, many poor provinces, such as the desolate western province of Qinghai, have few resources with which to invest in tourist attractions. Thus, structure, distribution, and volume affect the extent to which tourism contributes to economic growth and poverty reduction.

Tourism in Guizhou and Yunnan

Tourism in Yunnan and Guizhou is typified by a concentration of tourist sites in rural regions dominated by ethnic minorities. As we have seen, large numbers of minorities live in both Guizhou and Yunnan, and their unique cultures, including song and dance, rituals, architecture, and clothing, attract tourists, both foreign and Chinese. In Yunnan, where economic growth during the 1990s far outpaced poverty reduction, the tourist sites were well developed, with productive assets such as hotels, restaurants, and roads that contributed to economic growth. In addition, most tourist sites were distributed in nonpoor areas and were structured in ways that excluded poor people. In contrast, in Guizhou, where poverty reduction outpaced economic growth, tourism was generally smaller in scale, with few productive assets to spur growth. Most tourist sites, such as Langde, were centered in poor areas and generally were structured to encourage the participation of poor people.

That tourism emerges as part of the explanation for the puzzling pattern of economic growth and poverty reduction in Guizhou and Yunnan might astonish those familiar with China. After all, Yunnan, where the weather in most regions has been accurately described as "four seasons, all like spring," has for decades been one of the most popular tourist destinations in China. (Although Guizhou is less well-known, the mild temperatures that persist year-round in Guizhou have earned it the designation of being a "natural air conditioner.") An early backpacker haven known for its beautiful vistas, mysterious and exotic minority cultures, and inexpensive beer, the appeal of Yunnan has gradually diversified from overseas budget travelers to more traditional foreign tourists and great crowds of Chinese individual and group tourists. Moreover, the mainstay of Yunnan tourism remains its minority cultures, focused primarily in the countryside.[4] It is surprising then that tourism in Yunnan does not contribute that much to reducing poverty in the province. The number of foreign tourists visiting the province rose from a low of approximately 212,000 in 1991 to 742,000 in 1996 and climbed above 1 million in 2001 and 2 million in 2005. As these statistics demonstrate, an increasing number of the international tourists visiting China included Yunnan on their list of destinations. The volume of Chinese tourists is a difficult statistic to interpret;[5] it also apparently increased rapidly during this period, from 11.1 million in 1992 to 45 million in 2001. By the mid-1990s, Yunnan ranked as the sixth most popular tourist draw in China, outperforming such internationally known tourist provinces as Guangxi province, home to the inspiring karst geography of Guilin, and Shaanxi province with its internationally renowned Terracotta Army (State Statistical Bureau various years-b, various years-c).

The Guizhou tourist destinations were simply not as well known. Tourism was also opened there in the early 1980s, when the capital city of Guiyang and the Huangguoshu waterfall were opened to foreign tourists, but its tourism industry developed much more slowly than that in Yunnan. Whereas Yunnan had numerous famous sites, Guizhou had but one truly famous tourist area—Huangguoshu, the highest waterfall in China. Although Guizhou is extremely scenic and attractive, its neighbors trump its attractions in almost every way.[6] Guizhou boasts a diverse mix of fourteen ethnic groups with populations above 5,000, but Yunnan has twenty-five designated ethnic groups of that size and has a tourism industry that is better organized to present them. During its history, Guizhou developed a unique

4. The main Yunnan urban site is the capital city, Kunming, which includes scenic areas such as Lake Dian and more recent attractions such as the Botanical Exhibition. These drew, even by the early 1990s, hundreds of thousands of overseas tourists and millions of Chinese tourists.

5. Chinese tourists are difficult to count, especially compared to international tourists, who are almost invariably asked for their passports to register at hotels and until the mid-1990s used foreign exchange certificates instead of ordinary Chinese currency. The extraordinarily high numbers here reflect the fact that, especially before 1993, the Chinese domestic tourism statistics included day visitors and even local families, dropping by, say, Emerald Lake (a site in Kunming) for the afternoon (Xu 1999, 162–63).

6. Although Guizhou indeed has beautiful "mountains and water" scenery, featuring karst geography and the highest waterfall in China, the Stone Forest in Yunnan has been known as the "First Wonder of the World" since the Ming Dynasty (1368–1644 A.D.) and is listed among the most prominent scenic spots in China. Moreover, what can compare to the mysterious karst geography in Guilin, made famous by centuries of Chinese poetry and watercolor paintings? The karst geography in Guizhou is simply not as impressive.

style of opera and several art forms, but they are not nearly as well known as those in other areas of China. Moreover, Guizhou, as mentioned earlier, is a new province. For all its stunningly beautiful charms, Guizhou is cursed with the widespread perception of being the homely younger sister of more refined and elegant relatives, including Yunnan. To make matters worse, the relative lack of convenient expressways and international-class hotels in Guizhou, not to mention its reputation for having relatively high crime rates, exclude many less hardy travelers. Guizhou claimed only a fraction of the foreign visitors that flocked to Yunnan; it had 37,453 visits in 1990, increasing to 125,344 in 1996 (approximately half the overseas visitors to Yunnan in 1991). The province did not receive more than 200,000 visitors (a mark reached by Yunnan in 1991) until 2001. According to Chinese statistics, domestic visitors to Guizhou exceeded those to Yunnan (frankly, these official statistics are hard to believe) until the mid-1990s, after which, domestic visitors to Yunnan exceeded those to Guizhou. Although Guizhou each year attracts increasing numbers of tourists, both foreign and domestic, the splendors of Guizhou are for now destined to remain a relative secret.

Despite Yunnan's much larger tourism industry, the vast majority of the most famous Yunnan tourist sites were in nonpoor areas, where their popularity and continued expansion contributed primarily to economic growth and had a diminished role in reducing poverty (see table 5 for a list of main tourist sites in Yunnan and their locations). By design, the province limited the popularization and development of tourism to specific spots, and these, as early as 1986 when China designated counties as either poor or nonpoor, were located almost exclusively in nonpoor counties. By 1982, four years after China reopened to the Western world, the central government included three areas in Yunnan on its national list of approved tourism projects—the Stone Forest, Xishuangbanna, and Dali—and by 1985 had added a fourth, Lijiang. Starting in the early 1980s, the Yunnan government channeled financial and promotional resources primarily into Kunming, Xishuangbanna, Dali, and Lijiang, successfully promoting these as its primary tourist sites (see map 2).

By the early 1990s, Yunnan government strategy remained focused primarily on five large nonpoor areas (see chap. 2). Four of these (Kunming, Xishuangbanna, Dali, and Lijiang) had long been key elements of its tourism developmental strategy; the fifth, Ruili, was a nonpoor prefecture in western Yunnan. None of these five sites contained any of the poor counties on either the national or provincial lists in 1986. Moreover, when Yunnan leaders were given the opportunity in 1994 to expand the number of poor counties from forty-one to seventy-three, these five tourist areas were not classified as poor countries, although some counties near them were. In addition to tourism development, the province located much of its transportation infrastructure and many of its health-care facilities in these limited,

Table 5. Main tourist spots in Yunnan

Most popular or key point tourist sites	County designation (poor/nonpoor)
Key point tourist sites	
Kunming (Lake Dian, the Stone Forest)	Nonpoor
Dali	Nonpoor/poor (mixed)
Xishuangbanna	Nonpoor
Lijiang	Nonpoor
Other popular tourist sites	
Ruili	Nonpoor
Shangri-la	Poor
Other sites listed on China's national list of key tourist sites	
Jianshui	Nonpoor
Nine townships	Nonpoor
Tengchong	Poor
Three Rivers area	Poor
Nationally and provincially approved vacation spots	
Dali	Nonpoor
Dianchi	Nonpoor
Fuxian (Chengjiang county)	Nonpoor
Xishuangbanna	Nonpoor
Yangshihai (Yiliang county)	Nonpoor
Yulong Snow Mountain (Lijiang)	Nonpoor

nonpoor regions. What is more, of the ten tourist destinations approved by the central state between 1982 and 1994 (which included the more popular Yunnan sites, as well as some less popular ones), only two were in poor regions (the less well-known and less visited Three Rivers Pingliu Scenic Area and the Tengchong Volcano Area), whereas eight were in nonpoor areas (the Stone Forest, Dianchi Lake, Dali, Xishuangbanna, Lijiang, Jianshui, Ruili River, and Jiuxiang).

In contrast, many poor places with potential for development as tourist sites did not receive the governmental support needed to make them viable tourist spots. In fact, some of the seventy-three counties in Yunnan classified as poor contained attractive areas, yet few of these received either provincial or central government support for tourism development. For instance, the spectacular terraced rice fields of Yuanyang county in Honghe prefecture, designed 1,000 years ago during the Tang dynasty, are of a style rarely found in China. The view of them from the mountain above, reflections of sun and clouds in the pools of water of the intertwined mazelike rice fields extending for thousands of meters down the mountain, rivals the best of what China

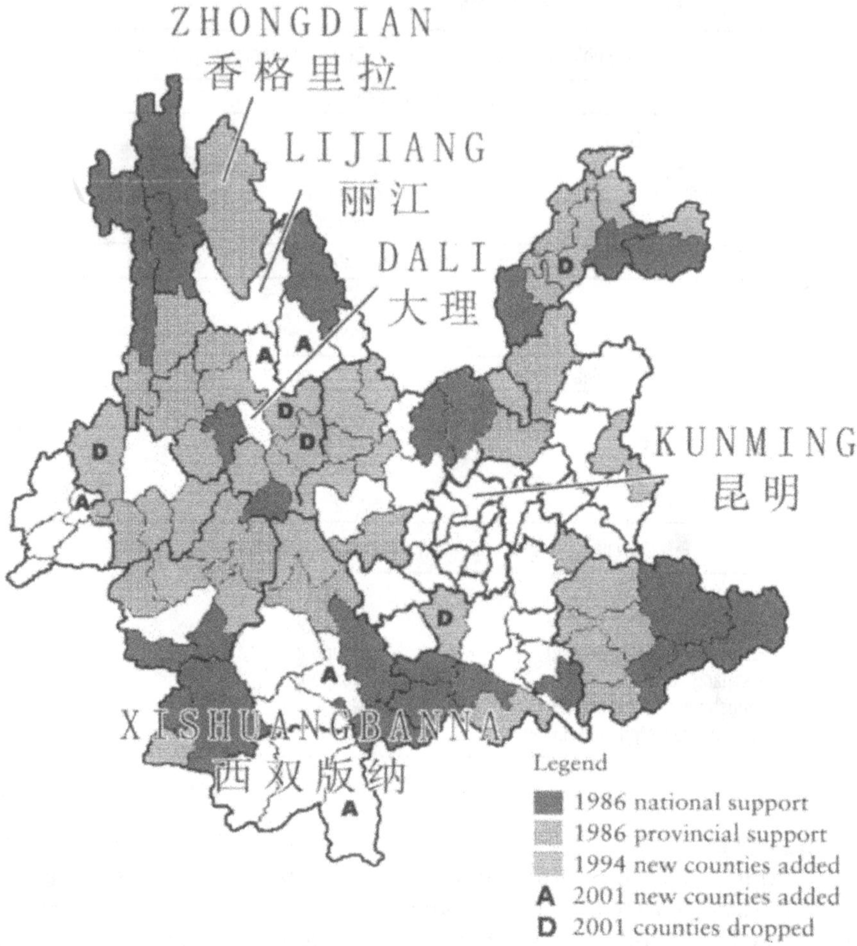

Map 2 Major Yunnan tourist sites (poor counties marked).

has to offer. Nevertheless, most people have never heard of the place. The area lacks development funds for promoting tourism and gets only a trickle of tourist traffic. Far from being oriented toward its poor, the county government of Yuanyang sought to expand by moving its offices from the picturesque if underdeveloped hillside town of Xinjie to the sweltering town of Nansha on the plains. Although this move achieved the country government goal of providing itself space for expansion, it used sorely needed development funds and encroached on some of the best farmland in Yuanyang. Moreover, in addition to building a town square, later the county built a handful of star-rated hotels, despite the relative dearth of overseas and domestic tourists. Facilities for backpackers, including inexpensive hotels and restaurants, were lacking and one of the backpacker hostels closed for lack of business. Even though the structure of the tourist facilities that exist in Yuanyang excludes, for the most part, the participation of its poor people, an increase in tourism would still probably benefit directly the rural residents of this poor county, with its natural scenery and ethnic cultures. After all, even without much promotion and with only a trickle of tourists, Yi and Hani minority children in scenic areas in Yuanyang county organize themselves after class to sell boiled goose eggs and to sing and dance for tips (Donaldson 2007). The provincial government, however, chose to invest in wealthier areas and invested inappropriately from the perspective of both tourism development and poverty reduction.

The story of Yuanyang was repeated in other potential tourist spots in poor areas, such as Tengchong, with its natural hot springs (which only in recent years have been effectively promoted); Nujiang, with its beautiful raging river and indigenous culture; and some poor counties near Dali. Such areas have the potential to decrease their poverty through tourism, but they lacked the resources needed to promote the local tourism industry. This belies the argument that the strategy of tourism development resulted from the province's dearth of resources. Areas of Yunnan also lacked resources, yet did not adopt this tourism strategy.

By contrast, in Guizhou many tourist facilities are in poor counties (see table 6 for a list of the main Guizhou tourist sites and their locations). According to my fieldwork and secondary sources, tourism in Guizhou is better distributed, with many tourist sites, including the most popular, distributed in poor counties. Of the eight sites selected as national tourist sites in Guizhou, three (Huangguoshu, the Zhijin Caves, and the Zhang River Scenic Area) are located in poor counties and three (Longgong Cave, Hongfeng Lake, and the Chishui Shaluo Nature Reserve) are in nonpoor counties,[7] and two (Wuyang River Scenic Area and Fanjing Mountain) straddle poor and nonpoor counties.[8] Whereas the Yunnan government restricted its tourism development to specific counties, Guizhou policymakers helped to develop tourist sites throughout the province (see map 3).

In addition to promoting these nationally and provincially sponsored tourist destinations, Guizhou leaders established a series of *nongjiale*-style ethnic minority villages as tourist sites—a centerpiece of their strategy. Beginning in the 1990s, the provincial government, led by the Guizhou Tourism Bureau, gradually developed several dozen of these, usually located in poor counties. The two most frequently visited ethnic villages in western

7. The entrance to the Longgong Cave, the second most famous scenic spot in Guizhou, is located in a nonpoor county but the site is adjacent to a poor county.

8. Tourism at Fanjing Mountain in Guizhou brought in revenues of RMB 45.7 million to the poor county of Yinjiang within five years after it had been developed in 1990, amounting to 17 percent of the total county production value, and sales of tourism commodities brought in profits of RMB 620,000, according to Wang and Zhang (2003, 588).

Table 6. Main tourist spots in Guizhou

Most popular or key point tourist sites	County designation (poor/nonpoor)
Key point tourist sites	
Huangguashu Waterfall	Poor
Longgong Cave	Nonpoor
Other sites listed on China's national list of key tourist sites	
Chishui Suoluo Nature Reserve	Nonpoor
Hongfeng Lake	Nonpoor
Wuyang River Scenic Area	Poor/Nonpoor (mixed)
Zhang River Scenic Area	Poor
Zhijin Caves	Poor
Fanjing Mountain	Poor/Nonpoor (mixed)
Ethnic minority tourist villages—west loop	
Caiguan (Anshun)	Nonpoor
Changlinggang	Poor
Gaopo	Poor
Heitu (Qingzhen)	Nonpoor
Huashishao	Poor
Loujiazhuang (Pingba)	Nonpoor
Shitouzhai (Anshun)	Nonpoor
Ethnic minority tourist villages—east	
Baojing (Zhenyuan)	Nonpoor
Chong'an (Huangping)	Poor
Fanpai (Taijiang)	Poor
Gaozeng (Congjiang)	Poor
Langde (Leishan)	Poor
Matang (Danzai)	Poor
Qingman	Poor
Shidong (Taijiang)	Poor
Tonggu (Majiang)	Poor
Wengxiang (Kaili)	Nonpoor
Xijiang (Leishan)	Poor
Zhaoxing (Liping)	Poor

Source: For ethnic minority Tourist Villages, Oakes (1998).

Guizhou, Heitu and Changlinggang, for instance, were developed with funds provided by the Guiyang branch of the Overseas Travel Corporation, a state-owned company (Oakes 1998, 177). The Guizhou tourism administration established the ethnic villages along two primary routes: a western spur of villages that could be visited along with Huangguoshu and other major tourist sites in Guizhou, and an eastern spur in some of the poorest rural areas in China. These and other government-investment villages succeeded in attracting tourism, and they became models for villages of other

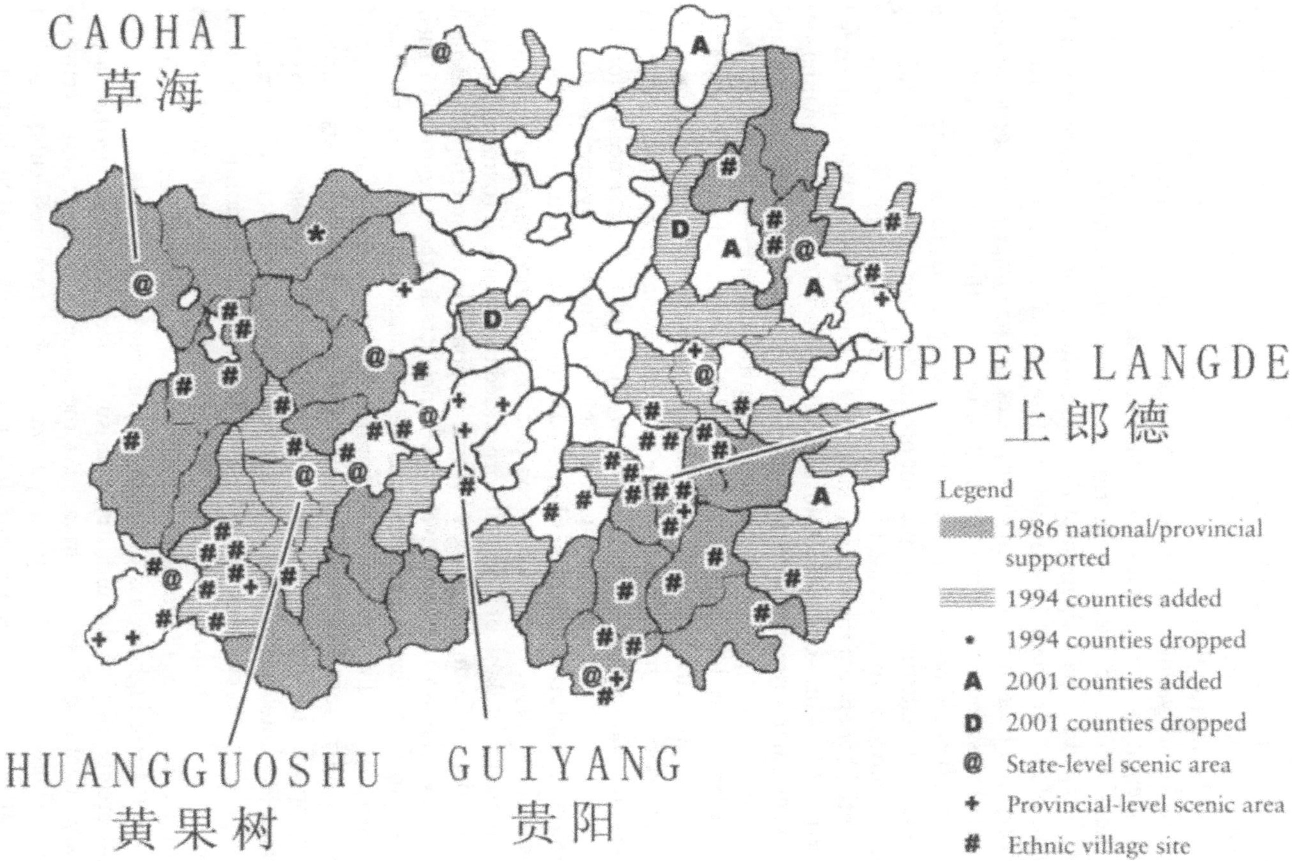

Map 3 Major Guizhou tourist sites (poor counties marked).

ethnicities that were subsequently established as tourist sites. By the mid-1990s, twelve such rural minority villages in eastern Guizhou and seven in western Guizhou developed for tourism quickly became among the most popular Guizhou tourist sites (Oakes 1998, 159–66). The majority of these were located in designated poor counties. For example, two of these villages, the Miao villages of Langde and Xijiang were both located in the Leishan county, one of the poorest counties in Guizhou, ranking eighty-first out of eighty-seven counties in net rural income in 1991.

Reinforcing the effects of distribution, the structure of Guizhou tourism encouraged the participation of the poor, whereas in Yunnan, poor people were often excluded. In the mid- to late 1980s, the Yunnan tourism industry had been structured in most places to encourage local participation. Nevertheless, even from the mid-1980s, much of the profits from the tourism industry did not benefit locals. In Xishuangbanna, for instance, tourism officials estimate that 15–40 percent of supplies used in the tourism industry were imported from outside the prefecture, dampening one of the primary potential benefits of the tourism industry for poor farmers (Wen and Tisdell 2001, 246). But, soon after tourist areas in Dali and Xishuangbanna became popular, primarily with foreign backpackers, local rural residents and governments stepped in to provide the infrastructure—roads, hotels, and restaurants—needed to attract greater volumes of other types of tourists. As early as 1988, Yunnan tourism officials refurbished and upgraded many of its tourist hotels to improve service (Yunnan Nianjian Bianjibu 1989). By 1989, official delegations were going to Thailand and other nearby foreign countries to attract more foreign tourists. The Yunnan government also established institutions to attract large-scale investment from the outside. For instance, in 1993, the Yunnan departments of finance and tourism, and the local branch of Bank of China, incorporated the Yunnan Provincial Tourism Development Company, which became responsible for steering investment into key Yunnan tourism development projects in these regions. In their efforts to formalize investment in these tourist spots, Yunnan tourism administrators realized the need for sensitivity to the needs of investors, and in the mid-1990s, they adopted, the principle of "whoever invests, whoever develops, is the one to profit." These investments were used to construct star-rated hotels and larger restaurants; organize Hollywood-ized performances of local customs; and complete large transportation projects, such as airports and major highways. These and other improvements meant that by the early 1990s the tourist facilities in these places had been increasingly tailored for a higher class of tourist. By increasing the scale, productivity, and profitability of the industry, tourism joined tobacco to become a primary economic base of Yunnan. At the same time, these improvements increasingly excluded the participation of local rural residents, who had primarily relied on tourism to supplement their income from farming; the profits went primarily to the Kunming-based coastal (and even overseas) investors that enabled this restructuring of Yunnan tourism.

By the early 1990s, infrastructure in the four primary Yunnan tourist areas increased in scale as the industry transitioned from backpacker tourism to a more formalized and structured tourism industry. In 1991, Yunnan had a total of 47 hotels, 10 of which were star-rated; by 1996, the province had constructed 168 tourist hotels (8 of them through foreign investment), 82 of which were star-rated, including 6 three-star and 4 four-star hotels.[9] As hotel construction continued briskly, these figures rose each year; by 2008, Yunnan boasted 904 star-rated hotels, including 11 five-star and 53 four-star hotels. Thus, Yunnan had more hotels than the comparable tourist provinces of Shaanxi (332 star-rated hotels, including 5 five-star and 30 four-star) and Guangxi (393 star-rated hotels, including 12 five-star and 38 four-star). Moreover, for the 1995–2000 period, Yunnan planned at least 1 three-star hotel for every prefecture capital and star-rated hotels in each of its 128 counties. Although local rural residents in some tourist areas continued to serve as cooks, waiters, and cleaners in some hotels and restaurants and food grown by poor farmers was purchased to feed the tourists, only relatively small portions of the profits trickled down to the poor. Even though rural residents still managed some of the smaller-scale hotels and restaurants, coastal investors and local governments became the largest beneficiaries of this growth in tourism. Moreover, as Yunnan tourism grew in sophistication, the industry demanded more elaborate skills, which in effect further excluded the poorly educated rural residents from tourism-related jobs.

In addition to the *nongjiale*-style ethnic villages, which were structured such that poor people could participate directly in tourism, other elements of Guizhou tourism were also structured to benefit the poor local residents. For instance, handicraft industry outlets typically purchased products directly from local peasants rather than hiring outside laborers to produce cultural items in a factory. Tim Oakes notes that "the majority of production occurs within village households on a contractual basis" and cites managers' estimates that 65–70 percent of production originated from contract producers (1998, 153).

Tourism as structured in Guizhou generally contributed to poverty reduction without the more costly infrastructure expenditures required for more elaborate forms of tourism. For instance, to smooth the transportation of tourists to tourist areas, local roads were expanded and often paved into two-lane roads—far less costly than building large-scale highways like those

9. For instance, in 1991 the Chinese national tourism administration invested RMB 700,000 in the Dali Hotel. Designed in the traditional Bai minority style, this two-star hotel was at the time considered the best hotel in western Yunnan.

Yunnan constructed to connect Kunming with its major tourist sites.[10] By 1996, Guizhou had just thirty-two hotels with star ratings, only two of which merited more than two stars, compared to the eighty-two star-rated hotels in Yunnan, ten with three stars and above. The total fixed assets of the Guizhou tourist hotels, RMB 552 million, were slightly more than one-quarter of the fixed assets of nearly RMB 2 billion of the Yunnan tourist hotels (Zhongguo Lvyou Nianjian Bianjibu 1997, 349, 372). By 2000, Guizhou had just fifty-nine star-rated hotels, including just thirteen with more than three stars and no five-star hotels. In 2008, Guizhou had two five-star hotels and twenty-four with four stars. That is, despite Guizhou's increasing its total number of star-rated hotels between 2000 and 2008 from 59 to 279, Yunnan still had more than three times the number.

The structure of the Guizhou tourism industry is also reflected in its tourism industry training system. In 1990, Guizhou tourism officials established a dispersed training system, with three tourism vocational institutes and one tourism training center teaching participants in the ethnic villages how to provide food, lodging, and other fundamental services (Zhongguo Lvyou Nianjian Bianjibu 1991, 424). Moreover, the provincial government signaled its commitment to using tourism as a part of its poverty reduction efforts when it sent a dozen prefecture and county-level leaders for training in Beijing in the mid-1990s under a national initiative that focused on poor, remote, and minority regions. Yunnan, by contrast, offered formal degree programs in tourism, including an associate's degree, in a Kunming-based vocational school, and a tourism institute in Lijiang that was at one time affiliated with Yunnan University.

Why are direct benefits from tourism important? After all, tourism has indirect effects such as providing employment in hotels, restaurants, and shops; increasing demand for food and other agricultural products; and attracting government revenues that sometimes fund poverty reduction initiatives. In reality, such indirect benefits are in many cases surprisingly limited. Although successful tourist areas do increase the demand for labor, often it is nonpoor people (including the friends and relatives of investors from outside the area) who benefit most, particularly in tourist sites located in nonpoor areas. By contrast, rural residents who participate in tourist sites near their homes tend to keep more of their earnings (particularly compared to migrants). Living at home typically reduces expenses and allows workers to continue farming, with the tourism revenues providing critical sources of cash. Being able to supplement incomes closer to home also avoids other problems, including the abuse and exploitation that rural-to-urban migrants

10. As noted previously, the Guizhou government did construct a 137-kilometer highway linking Guiyang with Huangguoshu—its most significant highway project for tourism. By contrast, most of the 3,458 kilometers of high-grade highway in Yunnan link Kunming with the major provincial tourism sites.

commonly face (e.g., Solinger 1999; see chap. 4).[11] Although rising demand for food can supplement to the incomes of those farmers who plant cash crops, these indirect benefits of tourism are often limited; Xishuangbanna, for example, imports much of its food and other supplies from outside. Finally, although some local government coffers have been filled with tourism taxes and receipts, this added revenue has rarely been invested in poverty reduction programs. Instead, many local governments invest in the urbanization of the prefecture capitals or county seats, as in Dali, and not in the countryside. Even when the poor benefit directly from tourism, powerful outsiders tend to control the development of the industry, as Oakes (1998) persuasively argues is true in Guizhou. Nevertheless, despite their lack of control, the poor do far more than merely perform on command for outside interests and local governments. Moreover, the power inequalities in Guizhou that Oakes highlights have been much more severe in Yunnan, where poor people are often effectively excluded from nearly any form of participation in tourism.

My secondary sources support that tourism efforts in Guizhou effectively reduced poverty. For instance, the provincial government claimed that it developed tourism in 648 ethnic villages, increasing incomes sufficiently to bring nearly 100,000 households and 330,000 people out of poverty by October 1996 (Guizhou Nianjian Bianjibu 1997, 589). The government data may be exaggerated, but anecdotal evidence from outside researchers supports the spirit of these claims. For example, Oakes (1998, 126, 181) reports that Heitu households annually earned an estimated RMB 571 from tourism, increasing the average per capita village income dramatically from RMB 167 in 1991 to RMB 670 in 1993, and that tourism fees alone in 1993 profited households in Changlinggang village RMB 1,746 on average. The Chinese Academy of Science notes that annual average per capita incomes rose from RMB 200 in 1992 to RMB 1200 by 1994 in Tianhetan village, and that taxes from tourism at Wuyang River made up one-third of the entire budget of Shibin county (Wang and Zhang 2003). By 2001, the benefits of the tourism industry in Shibin and other poor counties prompted Yang Shengming, director of the Guizhou Tourism Department, to laud the industry for bringing in opportunities for poor people outside of agriculture (Guizhou Nianjian Bianjibu 2002, 276).

Data from provincial statistical yearbooks for Guizhou and Yunnan allow us to generalize these examples and further support our argument. Poverty rates are not available below the Chinese provincial level; however, comparing the changes in the net rural incomes of each county with GDP underscores the different effects of the two styles of tourism development.

11. In Shangri-la, for instance, one hostel owner who was a young investor from Beijing delayed paying her three migrant workers their monthly salaries of RMB 300 for several weeks while she gambled nightly with the adult children of local officials.

For instance, in 1992–2002, the nominal GDP of Jinghong (capital of Xishuangbanna, in Yunnan), Dali, and Lijiang quintupled. The GDP of Zhenning county in Guizhou, which contains Huangguoshu Waterfall, also grew, but at about half this rate. The slowest growing of these three Yunnan tourist spots grew nearly two-thirds faster than the average tourist county in Guizhou. Moreover, not one county (poor or nonpoor) in Guizhou with tourism resources came close to matching the economic growth rate of the Yunnan tourist areas.

Despite this relatively modest growth in Guizhou, between 1993 and 2002 the per capita net rural income of the counties containing ethnic tourist villages increased on average by 291 percent. If we count just the poor counties with ethnic villages, the net rural income rose even further, by 337 percent, during that period.[12] The net rural income of Leishan, for instance, rose 422 percent (from RMB 248 in 1993 to RMB 1,294 in 2002), and the net rural income of the Dong county of Congjiang, with several ethnic tourist villages, increased by 336 percent. Although the GDP of the Yunnan tourism counties increased rapidly, the growth of the net rural incomes of these counties was much lower than in Guizhou tourism counties. In an indication of limited spread of the effects of the Yunnan tourism industry, the net rural incomes of the counties surrounding Dali and Lijiang (in Yunnan) increased at less than half the rate of the counties surrounding Huangguoshu (in Guizhou). The incomes of those counties also grew more slowly than that of the average poor county in Yunnan and increased at a rate significantly lower than half the average of poor tourism counties in Guizhou. These statistics are consistent with the evidence presented here from secondary sources, interviews and fieldwork. Overall, the benefits of Yunnan tourism were concentrated in nonpoor counties and were directed primarily toward increasing GDP, whereas the benefits of Guizhou tourism were more evenly spread.

Moreover, Guizhou tourism development is not likely to morph into Yunnan tourism. This contrasting pattern in the two provinces has persisted since the late 1980s, and it is likely to remain so unless one province changes its tourism development policies.

Case Studies

Case studies illustrate the importance of distribution and structure in understanding the effects of tourism on economic growth and rural poverty

12. Note that the net rural incomes of both the poor and nonpoor Guizhou counties with ethnic villages increased much faster than that of the average Guizhou poor county (268 percent).

reduction. I present here four sites in Yunnan (Xishuangbanna, Lijiang, Shangri-la, and Tengchong) and two sites in Guizhou (Upper Langde and Caohai).[13]

Xishuangbanna (Yunnan)

The Xishuangbanna Dai autonomous prefecture, consisting of three non-poor counties in the southern tip of Yunnan, is characterized by a lush tropical rainforest that supports a diverse range of protected plants and animals, including half of the endangered plants in China. The government encouraged tourism based on the natural and cultural endowments of the prefecture in the early to mid-1980s. Since the late 1980s, tourism flows to Xishuangbanna increased more than 20 percent annually. Between 1991 and 1996, the number of international tourists to the prefecture increased from 8,460 to more than 23,000, and the Chinese visitors doubled from 600,000 to more than 1.2 million. Tourism also became increasingly important to the local economy, accounting for 26 percent of the total GDP of the prefecture by 1994.

The National Tourism Bureau survey conducted in 1994 suggested that tourism in the prefecture is relatively decentralized; its eight hundred tourist sites are distributed among forty towns and organized around four popular tourist routes that are spread among its three counties. Tourists generally do not tarry in rural areas; instead, an estimated 99 percent of tourists make their base in, and take day trips from, Jinghong (the prefecture capital), a medium-size city where the majority of travel agents and hotels are located. Attempts to set up lodging in the vicinity of the nature reserves, such as Dai-style accommodations built in the Menglun Botanical Gardens, failed due to competition from the more established tourist facilities located in the prefecture capital. Thus rural tourist sites in the region "can only obtain tourist income from lunch and entrance fees plus small sales of tourist commodities" (Wen and Tisdell 2001, 216). Even here, many tourists are suspicious of the authenticity of wares sold there and prefer to buy minority clothing and other goods from Kunming-based shops. Thus, despite the abundance of tourism in Xishuangbanna, the structure of the tourism industry in this area reduces the direct benefits for its poor.

Lijiang (Yunnan)

Although it was officially opened to foreigners in 1985, Lijiang did not receive the resources needed to increase the scale of tourism until the tragic

13. Unless otherwise indicated, the information in this section is from my fieldwork. Much of the information on Xishuangbanna comes from Wen and Tisdell (2001, chap. 8).

1996 earthquake[14] and the subsequent listing of the city as a UNESCO World Heritage site in 1997 (UNESCO 2009). Drawn by the Yulong Snow Mountain and a well-preserved, albeit highly commercialized, Old Town area, the number of visitors to Lijiang exploded from 98,000 (principally foreign backpackers) in 1990 to nearly 3.4 million in 2005. Although the government is at pains to protect the Old Town from overdevelopment, the area is crowded; there are 2,600 shops in a 2.7 square kilometer area of the Old Town alone hawking handicrafts, Naxi clothing and souvenir T-shirts, Chinese traditional herbs, tea, and art.[15]

Despite this growth in volume, relatively little of the wealth generated in the area reaches poor rural people. In terms of distribution, five of the six county-level governments in the prefecture (including Lijiang Municipality itself) were designated non-poor counties in the original 1986 list and in the 1994 expanded list (and Yongsheng county was added during the 2001 readjustment). Moreover, although some additional sites have been opened, including nearby temples and a soon-to-be-opened site promoting Dongba culture, tourist activities still center on the Yulong Snow Mountain and the Old Town, both in the immediate Lijiang area where few poor rural residents reside.[16] Exacerbating the inequitable distribution, tourism is largely structured to impede the participation of poor people. Although the architecture of Old Town is maintained in the traditional Naxi style, many locals (who are classified as urban, in any case) rent their houses to entrepreneurs from outside the province, especially investors from the eastern coast of China and from neighboring Sichuan province. These and the seventy-five star-rated hotels in the area are largely out of the reach of poor residents. Even the backpacker hostels are largely owned and staffed by nonpoor people, many of them from outside the province. The handicrafts sold as authentic Naxi traditional pieces are also primarily manufactured outside the area.[17] Many of the agricultural products, such as popular *tianma* (a tall gastrodia tuber) and highly sought-after fungi, sold in the area are gathered or grown in surrounding nonpoor counties.

Yet poor people are not completely excluded from the tourism industry in Lijiang. Young people from the poorer surrounding rural areas do

14. The earthquake (7.0 on the Richter scale) killed 309 people and caused an estimated RMB 2.5 million in damage. The ancient buildings in the Old City, built using traditional techniques, largely survived the earthquake, unlike buildings in the newer areas of the city (Yunnan Nianjian Bianjibu 1997).

15. Interviews with the officials from the Lijiang Old Town Protection Committee, local residents, and residents of the countryside surrounding Lijiang.

16. Lugu Lake in Ninglang county, several hours drive northeast, is an exception to this; there poor people do directly participate in tourism.

17. Local interviews. For instance, one village in Heqing county in Dali prefecture, south of Lijiang, makes most of the silver handicrafts found in Lijiang, as well as many of the silver handicrafts of a variety of ethnic groups sold in many minority areas throughout southwestern China.

work in the Old Town shopping districts as shop assistants, earning an average of RMB 300 per month plus room and board, as well as benefiting from the increased demand for agricultural products. Nonetheless, even though the wealth created through rapid tourism development has contributed to the GDP of the area, the distribution and structure of the tourism industry in Lijiang funnels much of the returns to investors and other nonpoor beneficiaries from outside the area. And top local officials plan to increase further the scale of the industry, in the hope that Lijiang will be placed on the itineraries of most international tourists, along with Beijing, Shanghai, and Xi'an.

Shangri-la (Yunnan)

Unlike other Yunnan tourist areas, most important tourist sites in Shangri-la[18] are located in counties designated as poor in 1986. The area was opened for tourism in 1997, and four years later, the tourism revenues exceeded those of logging, previously the largest industry, by RMB 10 million. The name change in 2001, combined with the completion a major road and a tiny airport, further stimulated tourism in this poor rural Tibetan region (Hillman 2003, 175–88). Because this county is classified as poor and has been recently opened for tourism, it can be used as a test for the poverty reduction potential of tourism industry development in Yunnan.

Despite the favorable distribution of tourism, the structure of the industry in Shangri-la constrains the participation of the poor in most of the popular sites, including Songzanlin Monastery, Bita Hai, and Shudu Lake. One of the most popular sites, the three-centuries-old Songzanlin Monastery, 5 kilometers from the county seat, excludes the participation of most poor people. All commerce inside the monastery, such as selling incense sticks for honoring the Buddhist images, is controlled by the monastery. Of the dozens of souvenir stalls conducting business outside, only two or three are owned by local residents; entrepreneurs from the wealthier Chinese coastal areas or from Sichuan run most of those shops.[19] The adjoining four-star Songtsam Hotel, a Sino-Singaporean joint venture, employs some two dozen staff, half of whom come from the urban county seat and half of whom come from outside the area. Similarly, the Bita Hai, a protected nature reserve, also excludes poor

18. In December 2001, the Chinese State Council allowed the little-known, primarily Tibetan county, Zhongdian, in northwestern Yunnan to rename itself "Shangri-la," based on the legendary paradise and due to its similarity with the descriptions in James Hinton's fictional novel *Lost Horizon.* Tourism to this region stimulated an economy that had been devastated by the ban on logging in 1998. The process of this name change and its impact on the local culture are analyzed by Ben Hillman (2003).

19. Generally, it is more difficult for poor people to sell factory-produced goods from stalls, which require capital and know-how to manage, than to make traditional handicrafts at home and sell them either directly to tourists or on contract to distributors, as is often the case in Guizhou.

people. After alighting from a taxi or bus (no public transportation serves the greater Shangri-la area, deterring independent budget travelers) and purchasing a ticket (RMB 30 at the gate), tourists are ferried by an environmentally friendly bus (for a further RMB 30) to the nature reserve and lake a few kilometers down a paved road as one of a half-dozen tour guides introduces the area. No one except a few dozen park employees (mostly urbanites from the county seat) lives inside this protected area. All activities, including taking a boat across the river, the restaurant, and the small campground with cottages for guests, are controlled by the park. This site is similar in structure to others in Shangri-la; although poor people live adjacent to the sites, very few of them benefit significantly from it, even indirectly.

One exception to this pattern of exclusion is Napa Hai, where local Tibetans living in nearby poor villages guide guests on horses through this wetland. Although the area can be traversed in several minutes, many tourists pay the RMB 30 fee to ride the horses around the site. Of this fee, however, the investor in the site (who charges ticket prices of RMB 30 in addition to the cost of horse riding) pockets all but RMB 5 per rider. Moreover, the tourist season for the wetland is limited, with black-necked cranes and other protected species of birds nesting in the area only from May to August. During the off-season, the wetland birds depart and the water levels drop precipitously; tourism similarly declines to a trickle. Nevertheless, local residents do benefit directly, making this site exceptional in Shangri-la. In 2004, participants reported earning approximately RMB 300 (on-season) and RMB 100–200 (off-season) monthly, significant in an area where the annual per capita net rural income that year averaged RMB 1,256 (State Statistical Bureau 2002c; local interviews). Nevertheless, these benefits are limited by the structure of the site, which principally benefits outside investors. In addition, the poor at other attractions scattered throughout the county are denied even the limited benefits afforded at this site.

Tengchong (Yunnan)

Two of the key Yunnan tourist destinations are located in a poor county; Tengchong is one of them. Although poor people can participate in some elements of the tourism industry here, the industry is not large and, in many ways, is structured to prevent such participation.[20] Although the county boasts a noted town, settled by retired overseas Chinese and containing the largest rural library in China, Tengchong is most famous for two main volcanic areas. In the north, two dormant volcanoes can be climbed using a set of high stone staircases constructed for that purpose. In addition to the

20. Tucked in the southwestern corner of the province bordering Myanmar and opened during the Qing Dynasty, Tengchong was once important enough to justify a British Embassy, opened in 1899; see http://www.echinaromance.com/destinations/tengchong.htm.

stairs and the pagodas, the park has a museum and narrow stone pathways that lead visitors to other nearby attractions. A wide stone pathway to the volcano is lined with shops selling furniture and decorations made of volcanic stone. Although local rural residents participate by transporting people in horse-drawn carriages from the road, where tourist vehicles can stop, to the main gate (a relatively brief and manageable walk, especially compared to the stairs up the volcano), the tourist area itself is fenced in and thus excludes people, other than the shopkeepers, who might sell handicrafts or agricultural products to tourists.

In the southern part of Tengchong county lies a site with natural hot springs baths, which does employ local residents. It is structured in a way that poor people can participate, although not as directly as in many ethnic minority areas. But, even though Tengchong is a national site and has well-developed local infrastructure (and an improving road system), it is among the less renowned and least visited Yunnan tourist sites. Thus, counties such as Tengchong (and Yuanyang, discussed earlier in this chapter) could use tourism to decrease poverty, but have lacked, until recent years, sufficient resources to promote the local tourism industry. Moreover, the tourism resources they did develop were often structured in ways that precluded the participation of poor people.

Upper Langde (Guizhou)

In the poor county of Leishan lies the tourism town of Upper Langde, described at the beginning of this chapter. This area in central Guizhou exemplifies the dozens of ethnic minority villages in poor areas that the provincial government opened to tourists in the late 1980s and early 1990s (Oakes 1998, esp. 193–206). A Miao village, some 30 kilometers down a paved two-lane road from the prefecture capital of Kaili, Langde was promoted as a tourist destination in the *nongjiale* style. Tourists stay in rustic rural homes; eat food prepared by poor people; and enjoy ethnic singing, dance, and culture. Financed by the Tourism Bureau, the Provincial Minorities Committee, and the Cultural Bureau, with Langde natives who migrated to the Chinese coast, the government and locals here developed facilities for tourists while protecting the traditional architectural style of Miao culture. They also structured tourism in the villages in ways that foster the participation of poor people. Most commonly, tourists arrive in organized groups. For each group the prefecture China International Travel Service pays the village a set fee, with an estimated 20 percent going to pay for expenses and the remaining 80 percent being distributed among the villagers participating in the tourism industry (Oakes 1998, 180).[21] Traditional

21. According to Oakes (1998), the China International Travel Service initially paid RMB 40–50 per group, which soon increased to RMB 150 and then reached RMB 320 by 1994. He

meals are purchased directly from, prepared by, and eaten with local families in their homes, with the price of the meal going directly to that family. Overnight guests typically do not stay with families (as they do in some other *nongjiale*-style destinations) but in dormitory-style rooms furnished with clean beds. The village head estimated in 2004 that the average family earns approximately RMB 300 each month from tour-group fees, selling handicrafts, preparing meals, and receiving tips for performances and pictures. Tourism has become a primary and crucial source of cash in Upper Langde that supplements subsistence agriculture (the average household is endowed with only 0.5 *mu* per person) and some migrant remittances.[22]

Caohai (Guizhou)

Weining county, located in the northwest corner of Bijie prefecture on the border with Yunnan province, is among the poorest regions in Guizhou (ranking sixty-third of eighty-seven counties in net rural income in 1995) and also in China as a whole. Within Weining lies one of the most intriguing Guizhou tourist spots—the nature reserve and bird sanctuary known as Caohai ("Grass Sea"). The Caohai wetland, with a long history punctuated with occasional unfortunate periods,[23] is shallow, with an average depth of 2 meters. More than 100,000 birds of 185 species flock to the lake during the winter months. Seven species, including the black-necked crane, black stork, and white-tailed eagle, are endangered and are included on the national "first-class protected bird" list; an additional twenty species (including the Eurasian crane and white spoonbill) appear on the second-class protected list. A bird sanctuary has been established here, managed by a handful of professionals from an office on the lake.

The lake draws reasonable tourist traffic given its remote location, estimated at several hundred individual overseas tourists each year, along with several thousand Chinese tourists coming in groups or individually. Because farms in the vicinity extend to the edge of the marshy wetland, the only practical way to tour the lake is by a flat-bottom boat, which can be hired at the dock at a negotiated hourly rate. In addition, several boats in the middle of the lake sell food and drinks, including barbequed fish and meat, as well as various "specialties of Caohai." Groups of Chinese tourists can be seen, even in the off-season, taking advantage of these services, lounging in boats in the middle of the wetland, drinking, eating, and enjoying the view.

---

also notes that by 1993 two-thirds of the household incomes in the village came from tourism. This is also consistent with another estimate of RMB 300 per capita income from tourism in 1996. See also Wang and Zhang (2003).

22. Local interviews. A *mu* is approximately 0.16 of an acre.

23. The wetland was nearly destroyed during the Cultural Revolution, when it was drained in a failed attempt to use it as farmland. It has been slowly reconstructed over the years and now is approximately 20 square kilometers.

The people involved in this site (approximately 120 people in 2004) have formed an association. Tourists wishing to hire a punt negotiate a price at the dock with a scheduler; the punters themselves are not involved in the process. All proceeds received from renting the boats and selling refreshments are then divided fairly among all the people in the association. Interviews that I conducted with punters, schedulers, and farmers in the vicinity of the lake (who are not part of the association) uncovered no complaints about the fairness of the process. As a result, these rural residents essentially have a monopoly over boat rides on the lake, which prevents tourists from engaging them in a bidding war that would minimize the price. Because the punters receive only a RMB 0.1 bonus for taking people out onto Caohai and rely on the association to earn the bulk of their money, they have little incentive to undercut other punters and work hard to get their cut of the proceeds. This means that prices are checked primarily by tourist demand. Although the volume of tourists is not large, tourists come a long way to see the lake; thus, they rarely refuse to take the boat ride simply because of the price.

The money earned from this venture in the off-season by each participant is estimated to be RMB 150–180 per month. If we assume this as the earnings per month throughout the year (clearly an underestimation, given that on-season earnings should exceed off-season earnings), this would increase the incomes of the rural participants by RMB 1,800–2,160 per year. Combined with income from farming, migrants' remittances, and other sources, the money earned from tourism can be vital to helping those in poverty earn incomes that exceed the poverty line. Although this small tourism industry helps a limited number of households, the income from tourism for the participating households is crucial and greater than it would have been had the structure of tourism development been more top-down style, as seen in other provinces.

As we have seen, the main tourism industry in Yunnan is focused on the rich cultural diversity of the province and is centered in rural, predominantly minority regions. Moreover, tourism has grown rapidly there, and the province has become one of the most popular tourist destinations in China. The distribution and structure of the tourism industry in Yunnan primarily promotes economic growth, with a more limited effect on rural poverty reduction. Even though Yunnan has many potential tourist attractions in poor counties, the government has not allocated the attention and resources needed to turn their natural beauty and ethnic cultures into viable tourist spots, focusing instead on developing tourist destinations in the nonpoor counties. Although the initial growth of tourism in these regions may have helped lift local residents out of poverty, the continued investment in the 1990s contributed more to economic growth than to poverty reduction. Meanwhile, the resulting large-scale Yunnan tourism industry reduced in many ways the participation of poor people in the tourism sector. By the early 1990s, the main rural tourist destinations that had been previously developed largely exhausted their potential for poverty reduction. Further investment continued to develop these sites, and the tourism infrastructure in these places increased in quality and scale. As a result, although many poor people benefited from tourism in these places, the main beneficiaries of these large-scale activities were nonpoor residents and outside investors, many from the eastern coast.

In Guizhou, on the other hand, many tourist activities and sites are distributed in modest villages in poor counties and structured to be small in scale. As a result, poor rural residents benefit directly by hosting tourists, both foreign and domestic. Although the amounts of money involved—and thus the profits—are usually quite modest, they can make a big difference in the income of poor people. In addition, at the Huangguoshu Waterfall, and other sites that are larger in scale, the government promoted the participation of the poor, and linked these major tourism sites to a western tourism circuit of ethnic minority villages. In the *nongjiale*-style ethnic villages established during the early 1990s, poor rural residents directly participate in the tourism industry, providing the food, lodging, and entertainment. The provincial government, which helped to establish these areas and attract and organize tour groups.[24]

Thus, the examples of Guizhou and Yunnan demonstrate how the structure of an industry can affect economic growth and poverty reduction. The development of tourism in the two provinces, whether it is small or large in scale and whether it is labor- or capital-intensive, determined the extent to which it generated employment for local residents.

In the process of promoting their tourism industries, the two provincial governments played a crucial role in shaping the development and structure of tourism. For Yunnan, the central and provincial governments together selected the sites that were to be developed for tourism. When, in the 1990s, provincial and central leaders faced a choice between expanding the number of tourist sites to other areas with significant tourism resources or focusing on improving those sites that had already been developed, they ultimately chose the latter. Although this decision not to spread resources too thin probably allowed the rapid development of the tourism industry, this decision reduced the impact of tourism on poverty reduction, especially in the 1990s and beyond. The Guizhou government chose a different approach. In addition to developing the Huangguoshu Waterfall, it also developed ethnic-

24. Oakes (1998) argues that government organizations, in attracting tour groups and earning profits from them, are exploiting rural labor. This arrangement does meet the Marxian definition of *exploitation;* certainly, the ability to attract and organize tour groups is a form of power (Mowforth and Munt 2003, 172). Nevertheless, without the government playing this role, it is unlikely that rural residents would be able to organize their own tourist attractions successfully, let alone market them to distant tourists in China and abroad.

based tourism. It located these tourist sites in poor counties and spread the tourism industry to every prefecture in the province; in doing so, the Guizhou government enhanced the degree to which this investment reduced poverty in these areas. In addition, the government supported development that kept the scale of tourism small enough to facilitate the participation of poor people in the industry. Whereas Yunnan policymakers spent billions of yuan developing their tourist sites, Guizhou policymakers depended on relatively minor infrastructure investments and market-promotion activities.

6

Coal Mining

Black Gold

> Coal is the food of industry.
> —Vladimir Lenin, 1917

The man's story was as surprising as it was haunting. In a guesthouse in the Guizhou town of Bakai early in my travels, I sat transfixed as Mr. Liu described how he made his living. In the off-season, this farmer organized several of his neighbors to mine coal. This small group of men, armed with pickaxes and other simple tools, together went into a pit mine and extracted the coal, which they then sold directly to a local brickmaker. (This was not quite as informal as it sounds—they obtained the necessary licenses from the local township government and filed a mining plan.) In this way, these poor farmers supplemented their meager incomes from farming. Mr. Liu was well aware of the risks—mining coal in this way was unhealthy at best and could prove fatal at worst—fatal accidents were an all-too-common occurrence in informal mines. Nevertheless, during my subsequent travels, I discovered many instances of the general phenomenon—through its relatively relaxed regulations and policies, the Guizhou government had fostered opportunities for people like Mr. Liu and his neighbors to improve their livelihoods.

Coal mining, like tourism, is an industry that often helps directly reduce rural poverty. Although extraordinarily dangerous, coal mining is a relatively low-skilled activity in which many able-bodied poor people can participate. Coal is often found in developing countries and has been a catalyst for economic changes in many of them. For instance, one World Bank report lists sixty developing countries, China among them, in which mining either had already made or had the potential to make major economic contributions to economic growth, poverty reduction, or both. The report divides mining industries into three different categories based on scale: (1) industries that are sufficiently large to make a difference on an international scale, (2) smaller industries that can still have an impact on a national or regional scale, and (3) industries consisting of "small-scale or artisanal" mining that can benefit rural or remote communities (Weber-Fahr et al. 2002). Each of these types can affect poverty and development.

Mining can theoretically benefit poor people by directly increasing rural incomes, enhancing the tax base to fund local government service programs, and bringing in ancillary benefits such as improved infrastructure and cheaper supplies of energy. Although large-scale mines often produce more tax revenue and infrastructure, the benefits to poor people are indirect and sometimes limited. Despite their promises, governments often do not invest tax revenues in social services or employment generation programs, preferring to spend it on policies or perks that benefit nonpoor people. Infrastructure produced alongside the development of mines also help poor people but only if rural residents are permitted access to them in ways that enhances their income (Weber-Fahr et al. 2002). On the negative side, large mines can worsen the livelihoods of local poor residents by competing for scarce natural resources, denying access to local infrastructure on which the poor rely, and raising local prices as income spent by the wealthier mine workers increases demand for food and other basic commodities (Weber-Fahr et al. 2002). Despite their being generally more polluting and wasteful, smaller mines are often on a scale and have a structure that enable poorly educated and less-experienced people to work in them. Small-scale mines are often an outlet of last resort for rural residents and are an important source of poverty alleviation (McMahon et al. 2000).[1] Throughout the world, large-scale mining extracts 95 percent of the total world mineral production employing just 2.5 million people, whereas smaller-scale mining employs an estimated 13 million workers and directly or indirectly supports an estimated 80–100 million people (Weber-Fahr et al. 2002). Overall, large-scale mines require relatively advanced equipment and capital-intensive labor-saving techniques, whereas smaller-scale mines are more labor-intensive and generally employ cruder technology and tools that are accessible to less formally educated workers. Thus, smaller mines can make a greater difference in reducing poverty, whereas large ones can have a greater effect on economic productivity and growth. The effect of the coal industry on poverty and economic growth is thus contingent on the distribution and structure of the industry.

The link between coal mining and economic growth is contentious. On the one hand, economists of all stripes, from dependency theorists such as Raul Prebisch (1950) to more market-oriented scholars like Jeffrey Sachs (e.g., Sachs and Warner 1995) have established that resource-poor economies,

1. As a World Bank study on coal mining and poverty notes, "[M]ore often than not, small-scale mining is a default option chosen as a direct result of economic contraction in other sectors or geographic areas. In that case, miners and their families often expose themselves to harsh working conditions for minimal income in a high-risk context, endangering their health and often the surrounding environment" (Weber-Fahr et al. 2002, 449).

such as Japan, Sweden, Singapore, and South Korea, often outperform resource-rich ones such as Mexico, Nigeria, and Russia. This is true even after controlling for factors that are thought to be critical for economic growth, such as levels of initial per capita income, trade policy, and investment rates (Sachs and Warner 1995).[2] Potential explanations for this phenomenon range from boom-bust cycles (Gelb 1988; Black, McKinnish, and Sanders 2003) inherent in most extractive industries to the so-called "Dutch Disease" caused by the rise in value of the currency of the country (Auty 1995; Collier 2007). Two of these explanations are especially applicable to China. First, reliance on mining harms the economy of a country through a "scissors effect," caused by lower-cost raw materials being exported in exchange for higher-cost imports manufactured using the raw materials (Prebisch 1950). In China, this effect takes place internally, disadvantaging coal-rich regions over others. Second, few coal industries throughout world history have ever been profitable; the majority rely heavily on state subsidies to continue operating (Thomson 2003, 77–78).

On the other hand, as implied by the quotation from Lenin that begins this chapter, the development of coal can literally fuel other industries, promoting economic growth. The money spent on large-scale mining spreads into other sectors of the economy, to both refiners and suppliers in lateral and downstream activities (Weber-Fahr et al. 2002). A study by Gary McMahon and Felix Remy (2001) concludes that every US$1 spent in the mining sector generates, on average, US$2.80 in the local economy because mining encourages ancillary services. Moreover, most modern industrialized countries, including Germany, Britain, and the United States, depended on their endowments of natural resources for their early growth and development (DeLong and Williamson 1994; Thomson 2003).[3] Thus, in a developing country, investment in the mining industry can stimulate poor economies, increase productivity, provide employment, motivate the construction of infrastructure, and bring industrialization to primarily agrarian areas. Whether it actually does so depends on a range of factors, including the scale of mining, the price of coal, and domestic and international economic factors.

Coal Mining in China

In China, the coal industry, although rarely profitable, has undergirded national development. China relies on coal for more than two-thirds of its

2. Sachs and Warner (1995) find that only two of the eighteen resource-abundant countries they studied—Malaysia and Mauritius—had a sustained annual growth of greater than 2 percent. Although they suggest Botswana is also an example, they lack the data to establish this.

3. Sachs and Warner (1995, 3) respond that, with falling transportation costs, the availability of natural resources inside a given country during its development phase is not as important today as it was in previous eras. For instance, Japan and Korea became large-scale producers of steel despite their dependence on imports of iron ore.

overall energy and 80 percent of its electricity (Rui 2004, 3). Since 1989, China has reclaimed its position as the largest producer of coal in the world, a status it held between 1000 and 1769 A.D. and lost when James Watt invented the steam engine, sharply increasing the demand for coal in the West (Thomson 2003). In the beginning of the Chinese reform era of 1978, the central leaders perceived energy shortages to be among the most salient impediments to further economic growth. As a result, Gao Yangwen, the coal industry minister, spearheaded the effort to reform the coal industry, establishing new incentives to reward increased production, and generally to reduce the role of party officials in production decisions. Although the Third Front initiative between 1964 and 1971 was well known for increasing coal production—which rose from 278 million to 392 million tons[4] (Thomson 2003, 55)—even greater increases in coal production occurred during the reform era that commenced in 1978. Although in the twenty-nine years between 1949 and 1978 coal production rose rapidly (if unsteadily), adding 548 million tons to the annual production of China, the period between 1978 and 1997 saw an even more remarkable increase of 690 million tons.[5]

China categorizes its mines into three types, based on scale: (1) centrally controlled state-owned enterprise (SOE) mines; (2) locally managed SOE mines at provincial, prefecture, and county levels; and (3) town-and-village enterprise (TVE) mines, local non-state-owned mines under township, village, collective, or individual authority.[6] There is also a fourth, unofficial category, micro-scale mines, which are mined, often illegally, by groups of individuals, often on an ad hoc and seasonal basis.

After adopting a goal of producing 1.2 billion tons of coal by 2000 (a target reached six years early), the central government focused its attention on developing local mines, especially TVE mines, as the primary source of increased coal production. Although the central and provincial governments throughout the 1980s and early 1990s continued to support SOE mines, their strategy to increase growth centered on smaller-scale, locally owned mines because these were the easiest and least expensive to develop quickly. To stimulate the growth of TVE mines, the Chinese central government allowed any party that could credibly develop these mines to do so under licenses issued by local governments. As Gao said in 1983, "small mines can be run by communes, brigades and masses. . . . Cadres, technical personnel and workers can also run small mines individually or by raising funds. In a word, we welcome people from all walks of life to run small mines" (quoted in Thomson 2003, 117). In support of this effort, in 1981 the State Council

4. In this chapter, *tons* refers to metric tons.

5. The information from this section comes primarily from Thomson (2003).

6. Even though local TVE mines are technically considered to be outside the government, cadres and other government officials were allowed to invest in and manage these mines, and they often did (Thomson 2003).

approved four financial incentives to the operators of local mines, especially TVEs: subsidizing mines suffering from fiscal deficits, reducing or exempting them from industrial and commercial taxes, investing in capital construction and mechanization, and increasing the retention of depreciation funds (Thomson 2003, 117). The TVEs proved to be far more productive than the SOEs mines and the central government efforts at promoting these mines helped to significantly increase total coal production (Zheng, Yang, and Shao 2002). Moreover, because these mines relied on rural labor, the central government further hoped that the development of small-scale, non-state-owned local mines would reduce poverty and improve the welfare of local rural residents—an explicit goal of the policy.

Spurred by the government emphasis on small-scale mines, output from local mines increased 80 percent between 1980 and 2000, compared to 16 percent increases for centrally managed SOE mines. Most of the production gains, and most of the losses experienced between 1998 and 2000, were borne by these small-scale mines. The proportion of these smaller-scale mines increased from 15 percent in 1978 to 46 percent in 1995, before declining sharply. Meanwhile, the number of TVE mines also rose from 1.52 million firms in 1978 to 23.36 million in 1996, and the number of employees exploded from 28.27 million to 135.08 million. Simultaneously, the relative role of centrally controlled SOE mines declined from their dominant position in the pre-reform era (fig. 5), with the proportion of coal produced by central SOEs declining steadily from 53 percent of the industry total in 1978 to 38 percent in 1996. Similarly, the proportion controlled by local SOEs dropped from 29 percent in 1978 to 18 percent in 1996. In addition to central policies supporting the TVE mines, the smaller-scale mines also benefited from access to relatively prevalent and low-cost rural labor, as well as their relatively efficient (compared to SOE mines) production practices.[7] Further, provincial governments supplemented the central policies by adding their own incentives for the promotion of TVE mines. To this end, many provinces established their own laws and regulations shaping the development of TVE mines, which varied by province.

Whereas TVEs in other industries were especially crucial to the accelerated economic growth and prosperity in the rapidly growing Chinese coastal areas, TVE coal mines were particularly vital for poverty reduction in the inland and western provinces. Approximately 80 percent of all TVEs in coal-rich provinces in western, central, and northern China were associated with the coal industry. Moreover, because such industries were frequently positioned in poor areas, employment from coal mining proved

7. SOE mines were required to invest more in facilities, land recovery, environmental protection, and social welfare and pensions, which partially explains not only their relative inefficiency but also their overall losses. By the mid-1990s, SOE mines were among the industries deepest in red ink, with losses in 1998 totaling RMB 3.7 billion.

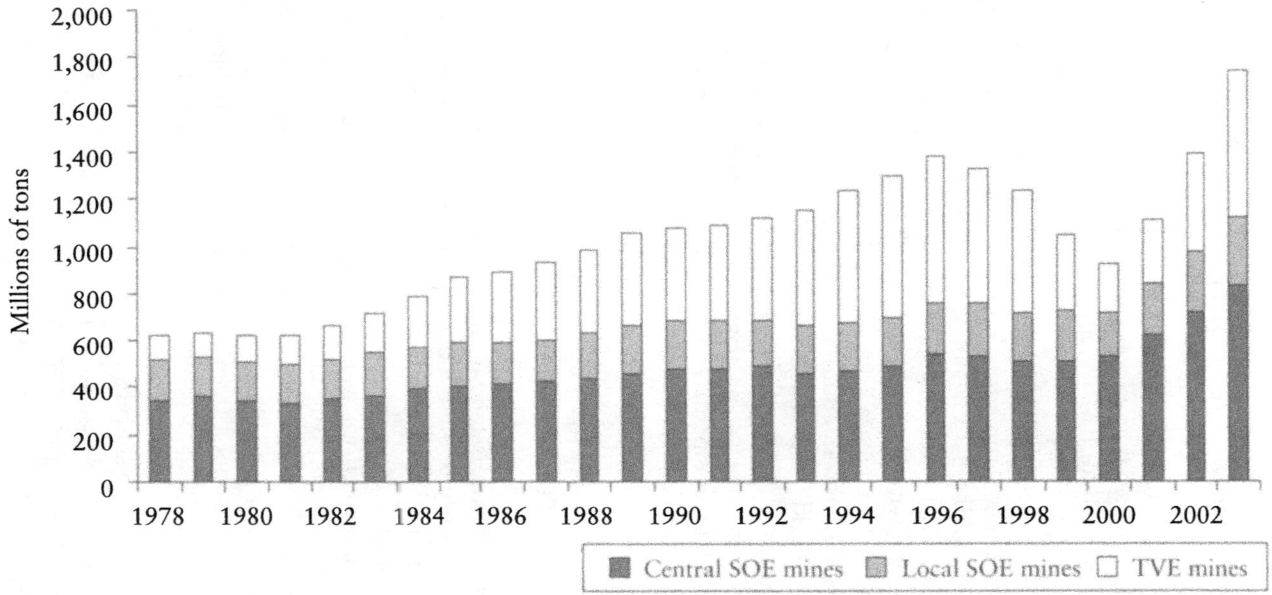

Fig. 5 Chinese coal production by type of mine ownership, 1978–2002. SOE, state-owned enterprise; TVE, township and village enterprise.
Source: Thomson (2003); Rui (2005).

to be vitally important for poor households. By the mid-1990s, the rural economy had become remarkably dependent on TVE mines, which employed almost 30 percent of the entire rural labor force (up from less than 10 percent in 1978) and were responsible for more than one-third of all rural income (up from 7.5 percent in 1978). Income from coal supported more than the individual miner (Rui 2004). One 2000 study of the mining industry in Shanxi revealed that migrants working in TVE coal mines remitted an average of more than RMB 3,000 annually to their families in their home villages (Zhang 2000).

The dominant position of the TVE mines shifted in the late 1990s due to the decision of the central government to protect SOEs from competition from overseas mines and Chinese TVE mines. Changes in the economy ramped up the pressure on SOEs of all kinds, including those in the coal sector. As reform deepened, and with layoffs in both the SOE mines and in the overall state sector spiking, the Chinese government aimed to minimize the social costs of closing SOE mines. In addition to pressures from reform, the entry of China into the World Trade Organization further motivated the central government. Because the most competitive coal mines in the global economy are those on the largest scale (Nolan 2001), the central government hoped to build up internationally competitive large-scale coal-producing enterprises. But declining prices for coal further exacerbated the SOE losses (Thomson 2003). Given the strategic and economic importance of the SOE mines, central government authorities sought additional protection for them by restricting and consolidating the TVE coal mines. Therefore, in November 1998 the Chinese central government implemented a two-pronged policy to "close coal mines and decrease output." In some areas, however, the local governments resisted, issuing licenses to local mines in contravention of central directives. Despite these local efforts, coal production as a whole temporarily declined and proportion of total coal production TVE mines dropped from 46 percent in 1995 to 24 percent in 2001. Although the goals of the central government efforts were ostensibly to reduce mining accidents and protect the environment, Rui (2004) links these measures with protecting and promoting larger-scale SOEs. During this time, the number of TVE coal mines declined from 23 million in 1996 to 21 million in 2001, and the number of employees dropped from 135 million to 120 million. Overall, the production of coal declined 30 percent, from 1.37 billion tons in 1996 to 951 million tons in 2000, whereas the proportion of coal produced by the central SOE mines rose sharply, from 40 percent in 1998 to 56 percent in 2001.[8] As a result of these consolidation efforts, the average output for each mining company increased from 17,000 tons per company in 1998 to 50,000 tons per company in 2002, and the share of the coal market of the

8. The production share of locally owned SOE mines increased more modestly, from 17 to 20 percent, during this period.

ten largest coal producers in China increased from 13 percent in 1997 to 21 percent in 2001.

These changes in production and in the relative importance of TVE mines were both relatively short-lived. In spite of the short-term success in achieving the government goals, the rapid economic expansion of China greatly increased the demand for fuel, compelling the government to reverse its earlier efforts to restrict coal production. By 2001, coal production had rallied, both generally and in the TVE mines in particular. Coal production in 2000–2003 exploded, rising 83 percent and reaching a historic high of 1.73 billion tons. Although the state-owned sector accounted for most of this trend, the proportion of coal produced by TVE mines rose during this period from 21 percent to 35 percent (although still well below its level in the mid-1990s). Moreover, whereas the government succeeded in closing many TVE mines, a portion of the local coal production shifted to the often illegal, micro-scale coal mines. The statistics published by Chinese authorities on the coal industry include SOE and TVE mines but not the micro-scale mines, making calculating their share of production difficult; nevertheless, some sources suggest that production from these mines was significant.[9] For example, a national conference at the end of 1995 found that half of all TVE mines were not licensed (Thomson 2003, 152).

On the whole, the size, scale, and distribution of the three types of Chinese mines—SOE, TVE, and micro-scale—have differing effects on economic growth and poverty reduction. Large SOE mines employ significant numbers of people, including some poor people, and on the whole they demand more skills, education, and experience than can be acquired by many poor rural residents. But, despite their relative inaccessibility to poor rural job-seekers, when SOE mines are located in poor counties, they can reduce poverty. They do so by employing poor people, producing ancillary industries (often TVE mines), and improving infrastructure. TVE mines are smaller in scale, make use of more labor-intensive mining tools, and typically hire untrained and poorly educated local rural residents or migrants (Wright 2004). In the smallest of these mines, poor rural residents can band together to form small ad hoc groups to exploit these resources. This is particularly true if the groups only require approval from township governments (the lowest level of formal Chinese government authority). If necessary, potential miners will forgo the licensing process entirely and mine illegally. Operators of micro-scale mines transport coal directly to market, and much of the profits go directly into the hands of poor people. Moreover, because these miners often mine close to home, their work in the off-season does not reduce the agriculture workforce.

9. Rui (2004) notes that in 1995 7,526 illegal mining groups extracted coal from SOE coalfields.

Tempering this rosy picture is the fact that Chinese mines "are the most dangerous in the world," according to one study on coal mining in China aptly subtitled *Your Rice Bowl or Your Life?* (Wright 2004, 631). Based on statistics that almost certainly understate the actual accident rate in Chinese mines, between 1992 and 2001, SOE mines were responsible for more than twice as many deaths per million tons of coal as were mines in India; this was nearly thirty times as many deaths as in U.S. coal mines in 1992–2002. Worse, two trends conspire to make TVE mines, the type of mine that has proven to be most helpful for poverty reduction in China, even more dangerous. First, there is a lack of strict management and safety standards, resulting in 7.7 times more fatalities in TVE mines than in the also dangerous, large SOE mines. Second, safety standards, which were improved in the 1980s, worsened in the 1990s just as the TVE mines were growing most rapidly. Despite the radically higher accident and death rates in TVE mines, many miners are compelled by economic necessity to continue working there, mainly because their families depend on the income from such mines. Rui argues,

> It is not because these mine-workers do not care about their lives, they simply have no alternatives. As found again and again in TVE mine accidents, most dead miners come from poor rural areas with high unemployment rates, they are willing to jeopardize their lives to earn a living. The survivors expressed themselves more directly: "This mine is dangerous. But where can I earn this RMB 200 per month if I leave here?"; and "without money, why should I need a life?" (2004, 12)

With each death a family loses a breadwinner, almost certainly adding to the number of poor. Nevertheless, these losses are unlikely to outweigh the benefits in terms of poverty reduction. At the mining death rates reported by Wright (2004), Guizhou is estimated to have lost approximately 125 miners in 1991, and 252 miners in 1996. This morbid calculation has to be weighed against the number of families that depend on mining for income, including the reported 300,000 workers formally employed in the mining industry in Guizhou in 1993 and many more who were employed informally in the industry (State Statistical Bureau 1994b, 54). The willingness of poor rural residents to work in these mines, despite their having the highest death rates in the world, underscores both the desperation of many residents of the Chinese hinterland and the importance of such mines in alleviating poverty.[10]

10. In studying the importance of Chinese TVE mines, two Chinese scholars concluded, in a somewhat exaggerated way, "in poor areas with large coal reserves, most towns and villages have escaped poverty and enriched themselves by depending on the contribution of TVE coal mines. [Such mines] have also made a great contribution to local infrastructure, education and social welfare" (Ye and Zhang 1998, 44–45).

Noting the importance of coal mining for poverty reduction should not be construed as promoting mining as a means of poverty reduction. Although mining is a prevalent low skill profession in southwest China, it is likely that there are many better ways of reducing poverty than through coal mining. The reality of being poor, however, implies a power differential that often means choosing among suboptimal alternatives. This sometimes means weighing the income that employment in coal mining might bring against the risk of injury or death. In the process of seeking alternative ways to alleviate poverty, I suspect we will discover that few solutions for poverty (originating from either the left or the right of the ideological spectrum) come without damning disadvantages. Almost every mechanism designed to reduce poverty brings with it negative consequences (as discussed in the conclusion to this book). My focus here is on the importance of the state's paying attention to the structure and distribution of industries to facilitate the access by poor people to any economic opportunities generated.

Guizhou and Yunnan Coal Mining

Southwestern China is an important source of coal. The region ranks third in China, with 8.6 percent of the total national reserves in 1986, behind the northern (50 percent) and northwestern (30 percent) regions.[11] In the pre-1949 era, the production of coal in the southwestern region was only a tiny proportion of the total Chinese production; during the Mao and, especially, the reform eras, the importance of coal from southwestern China increased gradually until by the mid-1990s it represented 15 percent of the total coal production of China.[12] Among the southwestern provinces, Guizhou and Yunnan contain the largest coal reserves, accounting for 59 percent and 28 percent, respectively. Guizhou possesses the fifth largest coal reserves in China, with 5.1 billion tons (approximately 5 percent of the national total), whereas Yunnan has the ninth largest reserves, with 2.4 billion tons (approximately 2.3 percent of the national total).

11. The northern region of China includes Hebei, Shanxi, Inner Mongolia, Beijing, and Tianjin. The northwestern region includes Shaanxi, Gansu, Qinghai, Ningxia, and Xinjiang. The southwestern region includes Yunnan, Guizhou, Guangxi, Sichuan, Chongqing, and Tibet.

12. According to the most accurate estimates, before 1949 coal production in the southwestern provinces was only approximately 0.4 percent of total Chinese production. This increased after 1949, and especially during the Third Front program, when railroads linking coal reserves with major cities in the region were built (especially linking Chongqing, Guiyang, and Kunming). By 1978, Guizhou produced 16.7 million tons of coal, approximately 2.7 percent of the total national production, whereas Yunnan produced approximately 14.8 million tons, approximately 2.4 percent of the national total. Local officials argued that many of the inefficiencies in the state-owned sector of the coal industry in both provinces are due to the Mao-era Third Front program. The vast majority of increases in coal production in the two provinces occurred after 1978 (Rui 2005; Thomson 2003).

The patterns of development of the coal industries in Yunnan and Guizhou differ markedly. Guizhou SOE mines are more concentrated than Yunnan SOEs, whereas Guizhou small-scale TVE mines are much more dispersed than Yunnan TVEs. Guizhou has large-scale, well-developed SOE mines concentrated in the four counties in the western prefecture of Liupanshui, which produces approximately one-third of all coal in the province. Much of the rest of the provincial production is from relatively small-scale TVE mines spread throughout the province. In contrast, five centrally administered and seven provincially administrated Yunnan SOE mines are distributed through seven counties in four prefectures and are therefore much less concentrated. Although Yunnan TVE mines produced the majority of its coal in the 1990s, these did not dominate the industry to the same extent that the Guizhou TVEs did.

Coal mining is one of the few major industries in which Guizhou enjoys a clear advantage over Yunnan. In the post-Mao reform era, the production capacity of Guizhou consistently exceeded that of Yunnan, and in most periods, it grew faster.[13] Overall, between 1978 and 1996 (before changes in central policy forced production cuts in both provinces), Guizhou coal production more than quadrupled (increasing 335 percent) compared to the growth of Yunnan production of 158 percent. In the first half of the 1990s, Guizhou coal production capacity increased 65 percent, from 37.23 million tons in 1991 to 61.54 million tons in 1996. During that same period, Yunnan coal production increased by a healthy, but more modest, 40 percent, rising from approximately 22 million tons in 1991 to 30.7 million tons in 1996. Expressed in per capita, the gap between Guizhou coal production capacity and Yunnan capacity is even starker, with the gap increasing especially rapidly in 1991–1996 and again in 2001–2004. The Guizhou productive capacity per capita was double that of Yunnan between 1993 and 1998. Central policy changes in the late 1990s also affected the industry in Guizhou more, especially initially. After 1998, while Guizhou production declined 39 percent, from 65.6 million to 40.3 million tons the next year, coal production in Yunnan declined 13 percent, from 30.9 million to 26.6 million tons. Nevertheless, the Guizhou coal industry was consistently larger than the Yunnan industry and apparently recovered from the cutbacks in the late 1990s; Guizhou production nearly tripled between 2001 and 2004.

Not only is the Guizhou coal industry larger than the Yunnan industry, but its distribution favors its poor areas. In 1996, 56 percent of the total Guizhou coal production came from poor counties, compared to 39 percent

13. This was not always the case in the pre-reform era. In 1952, production in Yunnan exceeded that in Guizhou by approximately 22 percent, whereas in 1965, Yunnan produced 61 percent more than Guizhou. In both years, the Yunnan production was trivial compared with the national production; in neither year did coal production in Yunnan exceed 1.7 percent of total Chinese production.

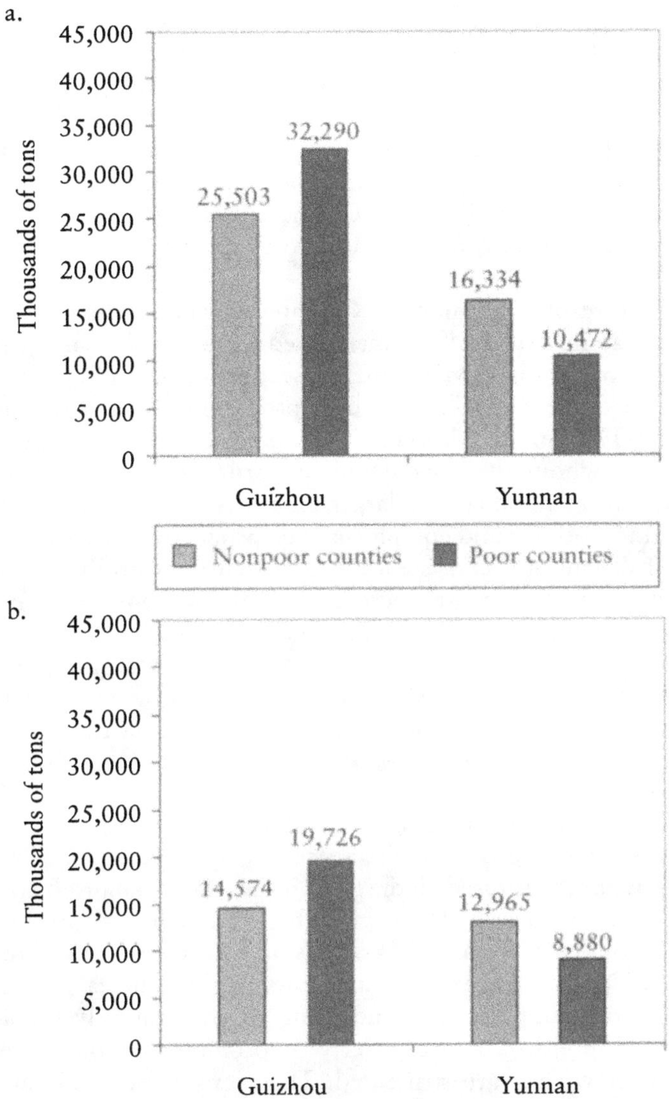

Fig. 6 Coal production—nonpoor versus poor counties in Guizhou and Yunnan. (a) 1996; (b) 2001.
Source: State Statistical Bureau (1997b, 2002b; 1997c, 2002c).

for Yunnan (see fig. 6).[14] Moreover, coal production in Guizhou poor counties was three times greater than production in Yunnan poor counties. Losses in the industry in the wake of changes in the central government

14. Coal production in Yunnan poor counties improved somewhat by 1996, when its poor counties produced approximately one-third of all coal in Yunnan (33.1 percent). Information about county-level coal production in Guizhou in 1991 is not available.

policy after 1998 dramatically reduced production in both provinces. Moreover, the losses in both provinces were spread evenly between the poor and nonpoor counties; during both 1996 and 2001, the proportion of coal production in poor counties was similar for the two provinces.[15] Despite losses in production, Guizhou poor counties in 2001 produced more than twice as much as Yunnan poor counties, a gap that expanded as production recovered. In 2003, for instance, Guizhou poor counties produced more than 43 million tons of coal, compared to 15 million tons for Yunnan poor counties.

The structure of coal mines in Guizhou is more conducive to poverty reduction than in Yunnan.[16] As mentioned earlier, in the early 1990s, one-third of the coal production in Guizhou was produced in SOE mines.[17] The remaining two-thirds of Guizhou coal production came from small-scale (often tiny) TVE mines. Although TVEs produced the majority of coal in Yunnan, throughout the 1990s a higher proportion of coal mines were organized into medium-size or larger enterprises with some degree of sophisticated technology and equipment. The proportion of coal produced by Guizhou TVE mines is consistently higher than that produced by Yunnan TVEs and, starting in 1991, increased faster. By 1996, TVE mines produced about two-thirds of the Yunnan coal output, whereas Guizhou TVEs produced four-fifths of its output. Moreover, as shown in figure 7, annual coal production in Guizhou TVE mines doubled between 1990 and 1996, increasing its annual production by nearly 2.5 million tons. This growth outpaced not only the production of Guizhou SOE mines (whose annual production dropped by 272,000 tons) but also the production of Yunnan TVEs (whose annual production increased by more than 750,000 tons) and SOEs (whose annual production increased by 930,000 tons). Therefore, although TVE mines captured all the gains in Guizhou coal production during this period, the relatively slower growth of Yunnan coal production was shared between its TVEs and SOEs. This may have been linked to the relatively loose Guizhou licensing requirements for TVE mines.

My fieldwork supports the conclusions of the scholarly literature that coal mines help either reduce poverty or promote economic growth, depending on how they are structured. There are numerous coal mines of all sorts in Yunnan and Guizhou. In Guizhou, I visited mines in several counties in Bijie prefecture in northwestern Guizhou, as well as in Qiannan prefecture to the south. In Yunnan, I visited several mines, primarily in

15. In Yunnan, coal production in poor counties increased to 41 percent, whereas, in Guizhou, it increased to 58 percent.

16. Unfortunately, available statistics do not allow us to analyze simultaneously distribution (poor vs. nonpoor counties) and structure (SOE mines vs. TVE mines).

17. The majority of these are centrally administered, responsible for approximately one-quarter of coal production in Guizhou; provincially owned SOEs control less than one-tenth of overall production.

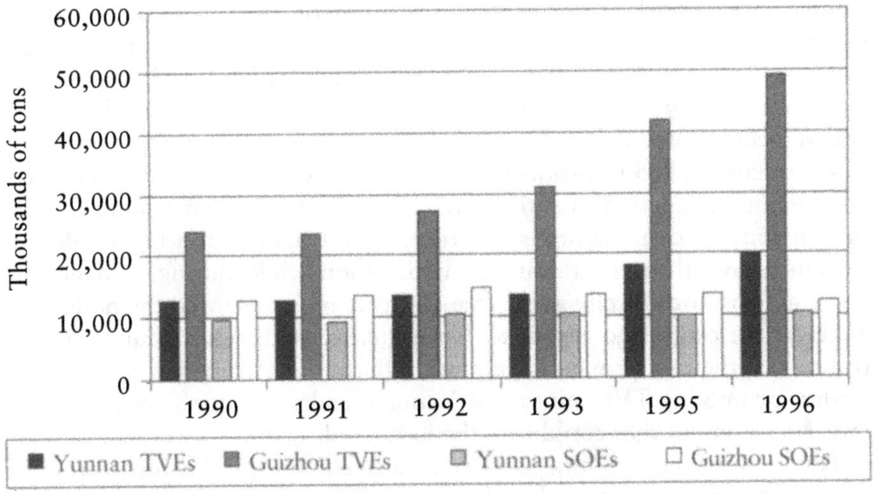

Fig. 7 Ownership structure of mines, 1990–1996. SOEs, state-owned enterprises; TVEs, township and village enterprises.
Source: State Statistical Bureau (various years-b, various years-c).

Zhaotong prefecture in the northeast. These prefectures are all quite poor. Two primary conclusions emerged from my study of the coal mines in these areas. First, there was a clear distinction between the coal mines in Yunnan and Guizhou, even among TVE mines. Yunnan TVE mines tended, on the whole, to be larger in scale, with broader boundaries, and larger, more formal management structures. Guizhou TVE mines tended to be less formally organized, with smaller teams organized in a less hierarchical, sometimes ad hoc fashion. In Yunnan, workers tended to be equipped with more effective tools; in Guizhou, miners generally relied on pickaxes and other simple hand tools. In Guizhou, numerous tiny mines were located directly by the side of the road, and people carried coal in baskets on their backs or in vehicles to the market to sell directly to other households for food or home heating. Second, TVE mines in Guizhou often were located near—sometimes directly adjacent to—small-scale TVEs of other kinds, such as brick kilns or other industries related to construction. The coal mines provided a steady supply of fuel for these other industries, which in turn supplied a steady market for the coal. These ancillary industries, moreover, provided additional small-scale employment opportunities for nearby rural residents. I saw fewer such enterprises in Yunnan. There the coal tended to be sold to larger entities, which transported it to urban centers or exported it to other provinces.

The conclusions of statistical evidence, my fieldwork, and secondary sources are that mining in Guizhou largely reduces poverty and to a greater extent than it does in Yunnan. Although many of the differences in the volume, distribution, and structure of the coal industries in Guizhou and

Yunnan are related to the natural attributes of the coal deposits of the provinces, the strategy adopted by each province to exploit those natural endowments nevertheless shaped the development of the coal industry differently. In the 1980s, the policies of the two provinces were similar in several respects. Both were (1) establishing a two-track pricing system, with lower prices applied to production up to a certain quota and higher prices applying to production over the quota; (2) enhancing the mechanization of production; (3) constructing supporting infrastructure; and (4) developing human capital through training and education while cutting management and staff positions. In this sense, the two provinces mirrored the policy and goals of the central government. Nevertheless, within the bounds of central policy, the two provinces adopted differing approaches, with Guizhou leaders promoting TVE mines and Yunnan leaders focusing on developing larger-scale mines that could feed the industrial sector.

The Guizhou coal mining industry, especially the production from TVE mines, was an important and explicit part of the provincial antipoverty policies beginning in the mid-1980s. The March 1986 Guizhou antipoverty directive explicitly made the production of coal and other natural resources an integral part of provincial development policy while concurrently eliminating taxation on coal mines in the poor counties. As early as the mid-1980s, the province had already established an infrastructure to support the development of TVE mines; these quickly became the leading producers of coal for Guizhou, the massive scale of production in the SOE mines in Liupanshui prefecture notwithstanding (Guizhou Nianjian Bianjibu, various years). According to one source, 100,000 Guizhou farmers were employed by the small-scale coal mines between 1985 and 1988 alone (Gao 2002, in Wen and Ren 2002, 210). The 1990 Guizhou policy similarly emphasized the development of pillar industries, including coal mining and, especially, TVE mines. In support of this effort, the provincial government explicitly directed relevant departments to help poor counties develop and exploit their natural resources in a way that could reduce poverty. In developing coal mining, the Guizhou government accomplished this by providing direct employment and income in an industry that the poor could access (Guizhou Nianjian Bianjibu 1991, 54). In 1996, the Guizhou government reiterated its intention to use the industry to reduce poverty and provide employment for laid-off workers, and this policy was effectively implemented. By 1996, thirty-six of the forty-eight Guizhou poor counties had at least some coal production (State Statistical Bureau 1997b, 2002b).

Also in the early 1990s, the Yunnan government crafted plans for its coal industry; however, its stated goal was not poverty reduction but economic growth. In its 1991 policy on coal production, the Yunnan government decided that the industry would "rely on technical advances, improve the quality of staff members, and develop the coal industry" as a part of the contribution of the coal industry to "ensuring the development of Yunnan's national product and the people's livelihood." This directive assigned a pivotal role to the local governments, requiring each department to "combine practicality, planning, decide on appropriate actions, and conscientiously carry out administrative work" (Yunnan Nianjian Bianjibu 1992, 193). In the mid-1990s, just as the Chinese central government reemphasized its goal of reducing and eliminating subsidies for the coal industry, Yunnan redoubled its commitment to subsidizing its SOE mines. On October 31, 1995, Yunnan adopted the policy of "two adds" (adding investment while increasing the speed of development) and "two unchangables" (continuing "the level of support" and "subsidizing losses") against the tide of reform and central directives to reduce dependency of the industry on government subsidies.

The regulatory environment toward TVE coal mines in the two provinces also differed in subtle but important ways (see table 7), with Guizhou being somewhat more permissive than Yunnan. In the years after the central government promulgated its 1983 measures for accelerating the development of TVE mines, both Guizhou and Yunnan implemented their own ordinances regulating them.[18] Both sets of laws encouraged the development of TVE mining in broadly similar ways, but the Yunnan law was more restrictive, encouraging larger-scale and more formal enterprises. In terms of the types of areas in which TVE mines could operate, both provinces permitted TVEs to mine in disparate areas and in mines that were not included in provincial plans. Moreover, both provincial governments permitted TVE mines within the borders of SOE mines. Although Guizhou officials permitted this without restriction, Yunnan restricted mining to remote areas along the borders of SOEs and required approval by government organs one level above those required for the SOEs. In terms of licensing, both provinces required that TVEs demonstrate the presence of coal resources, delineate clear boundaries for mining, and follow provincial safety and guidelines. In addition, the Yunnan regulations mandated that TVEs hire personnel with knowledge and expertise in mining procedures and extraction techniques; the Guizhou regulations were silent on this. For most TVE mines, both provinces required county-level approval before the licenses were granted, and Yunnan required that TVEs also obtain an additional "township-level opinion" before applying for licenses. Moreover, Guizhou released temporary and seasonal mining from the requirement of obtaining county-level approval; township-level approval was sufficient for this kind of mining. And, in addition to levying the taxes approved in the central government, Yunnan required TVE mines to pay a county-level management fee. Thus, the Yunnan TVE licensing

18. Guizhou passed its regulations, Guizhou Province Provisional Measures for the Management of TVE and Collective Mining Enterprises and Individual Mining (1986). Yunnan promulgated its Yunnan Province Provisional Regulations for the Management of TVE and Collective Mining Enterprise and Individual Mining (1987).

Table 7. Regulations and approvals process for TVE mines in Guizhou and Yunnan

Category	Guizhou	Yunnan
Governmental approval level for most TVEs	County	County, plus township opinion
Governmental approval level for temporary seasonal mining TVE	Township	County
Taxes, governmental level	Central government	Central government, plus county management fee
Regulations encouraging longer-term, more formal TVEs	No special regulation	Grants 15-year license
Approvals needed for TVEs operating within SOE borders	No special restriction	Must obtain approval of SOE and of government organ one level above
Licensing requirements	Must demonstrate coal resources and delineate boundaries	Must demonstrate coal resources and delineate boundaries; also must hire personnel with knowledge and experience

Notes: Promulgated by Guizhou in 1986 and by Yunnan in 1987. SOE, state-owned enterprise; TVE, township and village enterprise.

process during the early 1990s required additional approvals and requirements; the Guizhou process at this time was relatively relaxed. In addition, Yunnan policymakers encouraged longer-term and larger-scale operations, offering qualifying businesses longer-term fifteen-year licenses (Guizhou Nianjian Bianjibu various years; Yunnan Nianjian Bianjibu various years; Yunnan Provincial People's Government 1987; Guizhou Provincial People's Government 1986).

By 1994, both provinces changed their approaches to TVE coal mines. Yunnan officials set out to shut down unlicensed small-scale mines and standardize the remaining mines through licensing procedures. In contrast, Guizhou leaders started to incorporate their TVE mines into SOEs in a bid to improve safety and rationalize production. Whereas the new Yunnan approach reduced the ability of poor people to participate in mining, the Guizhou approach curtailed these opportunities less as officials attempted to improve conditions and productivity (Guizhou Nianjian Bianjibu 1995, 344; Yunnan Nianjian Bianjibu 1995, 207). These differences in the overall impact of the two ordinances are captured in the goals for the regulations. Whereas the Guizhou policy goals were listed as the "opening, vitalization and good management" of the coal industry, the Yunnan goal was stated to be more oriented toward "reasonable planning, correct leadership and strengthening management" (Yunnan Provincial People's Government 1987, Article 4; Guizhou Provincial People's Government 1986, Article 1). Although the regulations of both provinces became increasingly strict over time, in line with the national policy to "support, transform, consolidate, unite and improve" TVE coal mining (Coal Industry Ministry 1985,

Article 5), Guizhou leaders continued to actively encourage the development of TVE mines as a part of its poverty reduction policy. Thus, although the specific pattern of development of the Guizhou and Yunnan coal industries can be explained in part by geographical and other factors, the more rigid regulations in Yunnan played a large role in restraining the growth of smaller-scale TVE mines while encouraging larger, more capital-intensive mining operations.

Coal mining affected economic growth differently in the two provinces. Ironically, the larger coal industry in Guizhou appears to have hindered its economic growth, whereas the coal industry in Yunnan probably contributed to its economic development to a greater extent. Development in Chinese coal-producing regions was impeded because of the gap between the price of coal (a resource that was sent primarily to coastal provinces) and the price of manufactured goods (primarily shipped from coastal to inland areas). The Seventh Five-Year Plan (1986–1990) enshrined what was by then an already widespread practice in the coastal regions—obtaining reduced-priced raw materials, energy, and agricultural products in exchange for more expensive finished products. Under the plan, raw materials were purchased at below-market rates by the coastal provinces, which then manufactured value-added or high-tech goods, a portion of which were sold to the inland areas at higher prices (Lardy 1992, 45–46; Yang 1997, 63). This practice helped to spur the development of the coastal areas by providing stable supplies of centrally priced and subsidized coal; simultaneously, it impeded the development of the west. This "scissors gap" was further aggravated by the disparity between the financial resources of the two regions. As Cindy Fan, a geographer, argues,

> [T]he most heated criticisms are against the preferential price policy. Inland provinces that are dependent on the output of primary products sell them at low prices but have to purchase finished goods from coastal provinces at high prices.... Not only has this "scissors gap" in prices unduly benefited coastal provinces that have a stronger industrial base, it has also led to declining incentives in food and primary product production. (1997, 627)

This phenomenon not only increased the economic losses of the provincial governments in inland China but also directly impeded the development of many provinces that supplied China with natural resources. As Dali Yang contends,

> With low state-set prices for energy and other raw materials, the more the interior provinces expanded their extractive industries, the more they lost money and needed subsidies from the central government.... But the regional division of labor did not just accumulate losses for the interior; it had real consequences for interior development. More concretely, the emphasis on producing a certain

> quantity of coal and other resources has served to distort the incentives of interior producers, leading them away from the pursuit of profits. . . . Most importantly, the incentive structure facing the interior has made it difficult for interior provinces to accumulate the local funds needed for investment, miring many interior provinces in ties of dependence upon the central government and what might be termed a poverty trap. (1997, 66)

The logic behind the "scissors gap" assumes that coal is shipped to manufacturing bases elsewhere and that local governments do not use their resources of coal and other assets for the development of the local indigenous economy. This assumed pattern fits Guizhou more than it does Yunnan. Even though production in Guizhou is larger than in Yunnan, Guizhou consistently used less of its own coal each year than Yunnan for every year recorded (State Statistical Bureau various years-b, various years-c). This surplus in production means that much of the coal produced in Guizhou could be shipped to other provinces, primarily the coastal provinces of Guangxi and Guangdong but also to Yunnan, at a net cost largely borne by Guizhou (Thomson 2003, 207); thus, Guizhou leaders were compelled to exchange low-cost coal for higher-priced finished goods. In contrast, the manufacturing sector in Yunnan benefitted from its coal production to a greater extent. Yunnan consumed more coal than it produced, and this gap between supply and demand increased over time. This challenge, however, was relatively easy to overcome as long as the price of coal remained low.

Throughout much of the 1990s, the coal industries of both Guizhou and Yunnan lost billions of yuan, primarily because the cost of mining coal exceeded the price paid for it. According to World Bank research from the late 1980s, taking into account the losses accrued by the entire coal industry, coal consumption in China had essentially been subsidized (Albouy 1991). Prices paid by the coal consumers were fixed at low levels (an average of RMB 65 per ton in 1989), whereas the costs of production were much higher (RMB 100 per ton for China in general, and RMB 131 per ton for southwestern China). In addition, although central subsidies helped narrow this gap, they did not close it; the report calculates a gap of RMB 2 billion in 1989 alone. Thus, the pattern of subsidies actually increased the yawning gap between the richer coastal provinces and less well-off inland ones.

In Yunnan, because the province used the majority of the coal it produced within its own borders, those losses were acceptable. Throughout the 1990s, the Yunnan economy grew at a pace that averaged 14.6 percent annually, including 15.1 percent on average industrial growth, thanks in part to the relatively inexpensive coal, produced with the assistance of central subsidies.

Despite the contribution that coal made to Yunnan economic growth, its coal industry did not significantly reduce poverty in the province, largely due to the volume, distribution, and structure of the industry. In contrast, in Guizhou coal production probably impeded economic development, although it did reduce poverty, primarily through smaller-scale TVE mines based in the Guizhou poor counties. As we have seen, although the geographical distribution of coal resources contributed to this pattern, policy decisions made by the provinces and the central government were also crucial.

But the effects of coal mining on poverty reduction must be weighed against its substantial risks. The dangers inherent in the industry make it difficult to advocate a policy in which TVE coal mining is promoted to reduce poverty. Nevertheless, coal mining did help reduce poverty in Guizhou. The two provinces, both rich in coal resources, used their coal mining industries for different purposes and structured their industries in ways to achieve those goals. These policies help explain the puzzling pattern of economic growth and poverty reduction in Guizhou and Yunnan.

Conclusion

The Micro-Oriented State, Development, and Poverty

> Go to the practical people and learn from them, then synthesize their experience into principles and theories.
>
> —Mao Zedong, 1943

Scholars have long promoted numerous pathways to reducing poverty in the developing world, incorporating different state strategies, capacities, and roles. Some argue that poverty reduction is best accomplished when the state removes itself as much as possible from economic decision making while proactively facilitating the ability of the market to stimulate the economy and reduce poverty. Others counter that poverty reduction is best accomplished when the state adopts a leading role in establishing industries that provide employment for poor people, allowing them to shift from agriculture to the more productive industrial sector. Still others argue that poverty diminishes when the state adopts a dominant role in the economy, all but closing off the economy to allow time for domestic import-substituting industries to germinate and grow. Others argue that poverty reduction requires the establishment of a network of welfare programs that protect poor people from the perils of a frequently unpredictable market. A smaller group of scholars point out that, because most poor people are engaged in agriculture, the promotion of that sector will most efficiently reduce poverty. Yet others argue that the state must tackle injustice, redistribute wealth, invest in widespread grassroots education and health care, and empower the poor before poverty will decline. The conditions that allow these multiple—and frustratingly contingent—pathways to reduce poverty are not yet fully understood. Many of these pathways rely on generating economic growth to reduce poverty, but they also work through other mechanisms. Yunnan traversed one of these paths; the developmental state model best characterizes Yunnan economic policy. The Guizhou government adopted a different approach to poverty reduction, one that is less discussed nowadays—characterized by the micro-oriented state model.

As we have seen, the patterns of economic growth and poverty reduction in the two provinces can be partially explained through their distinct approaches to similar features of their rural economies: road building, migration, tourism, and coal mining. These four factors are not the only ones that were important to the economies of Guizhou and Yunnan. Indeed, other factors, such as industrial structure, culture, corruption, and tobacco production, also made a difference in the economies of Guizhou and Yunnan. Even so, as we have seen, these other areas do not explain the differences in economic growth and poverty reduction. Although these four factors proved to be important in both provinces, it is the variations of each of them that explains the different patterns of economic growth and poverty reduction in Yunnan and Guizhou. Thus, the policy choices of these provincial governments, not just cultural, geographical, and economic factors, created these puzzling patterns.

In this chapter, I analyze these areas synthetically to derive and explore the overall models that the leaders of the two provinces adopted to change and improve their economies. As listed in table 1 (in the introduction), the models of poverty reduction vary in the nature of the relationship between the state and market, primary goals (e.g., growth or poverty reduction), tactical approaches, scale of the activity, and mechanism through which poor people are expected to benefit.

The Yunnan Strategy

In Yunnan, the patterns in three of the four areas—road building, tourism, and coal mining—suggest that the Yunnan provincial government followed a form of the developmental state model.[1] By and large, the Yunnan government policies related to the tourism and coal mining industries were based on a strategy of market alteration. The provincial government adopted a key role in the tourism industry, especially in the 1990s, by selecting and promoting specific areas marked for tourism development. Government officials proactively established tourist sites and attractions, overseeing the construction and management of hotels and restaurants and the construction of the necessary infrastructure required for tourism. They took a lead role in the planning and development of the industry while allowing private companies to participate in most aspects of tourism. The government hotels and other facilities thus did not exclude the private sector, which took an increasingly important role over time. The government devoted significant resources to the development of the industry, altering the market decisions of consumers, investors, and other actors. In the coal industry, Yunnan

1. Migration is excluded here because during most of the 1990s and beyond Yunnan lacked a discernable migration policy of any kind.

leaders raised barriers for TVE coal mines and poor participants, adding additional requirements in the licensing process, such as higher levels of training and education, that were more difficult for poorer people to obtain. They also developed large-scale SOE coal mines and used the coal produced in Yunnan for the development of the province. The Yunnan infrastructure policy was designed as a foundation to further both these plans, as well as to stimulate border and internal trade and to promote the tobacco industry. In this way, through its development policies, the Yunnan government attempted to alter the market.

In each area, the primary economic goal of Yunnan was to stimulate economic growth. The highways built in Yunnan were designed to increase the flows of products and to enhance the tourism industry, thus promoting productivity and spurring growth. The tourism industry absorbed assets that increased the scale and productivity of the industry as a whole and stimulated the Yunnan service sector. In addition, Yunnan leaders encouraged longer-term participation in the coal industry, granting extended licenses to larger-scale operations of the kind that maximize value to achieve growth. They then used this inexpensive (central and provincial government-subsidized) supply of coal to fuel economic expansion, industrialization, and urbanization. Overall, through the three factors, Yunnan focused its relevant policies with the goal—explicit in most cases—of stimulating economic growth.

The Yunnan leadership also adopted a strategy of investing in key industries. They designed the highway network to stimulate and assist key industries—including tobacco, mining, and tourism—by reducing the transportation costs of the key inputs and final products. Similarly, tourism and coal mining were key industries in which the Yunnan government invested significant resources for development.

Moreover, the scale of development in each of these factors was large. The highways built were primarily either expressways or Class 1 and 2 highways. The tourism industry became larger in scale starting in the 1990s with the encouragement and investment of the Yunnan government, often in partnership with the private sector. The industry featured multistarred hotels, fancy restaurants, and modern entertainment sites, as well as more organized and structured tourist destinations. (As we have seen in chap. 5, the scale tends to exclude participation by poor residents.[2]) Finally, the Yunnan coal industry was of the largest scale possible, given the geographical constraints. Generally, mines applied relatively advanced technology and sought more educated and experienced workers, both characteristic of capital-intensive production.

2. An exception is Lugu Lake, located several hours from the famous attractions in Lijiang, which is structured so that poor locals there have benefited, a pattern more similar to Guizhou tourist sites.

Table 8. Yunnan government strategy

Characteristic[a]	Yunnan
Primary relationship with market	Market alteration (primarily)
Primary goal	Economic growth
Primary development strategies	Invest in key industries
Scale of industry	Large
Mechanisms for poverty reduction	Shift workers from agriculture to services and industry
Model adopted	Developmental state (outward-oriented)

[a] See also table 1 (in the introduction).

Overall, the strategy of Yunnan leaders best matches the model of the outward-oriented, developmental state (table 8). The Yunnan government approached development primarily by altering the market, investing resources in key industries, focusing on large-scale industrialization, and attempting to shift labor from agriculture to industry.

Further evidence of the Yunnan developmental approach emerges from its development priorities, level of spending, deemphasis of basic agriculture (commercial crops, especially tobacco, were strongly encouraged), and urban bias. First, development in other areas central to Yunnan development and poverty strategy, including its poverty alleviation policies and practices, demonstrate that Yunnan designed and implemented proactive development policies throughout the 1990s. From the 1980s, the Yunnan government implemented a development plan that focused on three leading industries—tobacco, sugar, and tea—and strengthened other pillar industries, including mining (especially coal and nonferrous metals), tropical products (rubber, seasonings, and fruits), the chemical industry (phosphorus and salt), the food industry, forestry, the construction and building materials industry, and tourism. The provincial government also focused on exploiting energy, transportation (primarily highways), and raw materials to fuel Yunnan development over the long term (Yunnan Nianjian Bianjibu 1987, 4).

During the mid-1990s, Yunnan continued to pursue the same development priorities, including mining, agriculture, and transportation infrastructure, and it redoubled its efforts in additional service industries, including communications and tourism. Yunnan officials remained focused on developing the economy, to catch up with the relatively advanced coastal provinces, by using agricultural production to feed its manufacturing and service industries. In doing so, provincial leaders applied higher-technology and capital-intensive technology to develop these sectors. Signaling the integration between Yunnan strategies for development and poverty reduction, the provincial poverty alleviation plans (such as the 1994 antipoverty plan) included specific regional development policies with detailed plans for each of its regions, targeting specific industries (including heavy industry), services, and agricultural products for development. As in most developmental states, Yunnan officials applied state resources to these efforts, taking a leading role in stimulating these industries.

Even more than tourism and heavy manufacturing, the Yunnan economy has been based on tobacco. It is difficult to overestimate the importance of tobacco and cigarette factories on the reform-era economy of Yunnan. Tobacco production in the province dates back to 1914, but it did not take off until the late 1970s. By the turn of the twenty-first century, Yunnan manufactured nine of thirteen premium brands of Chinese cigarettes. At that time, a 180,000-square-kilometer area in Yunnan became the largest tobacco-producing region in the world. By 1995, some 30 percent of the Yunnan GDP was linked to tobacco, and a massive 80 percent of government revenue came from tobacco production (Eng 1999). Perhaps not surprisingly, Yunnan tobacco production has been skewed toward its nonpoor counties (see fig. 2 in chap. 3). By 1996, whereas tobacco production in poor counties had increased approximately 43 percent in Yunnan (and 48 percent in Guizhou), production in the Yunnan nonpoor counties had increased 52 percent (compared to 16 percent in Guizhou). This pattern continued, despite severely reduced centrally mandated production quotas. Thus, like so much else in Yunnan, the production of tobacco was a great boon to its economic growth but was skewed toward its nonpoor counties. Despite its being an agricultural crop, tobacco was also part of the industrial strategy of Yunnan because those development plans included a great emphasis on cigarette manufacturing. By encouraging not just tobacco production but also cigarette manufacturing, Yunnan retained much of the value-added services within the province. This formed the backbone of Yunnan GDP growth, as well as much of its government revenue.

Second, Yunnan government expenditures were unusually high and consistently much higher than those of Guizhou throughout the reform era (see chap. 1). Yunnan government spending relative to its GDP was among the highest in China and led all provinces in 1992–2000. The province remained among the highest-spending Chinese provinces after 2000. Moreover, as we have seen, this spending was unusually skewed toward its nonpoor counties. Thus, both through a Keynesian effect and the targeted application of resources, Yunnan government spending contributed to the overall growth of the province, much of this growth in its nonpoor areas.

Third, Yunnan leaders successfully shifted the provincial economic and employment base out of the agricultural sector into the industrial and service sectors, in part through developing tourism and coal mining. The development of other industries (tobacco being a partial exception) also helped to shift the labor force. According to the Yunnan Statistical Yearbooks, in the early 1990s the industrial and service sectors of the province grew faster than the agricultural sector and began to account for a large proportion of its GDP. Between 1990 and 2002, the Yunnan secondary and tertiary sectors expanded sixfold while its primary sector grew relatively modestly (State Statistical Bureau various years-c). Agriculture, which accounted for 37 percent of the total GDP of Yunnan in 1990, declined to 24 percent by 1996 and continued to decline, dropping below 20 percent in 2003 and reaching 18 percent by 2008.[3] By contrast, during this time, the contribution of the Yunnan industrial sector to the total GDP rose from 35 percent in 1991 to 44 percent in 1996, before declining to 43 percent in 2008, and the contribution of the service sector increased from 28 percent in 1991 to 30 percent in 1996 to more than 39 percent in 2002. In addition, this industrialization trend was uneven, with the shift from agriculture affecting the Yunnan nonpoor counties to a greater extent than its poor ones. By 1996, nearly half the production structure of the Yunnan nonpoor counties was based on industry, whereas the economies of the poor counties continued to be dominated by agriculture. These trends have continued. Thus, the distribution of these industries (located disproportionately in nonpoor areas), the relative lack of internal migration in Yunnan, and the structure of these industries (which often constrained the participation of the poor) limited the gains of industrialization for the rural poor.

Finally, despite its focus on tourism and tobacco in rural areas, the Yunnan development strategy reveals an urban bias of the type articulated by Michael Lipton (1977). Yunnan focused on the development of its urban areas, at the county level and above. The province linked its prefecture-level cities via major highways and allocated its natural resources to fuel the growth of these areas, for example, by processing natural resources within those urban areas. As Yunnan industrialized, its major cities grew rapidly (see fig. 8; as the figure shows, Guizhou cities grew much more slowly).

Moreover, the Yunnan government spent five times more on fixed assets and capital construction in the nonpoor counties than in the poor ones (State Statistical Bureau various years). For instance, in 1991, Yunnan spent 6.5 times more on fixed assets in nonpoor counties compared to poor ones and more than four times more on capital construction. By the mid-1990s, the spending ratio in capital construction increased to nearly sixfold.[4] The Yunnan government invested more in urbanization and construction, targeting to a great degree the nonpoor areas.

One of the explicit intentions of this urbanization push was to spread the benefits of growing trade, tourism, and technology in these cities to other

3. The contribution of agriculture to the Guizhou GDP did not drop below 30 percent until 1999.

4. Compare this to the spending ratio of 2.5 in Guizhou. Although Guizhou shows a similar overall pattern of investing more on capital construction in its cities, the effect is much more muted.

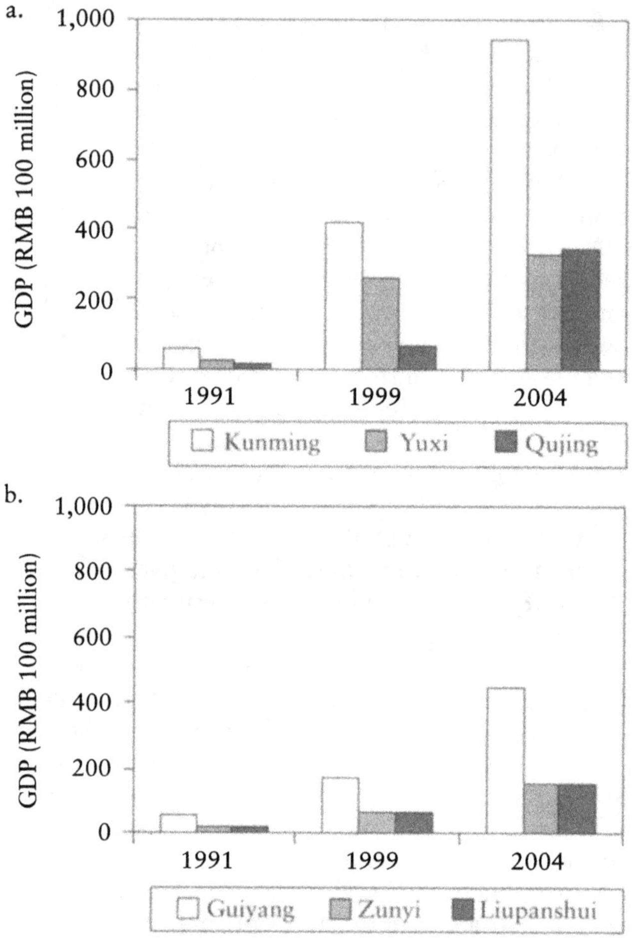

Fig. 8 GDP of major cities, 1991, 1999, 2004. (a) Yunnan; (b) Guizhou.
Source: China Research Society of Urban Development (1992, 2000, 2005); author's calculations.

areas. As Gao Yan, the Yunnan party secretary at the time, argued in his 1995 annual report,

> The construction of cities and towns is one of the most important steps for regional economic development. We must pay attention to city and town planning, and improve civil construction . . . following the route of using the land to generate money and using the money to build up the city. We must study and improve the people management system to transfer surplus rural labor toward the secondary and tertiary industries, and gradually connect large, medium and

> small-sized cities, to their mutual advantage, and to have integrated economies between cities and towns. (Yunnan Nianjian Bianjibu 1996, 7)

This plan was thus explicitly tied to transferring poor rural residents from agriculture to the manufacturing and service industries. Due, at least in part, to the lack of roadways between towns and villages, as well as to the lack of an appropriate structure and distribution of the various industries, the provincial plan attempting to generate such 'spread effects' to reduce poverty was largely ineffective. The plan did, however, succeed in developing the wealthier areas of Yunnan, including its cities and towns, as well as the tobacco- and tourist-rich areas of the countryside.

The urban bias of Yunnan is also revealed in its taxation policies. Until the central government canceled the agriculture tax on January 1, 2006 (Yunnan was one of the last five provinces to abolish the agriculture tax), the burden of taxation on Yunnan farmers far exceeded that borne by Guizhou farmers.[5] The Yunnan policies drove up the cost of farming to an even greater extent by taxing farmers at a high rate. Although Yunnan government officials taxed rural residents at a rate similar to other provinces (including Guizhou) in 1991, by 1994 the relative tax burden on Yunnan rural residents had increased precipitously. By the mid-1990s, the Yunnan agriculture tax was among the highest in China, ranking second only to Shanghai. This high rate of taxation, along with the tax revenues from tobacco, tourism, and coal mining, helped to finance the Yunnan development goals, concentrated mainly in urban areas, not antipoverty policies.

One other element related to finance and the urban bias is unfortunately, due to its political sensitivity, difficult to confirm through interviews or statistics—the extent to which development and antipoverty funds were squandered or funneled away from their intended use. Concrete evidence for either is difficult to find. There is only anecdotal evidence that much of these government sponsored economic activities in Yunnan rural areas, especially in the prefectures and counties, contributed neither to sustained economic growth nor to poverty reduction. This evidence can be considered indicative but not definitive. In many counties that I visited in Yunnan, the county towns were strikingly well developed, with larger and newer buildings, wider streets, fancier public squares, and even modern sports arenas. In many cases, the most developed buildings were conspicuously those occupied by the government. Although the construction of such facilities would deliver some short-term boost to the GDP statistics, they are not productive assets that would provide significant and sustained productivity and employment through the manufacturing and service industries.

5. It is certainly true, as Christine Wong (1997) notes, that Guizhou farmers were also taxed heavily. From a comparative view, however, they were not taxed as heavily as the farmers of other provinces, including and especially Yunnan.

They are impressive artifacts to show visiting central government inspection teams, but do little for either long-term growth or poverty reduction. Indeed, corrupt officials could easily use these sorts of prestige projects in kickback or embezzlement schemes. Moreover, many of the counties I visited had potential projects that if implemented could have been helpful for poverty reduction or development but that lacked investment funds. For instance, the government of Pingbian (a poor county in Honghe prefecture, Yunnan) had invested millions of yuan in development funds in building the county square and an adjoining soccer stadium, used but twice during its first year. Officials justified these projects as contributing to the cultural development of the county. Meanwhile, a partially developed national forest, which could potentially spur the tourism industry and provide opportunities for poor rural residents, remained starved for development funds. Also, the prefecture government in Honghe spent a reported RMB 800 million (US$97.6 million) on its new prefecture capital buildings and moving costs while the seven designated poor counties that it governs remain starved for development funds.[6] This positioning of a developed county town or prefecture city within an impoverished countryside was replicated in each area of Yunnan I visited, an impression shared by many of the academic scholars and reporters I interviewed. Additional research, however, is needed to systematize this anecdotal evidence and determine whether these differences are systematic.

Using this developmental state strategy, Yunnan officials succeeded in stimulating the growth rate of the province during the 1990s; Yunnan went from one of the weakest economies in China to one of the strongest among the noncoastal provinces. But Yunnan officials focused their resources on limited areas of the province (primarily the central areas, with tourism to the south and parts of the northwest and tobacco in the southwest) and on a limited range of industrial sectors, supported in part by the construction of an extensive highway system, concentrating their development efforts in a narrow band of mostly nonpoor areas. In doing so, they excluded large swaths of the poor regions, primarily in the southeast, northeast, and most of its west. They also structured the developed industries in ways that made participation by poor people difficult. Even when they focused on poor areas, such as building a highway through the poor prefecture of Zhaotong, the effect on rural poverty was dubious. Overall, the province emulated the central government strategy of allowing some areas and people to become wealthy first and then waiting for those benefits to trickle down to the poor rural residents or promising to distribute the fruits of that progress at a later, as yet unspecified date.

6. Prefecture officials reported the RMB 800 million during meetings I attended. Printed official reports are lower (RMB 700 million equivalent to US$85.4 million) though of a similar scale.

The Guizhou Strategy

In contrast with Yunnan, the patterns of development in Guizhou cannot be categorized as one of the six development strategies commonly outlined in the literature. Instead, they can best be characterized as fitting what I call the micro-oriented state model (see table 1, in the introduction). In the four areas we have identified as explaining the puzzle of economic growth and poverty reduction, the Guizhou government adopted multiple relationships toward the market. For tourism, Guizhou altered the market, not only by funding and developing its premier tourist site, the Huangguoshu Waterfall, but also by taking a primary role in establishing tourist sites in ethnic minority villages spread throughout some of the most impoverished areas in Guizhou. Starting in the mid-1980s, the Guizhou government also altered the market by supporting and encouraging the migration that was already occurring through economic necessity, by training rural workers and helping them find jobs in coastal areas. The province planned the development of large-scale industries along the lines of the pre-reform planning system, setting targets for production and allocating resources in a way that appears closer to market replacement. The role of state-determined prices and planned logistics designed to send the coal from Guizhou to the growing coastal areas largely precluded market allocation in the SOE portion of the coal mining industry. But, for the smaller-scale TVEs, the province adopted flexible policies designed to maximize the participation of rural residents. Although the province required that potential mine operators obtain county-level approval, it adopted minimal requirements for the granting of licenses and it allowed seasonal miners—those most likely to mine during the farming off-season—to obtain permission at the township level. By providing subsidies and tax incentives in the coal industry, it also facilitated the market. Finally, road construction, distributed in rural areas and structured via accessible road networks linking village to town, appears to be designed to alter the market in its selection of priorities. The province also intended to facilitate the market by providing the means for poor rural residents to enter market towns to sell surplus goods and learn about job opportunities outside the area. In this way, Guizhou officials reinforced the economy centered around the traditional marketing town (as described in Skinner 1964) by adopting an innovative mix of state activities that facilitated, altered, and even replaced the market in different industries at different times.

As one of its primary goals, Guizhou adopted poverty reduction. This intent is explicitly linked to the four factors described here. Poverty reduction was the goal of the province's plan to construct rural roads connecting villages with townships and townships with counties. In the tourism industry, the province attempted to reduce poverty both by developing the Huangguoshu Waterfall and surrounding sites as attractions and by developing chains of ethnic villages throughout Guizhou. As early as 1992, Guizhou became the first Chinese province to explicitly link tourism with poverty reduction. The Guizhou government also encouraged migration to reduce rural surplus labor, thereby reducing poverty for the migrant workers and their families by stimulating remittance income. It did this via permissive migration policies and the overt promotion of rural-to-urban migration, both internally and cross-province. The provincial government also permitted poor people to open TVE coal mines by relaxing licensing during the early 1990s. Many poor rural residents responded, at least until the late 1990s, and exploited the plentiful coal resources in the hills surrounding their farms, typically by banding together into small temporary groups to mine the coal and sell it on the open market. With its SOE mines, the province explicitly tried to reduce poverty by reserving quotas of positions at these mines for people from poor counties and by allowing TVE mines to operate on SOE-mine land that were not being actively mined. In each of these areas, Guizhou leaders specifically focused on poverty reduction as its primary aim and focused less on economic growth.

The primary Guizhou development strategies are similarly difficult to place in clear-cut state-market categories; Guizhou in nearly every case developed through overt state action as well as by strengthening local markets. By creating opportunities in the tourism and coal industries, and by constructing accessible roads and promoting migration, Guizhou government policies enhanced the livelihoods of the rural residents, increasing their access to income outside agriculture as well as to local markets through which they sold surplus production. By constructing a rural road system centered on linkages among villages, townships, and counties, the provincial government also developed local markets in Guizhou.

The scale of each of these elements was comparatively small. The roads constructed in Guizhou were predominately small-scale rural roadways. The Guizhou migrant workers were relatively unskilled, and the remittances they sent back to their home villages, although sufficiently large to be helpful in reducing rural poverty, were often not large enough to allow investment in productive rural industries. Both the coal and tourism industries did have some large-scale enterprises: the infrastructure for Huangguoshu Waterfall and its surrounding tourist sites were set up to accept tourists in large numbers and the SOE coal mines in the Liupanshui area of Guizhou are among the largest in China. Nevertheless, in both industries, government efforts to develop smaller-scale production—TVE coal mines and small-scale ethnic tourist destinations—balanced and complemented the large-scale elements of these industries. Moreover, in both cases, the Guizhou policies mitigated the negative aspects of the scale of both tourism and coal mining by making special provisions for poor people. Poor people participated in the large-scale SOE coal mines through quotas and in TVEs mining within SOE boundaries; in the tourist sites surrounding Huangguoshu, poor residents sold handicrafts, served as punters, and arranged folk dances.

A core mechanism that Guizhou leaders adopted to reduce poverty was increasing options for rural residents to participate directly in opportunities that might supplement their incomes.[7] Unlike a progressive state, Guizhou did not provide any more direct aid than other Chinese provinces. Moreover, in contrast with the trickle-down approach of a liberal state, Guizhou officials encouraged opportunities that were directly accessible, through both structure and distribution, to poor people. At the same time, each of these opportunities required individual initiative for participation. In this way, the micro-oriented state approach also contrasts with the progressive state strategy of applying direct aid through food subsidies or through providing universal health care or education. This is not to say that providing aid directly to poor people is not laudable and often effective; Guizhou leaders simply adopted a different strategy.

In sum, the poverty reduction strategy adopted by Guizhou is the micro-oriented state model (see table 9). This model contrasts with the four top-down models for poverty reduction, summarized in table 1, in that the state adopts a variety of relationships with the market: facilitation, alteration, and replacement. The Guizhou government primarily altered the market in its economic policies, but it also facilitated the rural market in its road building policies. And in policies for the tourism and especially the coal industries, the provincial government at times appeared to replace the market. In addition, although both focus primarily on poverty reduction, the micro-oriented state differs from the progressive state; whereas the progressive state does so for ideological reasons related to redistributive justice, for the micro-oriented state, poverty reduction is the primary goal. Moreover, to the extent that Guizhou developed, it did so by growing its economy *via* poverty reduction. The micro-oriented state adopts neither the opening of the market (as does a liberal state) nor the redistribution of wealth (as does a progressive state). By instead adopting strategies focused on increasing opportunities for poor people, Guizhou grew its economy slowly, developing from the bottom up. Also, the activities promoted by the Guizhou government were small in scale. Finally, in contrast with other strategies for

7. Although setting up these opportunities is similar in some aspects to the strategy in developmental states of shifting rural labor to industry, it varies in two ways. First, the developmental state usually envisions a permanent shift of the workforce from agriculture to relatively large-scale industries. In Guizhou, in contrast, the new opportunities established through the provincial policies were supplementary to the primary foundation of rural economic life—agriculture. Tourism and coal mining employment opportunities in Guizhou were often part-time activities. Migration also sometimes occurred during off-periods in the agricultural cycle or was undertaken by individual members of a household. In this way, the patterns of these activities in Guizhou contrast with the more permanent, large-scale transfer envisioned by the developmental state model. Second, the developmental state model sparks development at the expense of agriculture, for instance by taxing agriculture and diverting the funds from agriculture to industry. In contrast, Guizhou lacked the urban bias, compared to other provinces, that would have drawn even more resources out of agriculture.

Table 9. Guizhou government strategy

Characteristic[a]	Guizhou
Primary relationship with market	Multiple relationships
Primary goal	Poverty reduction
Primary development strategies	Enhancing rural livelihoods; strengthening local and rural markets
Scale of industry	Small
Mechanisms for poverty reduction	Increasing opportunities for rural residents to directly participate in opportunities to supplement income
Model adopted	Micro-oriented state

[a] See also table 1 (in the introduction).

poverty reduction, the micro-oriented state does not rely on trickle-down effects or direct aid. Instead, it focuses on indirect mechanisms, primarily increasing opportunities for poor people to improve their livelihoods by participating in economic activities; this was the primary strategy adopted by Guizhou officials.

Considering Guizhou as a micro-oriented state is consistent with other elements of its strategy. From the mid-1980s, the Guizhou government focused not on opening up counties (as in Yunnan) but on connecting villages with nearby townships. Whereas Yunnan detailed plans for each of its regions, Guizhou encouraged each of its towns or townships to invest in its own pillar industry, usually related to agricultural processing, mining, or TVEs of various kinds. The Guizhou government recommended that townships focus on mid- to low-end industrial products that used labor-intensive production processes. To support this, the provincial government in both its 1990 and 1994 poverty plans allocated resources to build roads connecting villages and townships.

Not surprisingly, there are also many exceptions to these generalizations. For instance, the government of Libo (a poor county in Guizhou) spent resources on constructing a garish and expensive town square, complete with a fountain with spouting water that dances to a light and music show—a project that is inconsistent with a micro-oriented state. The same town, even though it was connected by highway to the international airport in Guiyang, constructed a woefully underutilized airport in an attempt to stimulate tourism (Pierson 2010). Perhaps no exception is more prominent than the Guizhou plan, centrally approved in 2000, to build a vast new campus for its administrative center, a large-scale affair that resembles an initiative that a developmental state might pursue. This plan was approved well after the general patterns in Guizhou had emerged and was pursued under the widely despised, former Guizhou party secretary, Liu Fangren, who was later jailed for life for corruption. Nevertheless, it is puzzling that a province committed to rural development and poverty reduction would support such an endeavor and that Hu Jintao himself would reportedly endorse it.

Despite these exceptions, the general pattern remains. In contrast to Yunnan, where growth increased without much poverty reduction, Guizhou implemented a different development strategy—the micro-oriented state. As a result, poverty declined much more than the growth rate of the province might lead us to expect.

Thus, Guizhou reveals that one path to reducing poverty is to provide economic opportunities in which poor people can participate. This typically involves industries and sectors that are small scale and low technology. In Guizhou, this was accomplished by building rural roads, encouraging migration, and promoting the tourism and mining industries in ways that facilitated the participation of the poor. By contrast, simply promoting rapid economic growth—even growth in rural regions—is not effective for poverty reduction if it is not distributed and structured in ways that poor people can benefit. Although straightforward, and perhaps even obvious, this thesis has largely been overshadowed by other, better-accepted theories of development.

Reexamining the Models

The micro-oriented state shares several key characteristics with the other models. For example, insofar as a micro-oriented state (such as Guizhou) focuses on encouraging alternative income sources to agriculture, it resembles the developmental state. Nevertheless, the differences in the models are greater than their similarities. In the micro-oriented state model, rural-based industries such as tourism and coal mining supplement, rather than replace, agriculture as a primary occupation. More obviously, whereas the developmental state model aims primarily to establish large-scale industries (Amsden 2001, 287), the micro-oriented state model pushes smaller-scale initiatives. Although such initiatives generally make only marginal differences in terms of GDP, they can contribute much to the livelihoods of rural residents. The developmental state seeks growth that helps the poor through trickle-down and spread effects, whereas the micro-oriented state seeks to reduce poverty by increasing accessible opportunities for poor people. Unlike the agriculture-oriented state, the micro-oriented state does not necessarily focus on spurring small-scale agriculture, though the opportunities it generate tend to supplement agricultural incomes by providing work opportunities during the off-season.

How do the two other bottom-up approaches compare with the micro-oriented model? Despite surface similarities, the micro-oriented model differs from the progressive states model in several ways. First, the progressive state, such the Indian state of Kerala, focuses on the direct provision of aid to the poor in the form of education, health care, and food aid. The micro-oriented state does not use direct aid to the poor or education and health-care initiatives as a primary part of its strategy. As we have seen, the Guizhou government instituted policies that increased opportunities that were structurally accessible to its poor rural residents but not directly administered by the government. Second, the progressive state model emphasizes redistributive justice as the primary motivation for government action. In Kerala, the programs that provide direct benefits to the poor were established as a result of pressure from societal groups. Another example is Cuba; the Cuban education and health-care programs originated in the wake of the communist revolution in that country, and even though Cuban civil society has weakened since the revolution, state ideology kept in place the health-care and education programs that are credited with reducing poverty in that country (Mehrotra 2002). By contrast, as we have seen in Guizhou, there has been no organized call for such state support, nor does the impetus for policy change originate from civil society. Although the Guizhou government, like all Chinese provincial governments, is tightly controlled by the CCP, there has been no unusual degree of provision of direct social services. The desire on the part of the CCP to keep at least a veneer of socialist ideology has been credited as a key reason that the central government pays some attention to the problem of poverty. Others counter that the CCP is no longer in any way a grassroots bottom-up movement responsive to the people. Either way, the Guizhou government does not vary from other Chinese provincial governments in this regard. Instead, the focus on poverty reduction under the micro-oriented approach (as in Guizhou) is based more on pragmatism, couched as a technical problem, rather than on ideological positions.

What implications does this new model have for the six previously identified models? One of my major goals here is to identify and elaborate alternative pathways to poverty reduction and lengthen the list of policy options. The Guizhou strategy is one such alternative. For the other six models, our evidence is still insufficient to reject their usefulness; different methods may be valid in different contexts. At the very least, my research indicates that several theories offered in the development literature are not *necessary* for achieving poverty reduction.

If my conclusion about the micro-oriented state model is so straightforward, how have development theorists missed it? In fact, they have not. The micro-oriented state can be seen in the TVE factories that dot the Chinese countryside, providing nonfarm, local, low-skilled employment in small-scale factories to millions of poorly educated Chinese workers (Oi 1995). The Wenzhou model of development, characterized by networks of family firms concentrating on a narrow range of small-scale manufacturing, also fits within this model (Liu 1992; Parris 1993).[8] Outside China, the

8. The Wenzhou model is often presented as an alternative to the polices of Guangdong province, with its reliance on foreign-funded small-scale factories, and to, especially, the Shanghai strategy of relying on large multinational corporations and domestic SOEs for its development.

micro-oriented state has been adopted by the Indian state of Gujarat, which has not only improved its agricultural production but has leveraged its network of far-flung migrants and immigrants to provide job opportunities for rural residents (Shah 2009). Both Taiwan and Hong Kong also developed their economies using small-scale, family-based enterprises and petty traders, who for decades provided a more equitable form of trickle-up growth (Cheng 2001; Chung and Yuen 2003).

In many (although not all) respects, the micro-oriented state reflects the thinking of Manfred Max-Neef, Michael Lipton, Paul Streeten, Robert Chambers, and others who focus on basic human needs approaches that avoid development-style approaches. The spirit of this approach has also captured popular imagination through works such as E. F. Schumacher's classic book, *Small Is Beautiful.* The micro-oriented approach is consistent with the conclusions drawn by a young Barack Obama working as a community organizer in the impoverished and neglected Chicago South Side.[9] Although such voices gained some degree of acceptance among academics and policymakers, especially in the 1960s and 1970s, they were largely drowned out in the 1980s by powerful political leaders espousing neoclassical economic theory, most notably U.S. President Ronald Reagan and UK Prime Minister Margaret Thatcher. Neoclassical economic theory forcefully advocates economic growth, large-scale production, and a minimalist state as being the most effective—indeed, the only—way to reduce poverty. It has dominated thinking about development since then.

Here my aim is to return currency to Schumacher's idea, eloquently evoked more than thirty-five years ago, that small is beautiful—or at least potentially effective at reducing poverty. As Schumacher argues, "Today, we suffer from an almost universal idolatry of gigantism. It is therefore necessary to insist on the virtues of smallness—where this applies" (1973, 62). This is equally true today. Despite the efforts of the many critics of the developmental state model, the commitment to large-scale growth and urbanization remains the overwhelmingly dominant policy approach. With its intoxicated praise of rapid industrialization and large scale ("density"), mass urbanization ("distance"), and market-based specialization (reducing "division"), the World Bank *World Development Report 2009* is just one of our most recent powerful reminders of this.[10]

9. In his discussion of the Altgeld Gardens public housing projects that he was helping to organize, Obama was very much in line with the micro-oriented approach. In his autobiography, Obama writes, "On the other hand, there did remain a part of the economy that could be called local, I thought, a second-level consumer economy—of shops, restaurants, theaters, and services—that in other areas of the city continued to function as an incubator of civic life. Places where families might invest their savings and make a go of a business, and where entry-level jobs might be had; places where the economy remained on a human scale, transparent enough for people to understand" (1995, 179).

10. In an ideal world, highly productive, growth-enhancing, large-scale industries could be combined with smaller-scale ones that are accessible to poor people. However, faced with

Nevertheless, despite its choosing this alternative pathway to poverty reduction, we should consider the Guizhou record cautiously. Indeed, the province has experienced significant poverty reduction, and this is impressive compared to the endemic poverty that persists throughout the world despite robust global growth and particularly in light of the modest economic growth in Guizhou. Yet, Guizhou has been and remains poor, with severe poverty persisting in many of its regions. Although the incomes of millions of poor Guizhou residents have risen above the poverty line, many of these remain just above that line—a precarious improvement in living standards. Even though life-threatening problems of hunger and malnutrition have become less pressing for some, and education and health care are more accessible, life in much of Guizhou remains a challenge.

Because the Guizhou economy is underdeveloped and remains among the weakest provincial economies as measured by per capita GDP, we should not be surprised that skepticism greets the claim that Guizhou has anything to offer as a model for poverty reduction. Most people living in cities in Yunnan are much better off compared to those in Guizhou, and many residents of the Yunnan tobacco and tourism regions earn relatively good incomes. Nevertheless, life in the impoverished areas of Yunnan can be much harsher than in most areas of Guizhou. Moreover, compared to its economic growth rate, the achievement of the Guizhou government in increasing incomes to a sufficient degree to pull millions of rural residents out of poverty is laudable. For these reasons, the Guizhou approach should be considered a viable strategy for poverty reduction.

The strengths of the micro-oriented state notwithstanding, this model, like the other six listed in table 1, is not ideal. Each of the four areas highlighted by Guizhou government policy—coal mining, road construction, migration, and tourism—contains negative edges that partially undermine their benefits. The serious health, safety, and environmental problems related to the coal industry are elaborated in chapter 6. Although roads also help reduce poverty, their construction can destroy fields, exacerbate soil erosion, and even bring in outside competition that undermines the local economy (larger roadways probably exacerbate each of these effects).

Even as rural-to-urban migration has been an effective mechanism in reducing poverty, such migration uproots people from their homes and often places them in insecure and dangerous positions. Changes in the Chinese legal structure that have relaxed barriers to housing, food, and jobs have only begun to diminish significantly the difficulties and discrimination that rural migrants experience in cities (Davin 1999; Solinger 1999). This lack

limited resources, governments often must choose between supporting economic growth and reducing poverty. Some governments are constrained by geography or other factors from enhancing economic growth. Moreover, in many cases the two strategies are in fact mutually exclusive.

of a legal status permits their exploitation, including the lack of guarantees of full salary payments and the lack of safeguards from and remunerations for accidents.[11]

The friendly face of tourism, for its part, also conceals the almost inevitable Hollywood-ization of cultures, as minorities modify their dances and songs—performances fundamental to their cultures—to conform to the taste of tourists (e.g., Britton 1991, 465–66).[12] Oakes (1998), in his study of tourism in Guizhou, argues that the industry has altered and decontextualized the cultures in that province. Tim Oakes argues that tourism creates contradictory forces, reinforcing traditional cultures by providing financial rewards for maintaining authentic practices and traditions even as the changes occurring in tourist villages threaten traditional ways of life. In addition, economic necessity sometimes drives poor rural residents in the tourism industry to perform duties that are dangerous or offensive to them. Oakes's study of tourism in Guizhou cites many examples of exploitation, including sweatshops making mass-produced "traditional" handicrafts.[13]

Thus, there are negative aspects to targeting each of these policies for poverty reduction. Remembering that poverty, properly defined, is broader than merely income level and includes personal safety and freedom from exploitation, these negative aspects mitigate the positive effects that the policies in these areas have on poverty. These are problems not just to be weighed against poverty reduction but that undermine to some degree claims about

11. Moreover, one migrant from Sichuan working in the Guiyang construction industry detailed how common it was for developers to disappear when construction was complete and before full wages had been paid to workers. When this occurs, migrant workers are sometimes given only enough money to return home.

12. This modification is obvious when one travels from ethnic villages developed for tourism to those that were not. In Congjiang county, I witnessed ceremonial dances marking social exchanges between Dong villages. The dance and song, although fascinating, lasted more than two hours with little variation in theme or rhythm—in stark contrast to minority performances for tourists.

13. Other duties, more conventional than prostitution or work in sweatshops, can also be offensive. For example, in Fugong county in northwestern Yunnan, young members of the Lisu minority working in the tiny tourism industry are compelled to drink alcohol with tourists. Alcoholism is a severe problem in the area—local residents report rates of alcoholism as high as 30 percent. Moreover, alcohol abuse competes with a form of Christianity that has predominated in the area for more than a century and has outlasted repressive periods such as the Cultural Revolution and other campaigns against religion. Faced with the endemic problem of alcoholism, local churches typically forbid drinking and shun anyone who uses alcohol. Tourists, unaware of this problem and believing that ethnic minorities in general are avid drinkers, often demand that their guides drink excessively with them, thus presenting a religious and social dilemma for economically desperate tourism workers. The guides I interviewed suggested it was impossible for them to refuse to drink while serving as a tour guide. Instead, they decided to band together in making a temporary pact—to withdraw from the church for a few years until they earned enough money from tourism that they could afford to leave the industry and return to church. While this example is from Yunnan, it nevertheless speaks to potential downsides of the form of tourism prevalent in Guizhou.

poverty reduction. Understanding the extent to which these shortcomings are unique to Guizhou or inherent in the micro-oriented state model is a question for further research. Because this model, unlike the progressive state model, is not based on a deep ideology of distributive justice and involves no shift in power, it is possible that these forms of exploitation and risks to security are inherent in it. Nevertheless, there is nothing inherent about a policy focus on coal, migration, tourism, and road building in this model; these areas mainly exemplify the importance of scale, distribution, and access.

Of course, this model is not unique for having downsides. Other antipoverty approaches have also proven to hurt the poor by undermining their traditional economies (e.g., Scott 1985), by compelling them to labor at exploitation wages, or by uprooting them from their social support network, among other realities of antipoverty programs. Moreover, many of the strategies adopted by Yunnan caused even worse after-effects in each of these dimensions. Strategies for alleviating poverty are rarely ideal. But, compared with the disruptions experienced by many counties that have been compelled by international organizations to implement the liberal state model, the micro-oriented state model can be much less traumatic. And compared with the stagnation and expense of an industrialization strategy through import-substitution (the protectionist state model) called for by dependency theorists, the micro-oriented state model can provide steady progress in poverty reduction that many countries may envy. The micro-oriented state model is far from benign, but its disadvantages should be weighed against the alternatives.

Further Insights

In addition to exploring the different ways in which two Chinese provinces approached economic development and poverty reduction, and to examining pathways for poverty reduction, I have also presented in this book some insights into the top leadership in China. Now that the Chinese central government has adopted serious steps to spread the benefits of its economic success and to close the yawning hole separating rich and poor, questions emerge as to the sincerity of their efforts. Are the leaders of China acting out of heartfelt concern or from fear of the protests and discontent that can arise out of inequity? Given Hu's experiences in poor areas, many scholars deduce that he is at least partly interested in reducing poverty. From his accomplishments in Guizhou, we can conclude that they are probably correct. Hu Jintao has already acted on those interests, and in a context where he could not assume that his policies would be acknowledged or rewarded.

What were the origin of his ideas? Every determined and thoughtful leader has advisors and theorists; Hu, in devising the Scientific Development

Concept with which he has been identified, is no exception. The staff of the Central Party School contributed to these ideas, and the fingerprints of Song Ping and Hu Yaobang, second-generation leaders, can be found on them. Hu's leadership in Guizhou also suggests that, in a genuine sense, these ideas are also his own. He had already developed them and implemented policies consistent with their spirit in Guizhou. And he did so at a time when many other local leaders—cautious to a fault—were looking toward Beijing and seeking to mimic their leaders and patrons, and waiting for approval when implementing anything that could possibly be criticized. So, even though Hu Jintao was clearly not the only figure behind the micro-oriented state approach of Guizhou, he was a crucial leader behind it. In formulating economic policy in Guizhou, Hu was thinking not only about how to expand an economy but also about how to create opportunities in which the poor could participate. He was considering how he could implement initiatives in this backwater province that, although they would not dazzle his superiors with scale and technology, would make a real different in people's lives. And, in one region of Guizhou at least, he displayed a pragmatic concern for the environment as early as the mid-1980s, before it was fashionable to do so elsewhere in the world.

In addition to these leadership insights, I have presented here insights of value for the development literature. First, I demonstrate that examining exceptions to the expected link between economic growth and poverty reduction is helpful, both empirically and theoretically. Although economic growth can explain many cases of poverty reduction, the numerous exceptions to this relationship justify further research. As noted earlier, even the most ardent advocates of economic growth do not claim that economic growth explains all or even most poverty reduction. After all, the accepted conclusion that poverty changes on a one-to-one basis with growth is founded on statistical averages that say little about any particular case. In addition, examining exceptions to the relationship between economic growth and poverty reduction deepens our understanding of the accepted rule because one way to understand *how* economic growth reduces poverty is to examine the cases in which it does not. More important, analyzing the exceptional cases suggests both which policies to endorse (by examining cases of poverty reduction without economic growth) and which to avoid (by examining cases of economic growth without poverty reduction) when attempting to reduce poverty (Donaldson 2008). This analysis should generate additional models that can guide the policies of poor areas. This method can also be applied elsewhere to explore puzzles in research areas unrelated to development and poverty.

A second development insight is that the analysis of exceptional Chinese provinces focuses attention on the importance of distribution and structure—not just volume—in understanding the effects of various factors and policy areas on poverty reduction. Most studies examine the relationship between economic growth and poverty reduction in the aggregate; however, the specific distribution and structure of economic growth, and the policies used to generate it, cannot be ignored. As we have seen, looking at the volume or density of roadways, coal mining, tourism, and other important areas was insufficient to understand their effects on poverty. It is commonly understood that, when economic growth is centered in wealthier regions in a country, its effect on poverty reduction will be low, particularly in the absence of migration. Nevertheless, studies of economic growth and poverty do not often focus on cases below the national level, which are crucial to understanding the distribution of benefits between poor and nonpoor regions. Structure is as important as distribution, particularly the degree of access that poor people have to potential opportunities. In many cases, barriers to the participation of poor people are endemic to the policies and changes that are intended to reduce poverty. For instance, as we have seen, many tourism sites in Yunnan (as in other places throughout the world) are structured in a way that limits the participation of poor people. The rural poor in developing countries also often have less education and experience, which prevents their access to opportunities in more modern industry. Generally, the smaller-scale, more labor-intensive industries seem to be more relevant to reducing rural poverty. In any case, analyzing the distribution and structure of industries, especially those intended to employ poor people, is necessary to understanding their effects on poverty reduction.

A final insight presented here relates to the state and market. My analysis increases the skepticism about the usefulness of distinguishing between the state and the market as actors promoting development and poverty reduction. The assumed dichotomy between state and market has been increasingly understood to be false because both the state and the market are involved in any economic policy. Despite this, few studies have incorporated both the state and the market in a manner that is analytically useful. I have redefined this issue here by focusing instead on the ways in which the state and the market can be related—through state facilitation, alteration, or replacement of the market. Although this conceptualization needs additional refinement, it is an approach that can be usefully applied elsewhere. For instance, Atul Kohli (2004), in his research on developmental states in South Korea, Nigeria, India, and Brazil, criticizes the false dichotomy between the state and the market, but provides few insights on how to proceed. If he had focused on the relationship between the state and market, Kohli could have further categorized the policies adopted by the four countries and deepened his analysis of their effects on industrialization.

More research also needs to be done on the micro-oriented state model and its relation to poverty reduction. Although the geography, economic structure, and depth of poverty in Guizhou are in many ways typical of other developing areas, in other ways Guizhou is unique—a province in a rapidly growing, resource-rich country that is at least partially oriented toward poverty reduction. Thus, further work is needed to test the applicability of the micro-oriented state model in other locales.

The importance of identifying additional approaches to poverty reduction cannot be undervalued, given that more than 1.3 billion people in the world today live on less than US$1.25 per day (Chen and Ravallion 2008). The sobering fact is that most government policies fail to reduce poverty, both rural and urban, in both developing and developed countries. One method of assessing which approaches and strategies are effective in reducing poverty is to examine the surprising and unexpected successes and failures. Guizhou is one such surprising success. Contrary to approaches that emphasize capital-intensive, large-scale development to spur economic growth, it is the smaller-scale approaches that can promote development that is distributed and structured to be accessible to poor people, and can better lead to reduced rural poverty.

Appendix

Methodology and Case Selection

> Faster growth is normally better for the poor than slower growth, and is not systematically offset by any change in distribution. But huge exceptions—and the possibility of clusters of countries where growth is much better for distribution, or much worse—mean that these findings are the beginning, not the end, of the inquiry. Residuals matter.
>
> —Robert Eastwood and Michael Lipton (2001)

The cases I use in this volume—Guizhou and Yunnan—were selected according to expectations about the hypothesized relationship between economic growth and poverty using the most complete and reliable data available—that provided by the World Bank. In this appendix, I outline the case selection process and other methodological issues. I first introduce and execute the regression analysis used to choose the two deviant cases. Because this regression is based on two data points, and is thus highly sensitive to data errors, considering possible sources of bias in the data is especially imperative. To reduce my reliance on a single data source, I also explore here alternative data sources that increase our confidence in the validity of the puzzle. Deriving data from multiple qualitative and quantitative sources allows us to cross-check and verify each source. Because my research explores numerous variables as potential explanations for only two cases, I also address the question of whether the research design violates the degrees-of-freedom problem.

Case Selection, Bias, and Regression Analysis

What is the best way to choose exceptional cases for study? There are numerous ways to select cases, most of which do not fulfill this goal (see table 10). First, many social science studies select cases for practical reasons, including previous expertise in the area, limited time, or limited financial support. Although this is understandable, cases selection using nonrigorous methods is often more biased than choosing cases more systematically. Second, there is random selection; this chooses typical cases, not atypical ones—the opposite of what we seek. Moreover, random selection is not appropriate in small-*N* studies because the risk of selecting a strange and nonuseful mix of cases increases as the number of cases decreases (Gerring 2007). Third, some scholars consult secondary research or panels of experts to select cases, an innovative method that increases the numbers of experts focused on finding relevant cases (e.g., Cimadamore et al. 2002). This method, however, risks following conventional wisdom and adopting the biases of others, thus potentially missing theoretically interesting cases that experts have overlooked. Fourth, cases can be selected because they have extreme values in their dependent variables, thereby indicating a high degree of success or failure. Selecting extreme cases of critical phenomena can be valuable in understanding the causes of rare but important events. But, if the extreme values occur with equally extreme values on potential explanatory factors, then conventional wisdom explains the phenomenon and nothing novel is uncovered. Fifth, cases can be selected using a typological design in which cases are divided into groups based on key criteria; cases are then selected because they fall into theoretically interesting categories (Bennett and George 2005), such as the studies of burden sharing during the first Persian Gulf War (Bennett, Lepgold, and Unger 1994). This method, although designed to select exceptional cases, often requires extensive knowledge of the relevant factors for each case, which is often unavailable or difficult to obtain. Moreover, by combining cases into categories, this method is most applicable when the data are in nominal or ordinal form. If reliable integer or continuous data exist, typological design may not be superior because it divides the independent variables into categories when continuous variables might be more accurate.

In my research, I combined the three remaining case selection methods listed in table 10. First, I followed the most-similar-cases design pioneered by Adam Przeworski and Henry Teune (1970), Arend Lijphart (1971), and Alexander George (1979), selecting paired cases that were similar in as many exogenous factors as possible and, thus, controlling for them. This method chooses cases that differ primarily in the factors of interest and that are similar in many factors not of interest, increasing rigor. Second, I simultaneously focused on diverse cases. Although the background conditions for each case are similar, the variables of interest diverge. Kohli's (2004) study of Korea, India, Brazil, and Nigeria also uses this method. In contrast with selecting cases with extreme values, selecting diverse cases allows a broad variance in both the independent and dependent variables. Neither of these two methods, selecting structured focused comparisons cases nor selecting diverse cases, however, ensures that the cases will actually be exceptions

Table 10. Methods for selecting cases for qualitative studies

Method	Advantages	Disadvantages
Nonsystematic methods (convenience, prior expertise)	Is expedient	Has a high risk of bias
Random selection	Minimizes bias related to human factors	Usually systematically selects typical cases
Consulting panel of experts (Cimadamore et al. 2002)	Increases number of involved experts from few to several	Risks following conventional wisdom, missing theoretically interesting but overlooked cases
Selecting cases with extreme values	If phenomenon is important but rare, can learn about causes because extremes likely to be exceptions	Is uninteresting because change in DV is explained by commonly extreme values in commonly accepted explanatory variable; risks selection bias
Typological design (Bennett and George 2002)	Finds exceptional cases	Presupposes extensive knowledge of cases
Focused comparison (Lijphart 1971)	Controls for a number of factors	May not select true exceptions
Diverse cases (Gerring 2007)	Matches extreme values on both IV and DV	May not select true exceptions
Deviant cases (Gerring 2007)	Enriches understanding of relationship between IV and DV by focusing on true exceptions; enhances explanatory power over IV	Generalizability to other cases suspect

Notes. DV, dependent variable; IV, independent variable.

or puzzling. Therefore, third, I also focused on deviant cases, those cases that are actual exceptions to the purported relationship between economic growth and poverty reduction. Deviant cases are particularly helpful for seeking "new—but as yet unspecified—explanations" (Gerring 2007, 106) to test in other contexts.

I selected deviant cases by regressing changes in the poverty rates against three factors that economists commonly believe cause poverty. In this selection method, deviant cases are then identified as the points that fall furthest from the regression line—those were the cases most likely to be exceptions to the expected relationship between economic growth and poverty reduction. Confidence that the points furthest from the regression line are true exceptions is increased by calculating the probability that the position of any given point is random. If a point is relatively near the regression line, the probability that its residual value (the distance from the regression line) is generated by random factors is relatively high. That probability decreases when data points fall further away from the regression line. Similarly, using *z* values we can calculate the probability of each residual value being random.

By selecting cases with low *z* values (say with a *p* value less than 0.05 in each direction), we can select the cases that are likely to be nonrandom exceptions. By choosing one case from each side of the regression line, I selected cases that defy economists' expectations in both directions: one case in which poverty declined in a relatively stagnant economy and one case in which poverty persisted with rapid economic growth.[1]

Although this selection method avoids many pitfalls, it has at least three drawbacks. First, this method is sensitive to data quality. A few misplaced data points will not normally affect a regression analysis much, as long as the number of cases is large. But, if those flawed points are selected as exceptions, many months of qualitative research can be wasted in chasing a chimera. Because case selection is the first step in an intense, time-consuming, and sometimes expensive qualitative research project, it is important to ensure that the data are reliable.

Second, it is possible that even true exceptions can be caused by systematic but theoretically uninteresting factors, such as the environment (e.g., rainfall or earthquakes), geology (e.g., soil quality or insufficient water), or another nonpolicy omitted variable. Moreover, the nature of the explanatory factors can only be discovered after considerable research. Fortunately, as discussed in chapter 1, the case selection method I used selected two provinces that share several possibly significant but theoretically uninteresting factors, thereby allowing me to control for them. We cannot always count on such a fortunate occurrence to provide a most-similar-cases design because this method can potentially pick cases that are so different from one another that they are difficult to compare.[2]

Third, selecting deviant cases can reduce the potential application of the researchers' conclusions to other areas. Many contemporary political science studies generate generally applicable conclusions by discovering, using regression analysis, nonrandom associations between variables, as well as reducing complex policies and even entire political systems to dummy

1. The use of this method was suggested by Professor Hal Wolman. The use of *z* values to test these probabilities was suggested by Professor Kristopher Ramsay.

2. Does selecting cases with extreme values on the dependent variable create a form of selection bias? As Collier and Mahoney argue, "selecting extreme cases on the dependent variable leads the analyst to focus on cases that, in predictable ways, produce biased estimates of causal effects" (1996, 59). The case selection process does indeed incorporate one form of bias because we are looking for atypical cases. The only problem with this, however, is that selecting cases with extreme values reduces our ability, as Collier and Mahoney note, to generalize the conclusions. By selecting extreme cases from both ends of a range, however, the case selection process does comply with a "basic and obvious rule: selection should allow for the possibility of at least some variation on the dependent variable" (King, Keohane, and Verba 1994, 129). By selecting on the dependent variable, however, I did not bias the results by choosing cases that I knew in advance confirmed a favored hypothesis (for a discussion, see King, Keohane, and Verba 1994, 128, 141–42); at the time of the selection, I did not know the policies or detailed circumstances in the cases I selected. Therefore, the cases are not biased against the pathways to poverty reduction discussed in the introduction.

or interval data. To the extent that researchers focus on a random sample among a universe of cases, the conclusions of their study are likely to apply to most cases (the study in Dollar and Kraay [2002] falls into this category). But, even at its best, that kind of study seeks general associations and discards exceptions to discovered relationships between variables. As a result, it provides few conclusions applicable to regions facing major obstacles to economic growth.

My case selection did essentially the opposite of this. I used a regression not to draw conclusions about average cases but to identify deviant cases, which might or might not represent a class to which multiple cases belong. In doing this, I did not assume or seek a single general covering law explaining poverty reduction (a goal to which some regression analyses implicitly aspire) but assumed instead that there are multiple pathways to poverty reduction that the regression analysis might obscure (Goertz 2006). Moreover, the similarities (geographical and demographic) of the two provinces to other developing economies increase the likelihood that insights from these cases can be applied to other areas. Of course, the degree to which my conclusions from these cases are applicable to other cases remains a question for future research. Nonetheless, the further exploration of purported pathways to poverty reduction (and finding new ones) by scrutinizing the extreme examples of success and failure is in many ways at least as important as understanding how the average economy reduced poverty.

Three advantages outweigh the three pitfalls of this approach. First, systematically selecting exceptional cases reduces the likelihood of choosing typical cases (as with random selection) or cases with certain forms of bias (as with nonsystematic selection methods). Second, by selecting cases using quantitative methods and studying them using qualitative ones, we leverage the strengths of both methods. Most quantitative studies test theoretically interesting factors for statistically significant correlations. Instead, I elected to conduct a structured comparative case study, which allows the collection of a rich array of data directly from a variety of primary sources. In this way, I avoided some of the problems associated with case selection using qualitative methods, but was able to use the deeper analysis of causes provided by such methods. Third, through identifying and scrutinizing exceptional cases, we can flesh out and modify the causal processes of old explanations, as well as potentially discover previously unidentified models that show how (or how not) to reduce poverty. Thus, we might find that each exceptional case traversed one or a combination of these pathways and learn more about the conditions under which these pathways did (or did not) work, as well as which specific mechanisms were used to reduce poverty (or not). Even more exciting, one or more cases might have traversed a new pathway that we can identify and detail.

Selecting cases requires constructing a regression model using factors that reflect the expectations of economists and other experts as the independent

Table 11. Variables used in case selection regression analysis

	Variable	How calculated	Expected sign
DV	Change in poverty rates	Poverty rate in 1996 – Poverty rate in 1991	Not applicable (DV)
IV1	Initial levels of poverty	Poverty rates in 1991	Positive or negative
IV2	Growth rate per capita	(GDP per capita in 1996 – GDP per capita in 1991) ÷ GDP in 1991	Negative (increased growth implies decreased poverty)
IV3	Location	Coast > inland > west[a]	Negative (coast); (inland); Positive (west)

Notes: DV, dependent variable; GDP, gross domestic product; IV, independent variable.
[a]Taken from Fan (1997).

variables. Three factors are typically expected to be important: initial levels of poverty, economic growth rate, and geographical location (see table 11). First, economists expect that poverty in areas with higher initial levels of poverty will change at different rates than those with lower levels of poverty. They disagree, however, on the direction the change, with some arguing that, other things being equal, poorer areas will become poorer over time (and richer areas will become richer), whereas others argue that a convergence in poverty rates should occur through mechanisms such as spread effects.

Second, economists expect that—except under relatively uncommon circumstances—economic growth will reduce poverty rates, and that the faster the growth, the more rapid will be the decrease in poverty. Advocates of the liberal, developmental, and progressive state models not only believe that economic growth reduces income poverty but also advocate policies that reduce poverty directly, without producing economic growth. Thus, controlling for economic growth did not prejudice my case selection against any of these positions; instead, it allowed the identification of factors, other than economic growth, that may be important for reducing poverty.

Third, economists expect that, for historical reasons, there will be regional differences in poverty rates. China scholars have detected a clear pattern of unequal development, with the richer coastal areas outpacing the growth rate and development of central provinces, which in turn have outpaced the growth and development of western provinces. Moreover, some central government policies have been applied differently to these different regions—western, central, and coastal (e.g., Fan 1997). Furthermore, areas in these regions are similar, in the broadest terms, both geographically and demographically. For these reasons, most experts expect that poverty in the Chinese coastal provinces will decline faster than poverty in the inland provinces, which in turn should decline faster than poverty in western provinces.

With data collected from the Chinese National Bureau of Statistics (NBS) and the World Bank, I calculated a regression line based on a model derived

Table 12. Regression results: initial levels of poverty, economic growth, and location against changes in poverty rates

Source	SS	df	MS	
Model	2149.05211	4	537.263029	$N = 25$; $F(4, 20) = 20.99$;
Residual	511.869347	20	25.5934674	Prob > $F = 0.0000$; $R^2 = 0.8076$;
Total	2660.92146	24	110.871728	Adjusted $R^2 = 0.7692$; Root MSE = 5.059

povt2t1intl	Coefficient	Std. Err.	*t*	$P>\|t\|$	95% Confidence interval	
pov91intl	−0.6909107	0.0934758	−7.39	0.000	−0.8858978	−0.4959236
gdpcapgrwth	−0.0506892	0.0276951	−1.83	0.082	−0.1084602	0.0070818
coast	−10.47261	4.72723	−2.22	0.039	−20.33344	−0.6117824
inland	−14.03452	3.205835	−4.38	0.000	−20.72177	−7.347266
_cons	25.87969	6.803142	3.80	0.001	11.68859	40.0708

Notes: df, degrees of freedom; MS, mean squares; MSE, mean sqaure error; SS, sum of squares; Std. Err., standard error.

from three independent variables (see table 12). The dependent variable was the change in the poverty rates between 1991 and 1996 (disaggregated at the provincial level) calculated by World Bank economists based on NBS grouped data (Piazza et al. 2001), the most reliable complete set of poverty data for each of the Chinese provinces currently available to the public. I excluded from the data set three of provincial-level cities (Beijing, Tianjin, and Shanghai) because of their tiny rural populations. Because the fourth provincial-level municipality in China, Chongqing, did not become an independent provincial-level city until 1997 (it was part of Sichuan), I included the 1996 Chongqing data in the data for Sichuan. In addition, fearing inaccurate data, I omitted two provincial-level autonomous regions, Tibet and Xinjiang. Because these two autonomous regions contain large independence movements with international support, the Chinese central government has particular reasons for not reporting accurate economic growth and poverty data for them. Eliminating these six provincial-level governments leaves a total *N* of twenty-five for each of the two years.

If this were a hypothesis-testing exercise, this regression would be misspecified and inaccurate.[3] But this exercise was not intended to test the economic model but, instead, tried to be as fair to the model as possible. The model served to predict, but not explain, as much of the variation in poverty rates as possible through nonpolicy factors. Because correlation between

3. The independent variables are not truly independent of one another. GDP growth, we know from extensive research, has been fastest in the Chinese coastal provinces, and indeed two variables (GDP growth and the Coast dummy variable) have a 0.64 correlation. Similarly, initial levels of poverty should be related both to location (the Poverty variable has a 0.62 correlation with the West dummy variable) and to GDP growth (with a 0.54 correlation).

variables increased the likelihood of finding a significant result, using correlated factors as independent variables was both fair to the model and not inaccurate as long as we attach little importance to a significant finding. Moreover, it is difficult to imagine omitting one of the variables simply because another variable could serve as proxy; the result would be a less accurate reflection of economists' expectations, even if the model might come up with similar results.[4] Similarly, there was no need to test for heteroscedasticity. Even if the variation changed across the entire range, it would have no bearing on finding residuals. Nor did I test for a nonlinear relationship between the independent and dependent variables because the model I simulated argues that there is a one-to-one correlation between economic growth and poverty reduction. Economists such as Dollar and Kraay would expect a straight regression line (Dollar and Kraay 2002).

The model as a whole is statistically significant (although little weight can be attached to this result). The first factor, initial levels of poverty, is significant at the 0.05 confidence level. The negative sign indicates that poverty declined more in the provinces with higher initial poverty rates, consistent with the convergence hypothesis. The second factor, per capita GDP growth, is significant at the 0.1 confidence level and has a negative sign, meaning that poverty rates in the provinces with higher rates of economic growth declined more than poverty rates in provinces with lower rates of growth. This is consistent with the view that poverty in provinces with a higher growth rate per capita declines faster than it does in provinces with a low growth rate per capita. Location, the final factor, is similarly significant, with signs in the expected direction.

The model is also an accurate predictor of changes in poverty. The adjusted R^2 for the model is nearly 0.77, implying that the three nonpolicy-determined factors selected explain more than three-quarters of the variance in the provincial poverty rates, although this is largely caused by the way the model was constructed. Despite the discussion on model specification, stopping at this point is nevertheless tempting. Given such a close fit, the results of this model are consistent with the expectations of mainstream economists. Economic growth, combined with location and initial levels of poverty, helped to reduce poverty in China between 1991 and 1996.

A closer examination, however, reveals that, although the changes in the poverty rates of no less than six of the twenty-five provinces were within

4. For instance, location not only captures economic growth but, more important, controls for central policy and spread effects. Running the same regression without controls for location gives similar results—statistically significant ($p < 0.0000$) with a smaller R^2 of 0.6. Although Yunnan remains the most extreme exception in one direction (in fact, the residual for Yunnan increases to 18) when the location dummy variables are omitted, Guizhou is not chosen. Instead, the central province of Anhui (which also experienced a high degree of poverty reduction) is chosen. Anhui, however, borders two rapidly growing provinces, Jiangsu and Zhejiang, and so this result can be superficially explained by spread effects, a factor for which the location dummy variables control.

Table 13. Provinces, in order of residuals

(1) Province	(2) Predicted poverty change	(3) Reported poverty change	(4) Residual (reported – predicted)	(5) Outlier	(6) Difference in human terms (residual × rural population)
Guizhou	**–21.94**	**–30.83**	**–8.89**	**0.03**	**–2,650,285**
Sichuan	**–11.01**	**–19.21**	**–8.20**	**0.04**	**–7,614,187**
Anhui	–44.57	–50.84	–6.27	0.09	–3,116,533
Guangdong	–0.92	–5.58	–4.66	0.16	–2,233,282
Jiangsu	–11.37	–14.55	–3.18	0.25	–1,627,759
Hebei	–19.65	–22.74	–3.09	0.25	–1,642,810
Jiangxi	–9.04	–11.77	–2.73	0.28	–856,231
Liaoning	–5.23	–7.51	–2.28	0.31	–510,861
Shandong	–11.67	–13.02	–1.35	0.39	–875,742
Henan	–34.47	–35.17	–0.70	0.44	–534,195
Ningxia	–13.16	–13.66	–0.50	0.46	–18,929
Hubei	–20.02	–20.32	–0.30	0.47	–125,034
Zhejiang	–6.84	–7.02	–0.18	0.48	–66,009
Fujian	–11.32	–11.23	0.09	0.51	24,385
Hunan	–14.10	–13.77	0.33	0.53	173,757
Heilongjiang	–18.77	–17.69	1.08	0.59	214,620
Qinghai	–12.73	–11.4	1.33	0.61	44,264
Jilin	–14.24	–12.54	1.70	0.64	252,053
Shaanxi	–14.60	–12.45	2.15	0.68	586,826
Shanxi	–28.03	–25.58	2.45	0.70	562,961
Gansu	–27.22	–23.74	3.48	0.77	690,920
Inner Mongolia	–23.34	–18.91	4.43	0.83	672,480
Guangxi	–18.60	–11.69	6.91	0.93	2,606,050
Hainan	**–12.13**	**–4.38**	**7.75**	**0.95**	**418,950**
Yunnan	**–15.83**	**–5.19**	**10.64**	**0.98**	**3,578,028**

Note: The outliers appear in boldface.

1 percentage point of that predicted by the model—exceptionally accurate—and the majority (fourteen) are within 3 points (see table 13), the model has no fewer than four outliers.

I determined the outliers of this regression by computing the residuals (the distance of each point from the regression line) and then calculating the chance that the distance was random. When the chance of that was less than 5 percent in either direction, I labeled that point an outlier. Specifically, I subtracted the change in poverty rates predicted by the model (table 13, col. 2) from the value reported by the data (col. 3); this residual value appears in column 4. Column 5 records the probability (p value) that the position of the data point corresponding to each province is caused by random variation. This is estimated by calculating the p values of the z values of the residual. I considered any province with a p value lower than 5 percent or higher than 95 percent to be an outlier (an equivalent p value of 0.1 in a two-tailed test). These four provinces appear in boldface in table 13. Column 6 is calculated by multiplying the residual times the rural population of each province; it expresses the difference between the predicted value and the actual value of rural poverty. In other words, this column estimates how many more or fewer people would be in poverty in each province if economic growth had had the effect on poverty that the model predicted (i.e., if all data points were on the regression line).

Although the model does explain the overall pattern of poverty reduction in China, for the four outliers, the difference between the expectations of the model and the actual change is significant (as calculated by z values) and considerable. Between 1991 and 1996, poverty reduction in Guizhou and Sichuan outperformed the model predictions based on the three independent variables. The Guizhou poverty rate declined 8.89 percentage points more than the model predicts, meaning that an additional 2.65 million people were not poor in 1996 than expected by the model. Similarly, the Sichuan poverty rate declined 8.2 percentage points more than expected, meaning that an additional 7.6 million people emerged from poverty. Yunnan and Hainan are outliers in the other direction: their poverty rates declined far less than the model predicted. The Yunnan poverty rate declined 10.64 percentage points less than expected, implying an additional 3.58 million people were in poverty in 1996 than the model predicted. The Hainan poverty rate declined 7.75 percentage points less than expected, translating to an additional 419,000 people in poverty. Overall, this methodology is in the spirit of Martin Ravallion's argument that "People are often hurting behind the averages," (2001, 1811) as well as Lipton and Eastwood's "Residuals matter" (quoted at the beginning of this appendix). In typical regression analyses, residual cases are dismissed. In this study, they are of central importance.

Data Sources and Reliability

This case selection regression analysis presumed that the data were generally accurate, or at least that bias was similar across the cases; this assumption is unwarranted. Unlike most large-*N* regression analyses, in which measurement errors in a small number of data points probably do not seriously taint the results, for case selection, we need the data to be accurate, especially the data for the provinces identified as outliers. This is a sobering prospect because statistics for China are notoriously suspect and are never to be taken at face value (although they often are). As two economists assessing the Chinese rural survey system caution, the data collection process in China is "highly politicized. Government leaders are quite sensitive to perceptions that they have failed to eradicate widespread poverty, which could undermine the government's legitimacy in light of its socialist ideology" (Park and Wang 2001, 385). The central government pressures in this regard have been passed down the administrative chain to provincial leaders (who since

1993 have been held personally responsible for achieving poverty alleviation goals) and then passed down to local leaders (Park and Wang 2001). Nevertheless, many scholars use Chinese statistics without explicitly considering how potential biases might affect the results.

Rural household economic data are collected from all Chinese provinces in two annual national surveys, each of which amasses extensive income, expenditure, and demographic information from rural households in the expansive and often rugged countryside.[5] In the first survey, the National Rural Household Survey (NRHS), introduced in 1984, data are collected in a top-down manner; the central government dispatches agents to local levels to collect survey data from a sample of 68,000 rural households in 7,100 villages in 857 of the more than 2,800 counties in China. For this survey, which is modeled after the UN Household Survey Capability Program, participating households are asked to maintain detailed diaries of all income and expenses. Assistance in completing the diaries is provided for illiterate households, and random visits are scheduled. To reduce local interference and promote accuracy, the central Rural Survey Organization of the NBS supervises the data collection. The data gathered include community information related to rural infrastructure and basic social services, as well as household information, such as agricultural production, conditions of housing, income, consumption, expenditures, and value of durable goods (National Bureau of Statistics 2004). These data are used to calculate poverty rates at the national and provincial levels (Bramall 2001). Experts praise the survey for being broad-based, comprehensive, and of a scale that allows generalization at both the national and provincial levels. In addition, unlike surveys in some countries that rely on one-off interviews, the NBS trains and monitors the participants as they maintain their diary of income and expenditures throughout the year. To deal with life-cycle problems, the NBS has since 1990 annually rotated off and replaced a portion of the survey participants (Park and Wang 2001). Although this survey is considered to be more accurate than other nationally based surveys in China, it is also limited. For instance, it is unable to measure broader forms of poverty beyond those measured by income and expenditure, evaluate antipoverty programs, and estimate poverty rates on the subcounty level (United Nations Economic and Social Commission for Asia and the Pacific [UNESCAP] 2005).

In addition, the results of the NRHS are restricted. Although the NBS claims that the data are published in several reports (National Bureau of

5. An additional survey, the National Rural Poverty Monitoring Survey (NRPMS), has gathered information, since 1997, from each of the 592 designated poor counties in China (National Bureau of Statistics 2004). Although this survey provides some crucial information, it leaves analysts unable to compare the rich and poor areas of a province. Moreover, because a minority of the people living in designated poor counties are not poor and because most poor people live in scattered areas outside the poor areas, this survey can tell us little about the poverty rate of a particular province.

Statistics 2004), the key provincial-level poverty rates are not openly disseminated. Fortunately, the World Bank, in researching its *China: Overcoming Rural Poverty* (Piazza et al. 2001), obtained access to these statistics from the NBS on the condition that the data be reported only in grouped form. In spite of these restrictions, World Bank researchers were able to compile perhaps the most accurate and complete set of rural poverty data available to the public for each of the Chinese provinces, data (available for 1989, 1990, 1991, and 1996) that I could use to select cases. Although the four years of the data are published together without comment, according to Chen Shaohua, an economist and one of the authors of the report, the provincial-level poverty data for two years (1991 and 1996) are reliable, whereas the data from the other two years (1989 and 1990) are best used for "reference purposes" only.[6] Moreover, although the report borrows from the legitimacy of its publisher, the World Bank, it nevertheless relies on the accuracy of the rural household survey that Chinese authorities collected. Although experts consider this centrally administered NRHS to be the more accurate of the two national surveys, it comes with numerous technical, political, and methodological challenges.

The second survey is the only source of detailed information from every one of the more than 2,800 county-level units in China as of the end of 2007.[7] The data are gathered from the bottom up, with local governments from each of the Chinese counties passing survey information upward to successive administrative levels until it reaches the central government. Although the survey results are compiled and published in the provincial and other local yearbooks for public consumption, neither the poverty figures nor sufficient data to derive such figures are reported. Moreover, at each level, officials have the opportunity to manipulate the statistics before passing them up to higher levels, access they lack in the centrally administered survey. According to my interviews with scholars and local officials, this manipulation can occur in two conflicting directions. Sometimes, to substantiate their appeals for additional aid, local officials are said to arbitrarily deflate economic statistics in an attempt to make the economic situation appear more serious than it actually is. At other times, officials desiring reward and promotion are said to inflate the statistics, making the economic situation appear better than it is. Although some local officials insist that these statistics are reliable, most officials and scholars use them cautiously.[8] In truth, it is very difficult, even for higher-level officials, to determine which

6. Interview with Chen Shaohua, World Bank economist, Washington, D.C., August 2002.

7. Sources refer to this survey in different ways, including "Regional Statistics through Administrative Reports" (in National Bureau of Statistics 2004) and "District Economic Statistics" (in UNESCAP 2005).

8. One township official at the forestry station in a mountainous poor county, responding to my questions about the forestry coverage rate in the county, reported an undoubtedly exaggerated rate of 70 percent. Realizing that this county, due to poverty and a lack of farm-

statistics have been manipulated (if any), to what extent, and in which direction by lower-level officials. Many of the scholars and even some of the local and central officials whom I consulted cautioned against taking the statistics overly seriously, although most informants maintained that the overall trends and relative comparisons, were relatively reliable; this is how the information from this survey was used in my case selection. For both surveys, the collected data are compared with the official Chinese poverty line, which is much lower than the international poverty line.

Chinese poverty statistics, like nearly all statistics, are to some degree inaccurate. Are those inaccuracies severe enough to proscribe the use of such statistics? Focusing on the more accurate of the two surveys—the top-down NRHS—Albert Park and Sangui Wang (2001) point to numerous, and sometimes countervailing, sources of bias that, they argue, generally overestimate income and thus underestimate poverty rates in China (see table 14 for a summary and how each source affects my study).

According to these researchers, two sources of bias tend to overestimate poverty rates:

- Ia. The official Chinese poverty line has a high standard for daily caloric intake of 2,400 calories, compared to the norm of 2,000–2,150 calories.
- Ib. Other surveys, such as Khan and Riskin's (2001), reveal that NBS data undercount income; for example, by not counting the rental value of housing.

Four sources of bias tend to underestimate poverty rates:

- IIa. NBS, in calculating its standard food bundle to generate a poverty line, sets grain at 88 percent of expenditures, when grain more typically accounts for only 70 percent of actual food expenditures of impoverished families, with the rest taken up by more expensive items.
- IIb. The inflation rate that is implied by annual increases in the poverty line is significantly lower than the official inflation rate.
- IIc. Remote and illiterate households are included less than is proportional to their numbers, despite a policy that explicitly tries to include them.
- IId. The 1998 slashing of the nonfood expenditures proportion of the poverty line from 40 percent of the total to 17 percent probably underestimates poverty after that date.

---

land, had been heavily denuded of forest land, the official paused to look at me apologetically. "Anyway," he said dryly, "these are the official statistics."

In addition, three sources of bias are ambiguous or both underestimate and overestimate poverty:

IIIa. Before 1990, planned (rather than market) prices were used to count self-produced consumption goods. (This is ambiguous because it affected both the poverty line and measured income.)

IIIb. NBS reports income, not expenditure, data, which fluctuates more (thus overstating poverty rates). But also exaggerates welfare because incomes tend to be 10–20 percent higher than consumption (thus understating poverty rates).

IIIc. Regional price differences probably underestimate poverty in provinces with more expensive goods while overestimating poverty in provinces with less expensive goods.[9]

Weighing each of these factors, Park and Wang conclude that two of the sources of bias are most important: (IIb), the low inflation rate, which causes poverty lines to be too low; and the first part of (IIIc), the use of income, rather than expenditure, which exaggerates income by 10–20 percent. These combine to underestimate poverty in China.

To this list we should add political pressures, as already above. If Chinese administrators exaggerate only the rates at which poverty has been reduced (by arbitrarily inflating income statistics), this will lead to a significant underestimation of poverty. But this source of bias has to be weighed against a countervailing one; whatever local officials gain by reporting rosy income figures, by doing so they lose central funding for antipoverty programs. Local officials engage in a continuous ritual, pleading poverty to gain additional funding, which creates pressures to exaggerate the extent of the problem; in this way, local poverty rates are overstated.

We should consider these sources of bias in context. Over the past two decades, Chinese data collection techniques and procedures have improved dramatically, as the CCP has shifted the goals of collecting the statistics from nearly pure propaganda toward more legitimate goals, such as research, assessment, and planning. In addition to these improved measurement tools and procedures, the monitoring of the overall process also has been enhanced (Bramall 2001). Even the most cynical experts do not believe that the numbers are completely invented. The central government, by and large, seeks at least one set of reliable statistics (the restricted NRHS survey) with which to inform its decisions, monitor the accomplishments of

9. Park and Wang (2001) also note two additional ambiguous factors. The first is based on differences from using aggregate data, as opposed to grouped data, which leads to unpredictable bias. The World Bank uses grouped data, whereas much of the other data I used are aggregates. The second factor is based on observations that total poverty headcounts include both transitional and chronic poverty, thus understating chronic poverty; this only applies if one is researching chronic poverty exclusively.

Table 14. Sources of bias in NRHS poverty statistics for China

Sources of bias	My response
I. Overstates poverty	
a. Using calorie standard	Applies only to China's poverty line
b. Undercounting income	Applies equally to all provinces Rental value of housing applies more to relative poverty and inequality, less to absolute poverty
II. Understates poverty	
a. Overcounting grain in food bundles	Applies only to China's poverty line
b. Using inflation rate	Applies only to China's poverty line Applies equally to Yunnan and Guizhou
c. Sampling biased against remote, illiterate households	Applies similarly to Yunnan and Guizhou
d. Slashing nonfood expenditure proportion of poverty line	Applies only to China's poverty line and only after 1998
III. Ambiguous/both directions	
a. Using planned prices	Applies only before 1990
b. Reporting income, not expenditure data	Applies to all provinces equally (to the extent that the ratios of income to consumption are similar for all provinces)
c. Using regional price differences	Underestimates Yunnan and Guizhou probably to similar degrees
d. Politically motivated bias	Countervailing Should apply roughly equally in all provinces

Source: Park and Wang (2001).
Note: NRHS, National Rural Household Survey.

subordinates, and warn of potential crises. Because the central government holds local officials accountable for reaching economic goals, including poverty reduction, the accurate collection of data is also considered in their evaluation. To attempt to ensure accuracy, central government auditors are also dispatched to a portion of the areas to verify these statistics. This serves as an imperfect check on local officials, largely preventing them from exaggerating wildly their reports. Moreover, a small number of intentionally misleading figures, if not too numerous, will be washed out in the averages, although their influence will increase as the unit of analysis becomes more local. After all, independent surveys, both Western and Chinese, generally confirm the overall trends, even when the absolute figures differ.

Nevertheless, we cannot rely solely on the accuracy of these figures. Fortunately, the puzzle I address in this book does not require such a high standard. Four issues minimize the degree to which these sources of bias in the data influence the present study (see table 14). First, some of the sources of bias are time-limited. The planned prices used before 1990, for instance, do not affect my quantitative data, which begins with 1991. Second, other sources of bias pertain to the calculation of the (too-low) Chinese poverty line, including (Ia) the calorie standard, (IIa) the over counting of grain in food bundles, (IIb) the inflation rate, and (IId) the slashing of nonfood expenditures. I avoid this by adopting the then prevailing international poverty line of US$1 per person per day.[10] Third, the comparative method helps us manage other sources of bias. That is, the puzzle of economic growth versus poverty reduction identified in the data will still be valid as long as the same biases apply to all the provinces, or at least to both Yunnan and Guizhou. For instance, the undercounting of income (Ib) and the political biases (IIId) should apply in roughly equal degrees to each province. Even where other sources of bias vary by province, several of them, including the inflation rate (IIb), the sampling bias against remote or illiterate households (IIc), and the regional price differences (IIIc), should apply similarly to Guizhou and Yunnan because inflation rates, illiteracy rates, and price differences in the two provinces are similar. If biases apply equally across provinces, the relative positions of the statistics for each province, as well as the trends, are reliable, even if the statistics are not trustworthy enough to compare them outside China, where data are likely to be biased in dissimilar ways. Fourth, that the results of the regression exercise were in line with economists' expectations (that poverty and growth are related) increases our confidence in the data. Although the main variables are from the Chinese government, the variables I used in the regression analysis were from different, independently collected sources: GDP data from annual bottom-up surveys, poverty rates from the top-down NRHS survey data processed by World Bank economists into grouped data, and location data based on politicians' and geographers' classifications. It is improbable that officials wishing to manipulate the data actually systematically coordinate these variables. Perhaps all the data are simply exaggerated, with inflated growth rates and underestimated poverty rates. Even this, however, cannot explain why the economic growth and poverty data of the four provinces—the outliers from the regression analysis—moved in unexpected directions while the data in the majority of the provinces moved in the expected directions.

Still, the numerous sources of bias leave doubt. Moreover, my interviews with Guizhou scholars revealed that many did not believe that Guizhou is doing as well as the data suggest. Few experts in Guizhou development and poverty, however, have compared it with Yunnan. After all, even the dramatic decline in the Guizhou poverty rate does not imply that people are doing well—life just above the poverty line, even if qualitatively better than life below it, remains marginal and fraught with struggle and uncertainty.

10. The problem of inflation still pertains here, however, because the international poverty line (US$1 per person per day) ironically takes on the U.S. inflation rate, which is in most years much lower than the Chinese inflation rate. Because Guizhou and Yunnan had similar average inflation rates between 1991 and 1996, this problem probably affects both provinces equally.

Interestingly, few Yunnan scholars who I interviewed doubted the statistics about Yunnan; they are aware of the extent of poverty in Yunnan, even in the face of the relative overall prosperity.

This reservation held by Chinese social scientists (grinding poverty in Guizhou casts doubt on its status as a positive exception) demands the exploration of other sources of information that can confirm or disconfirm that the puzzle of economic growth versus poverty reduction exists. After all, getting the puzzle right is the critical first step in finding out which poverty reduction strategies work best. Although the central government restricts access to provincial poverty statistics, there is no lack of other data that proximate poverty, estimates based on separate surveys or data based on peeks at restricted data. In addition to verifying the existence of the puzzle, perhaps we can find data that also extend the puzzle past 1996.

As mentioned earlier, to my knowledge, no publicly available source of poverty reduction data covering each of the Chinese rural provinces exists, other than the two years processed by the World Bank. Nevertheless, an alternative measure of poverty is available—per capita net rural income, which is collected bottom up from each county and published in provincial yearbooks. Of course, average per capita net rural income cannot replace income poverty data. Because this statistic is aggregated (although at a lower, county level), it conceals the actual number of poor people. The statistic, however, does measure income minus expenses in rural areas for each county in each province, a relatively disaggregated unit of analysis, and it may be one of the best available alternative variables to rural poverty rates. County-level net rural income data in China is collected (in the same bottom-up fashion described earlier) by local governments in China for publication in publicly available annual provincial statistical yearbooks. It is thus a separate source from the World Bank NRHS survey data.

Figure 9 compares the nominal GDPs of Yunnan and Guizhou. As we can see, although the Yunnan economy did grow remarkably faster than the Guizhou economy between 1990 and 2007, the overall average Guizhou per capita net rural income during those years kept pace with, and at times even exceeded, that of Yunnan.

The contrast between growth and net income in the two provinces is even starker when we separate the data on net rural income for poor and nonpoor counties. In 1986, the Chinese State Council categorized each of the more than 2,800 counties as either "poor" or "nonpoor," with provinces having the opportunity to delineate their own lists (Park, Wang, and Wu 2002; Zhang, Huang, and Rozelle 2003). Although this process, like the collection of poverty data, had several methodological and political problems (see Park, Wang, and Wu 2002), any biases probably affected Yunnan and Guizhou similarly. The average per capita net rural incomes of poor and nonpoor counties in Yunnan and Guizhou can be measured separately, giving us four lines to compare. For these data to confirm the puzzle, we expect

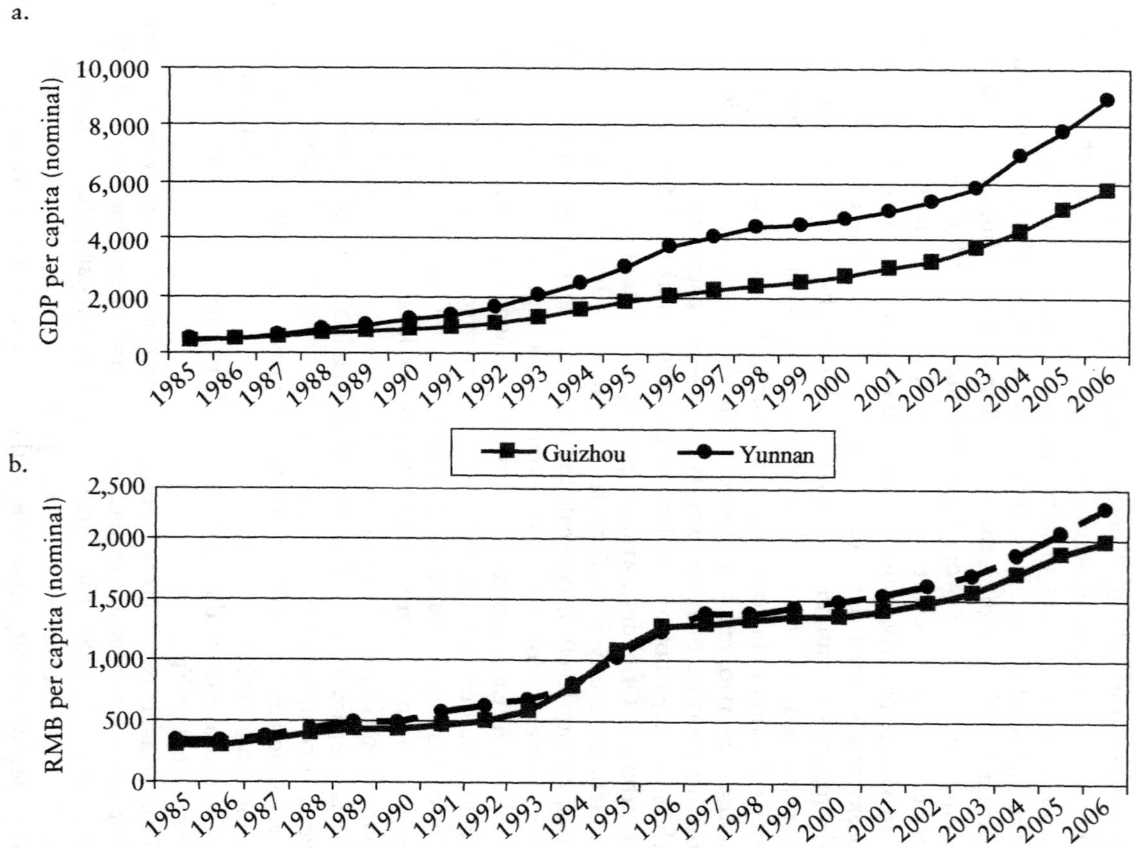

Fig. 9 (a) GDP per capita and (b) net income per capita in Guizhou and Yunnan, 1985–2006.
Source: Guizhou Nianjian Bianjibu (1986–2007); Yunnan Nianjian Bianjibu (1986–2007).

the per capita net rural income of the Yunnan nonpoor counties to exceed the per capita net rural income of the nonpoor counties of Guizhou, reflecting that the superior performance of Yunnan in GDP growth primarily benefited its nonpoor counties.[11] We also expect the per capita net rural income in Guizhou poor counties to exceed that in Yunnan—reflecting better performance in poverty reduction by Guizhou. As figure 1 (in the introduction) demonstrates, that is precisely the pattern we find. Thus, sources based on both of major comprehensive income surveys of China confirm the general pattern and reinforce our confidence in the existence of the puzzle.

Other sources provide independent, although less complete, evidence generally confirming the puzzle. For instance, as a part of its 1995–2000 Southwest Poverty Reduction Project, the World Bank, through Chinese government agencies, conducted independent income surveys in most of the targeted counties of the three provinces participating in the program (Yunnan, Guizhou, and Guangxi). The surveys are not as extensive (six counties for each of the two provinces) and are based on different poverty lines (the one for Yunnan is slightly higher than for Guizhou, presumably reflecting different costs of living). In any case, the results of the survey are largely consistent with the puzzle. According to this survey, the poverty rate in the project counties surveyed in Guizhou declined steadily, from a high of 34.5 percent in 1995 to 20.1 percent in 1999. For Yunnan, however, the results were U-shaped, beginning at 33.4 percent in 1995, dropping to 20 percent in 1997, and then increasing again to 27.3 percent in 1999. As with the other two data sources, Guizhou started the period with a higher poverty rate than Yunnan, but ended with a lower one. The main difference between the data sources is temporal—the reversal in position of the relative poverty rates in the two provinces occurred in the previous surveys before 1996, and in these after 1998.[12]

In addition, a group of economists obtained two years of data, 1995 and 1998, from the Chinese Academy of Social Science and the Ministry of Agriculture, respectively (not from the NBS). Their resulting table presents poverty headcount rates for nineteen Chinese provinces, including Guizhou and Yunnan, measured using both the official Chinese and the international poverty lines. Measured against the higher international poverty line, the pattern is roughly consistent with that in the World Bank data. The Guizhou poverty rate starts out slightly lower (30.11 percent) than the Yunnan rate

11. Finding such a pattern would not preclude the possibility that, for instance, most poverty reduction in Yunnan occurred in its nonpoor counties, whereas the opposite was true for Guizhou. Although this is possible, a finding that the net rural income in Guizhou poor counties exceeded that in Yunnan poor counties (and vice versa for nonpoor counties) would nevertheless be consistent with the puzzle.

12. See the report by the General Organization of Rural Social-Economic Survey of National Bureau of Statistics and Foreign Capital Project Management Center of State Council Leading Group Office of Poverty Alleviation and Development (1999, esp. 44).

(39.79 percent) and decreases more than 10 percentage points, compared to a decrease of 3 percentage points for Yunnan. Measured against the lower official Chinese poverty line, however, the poverty rates for both provinces increase, indicating that the poorest of the poor increased in number in both provinces—a pattern consistent with the World Bank data for Yunnan but not for Guizhou. Moreover, the Yunnan poverty rate begins higher (15.99 percent) than the Guizhou rate (12.16 percent) and also increases faster (10 percentage points for Yunnan compared to 3 for Guizhou).

Also consistent with the puzzle are data from an unidentified source that appears in a table included in a report by two internationally recognized Chinese sociologists, Wang Shaoguang and Hu Angang (1999). According to the 1993 poverty rates listed there, which were calculated based on an unspecified standard, the Yunnan poverty rate was higher than the Guizhou rate (23.67 vs. 21.89 percent).

In contrast, the results of one important survey (Khan and Riskin 2001) are inconsistent with the pattern that generated the puzzle. The joint Chinese-foreign rural surveys, conducted in 1988 and 1995, were spearheaded by Azizur Khan and Carl Riskin, two economists. Their sample, a subsample of the NBS panel, is far smaller than the NBS samples, incorporating 10,258 households in 1998 and 7,998 households in 1995 (compared to 67,000 households in the full sample). The 1988 survey of twenty-eight provinces excludes two provinces (Xinjiang and Tibet), whereas the 1995 survey excludes nine additional provinces, bringing the total provinces surveyed to nineteen. Guizhou and Yunnan are included in both surveys. According to these surveys the poverty rates of both provinces barely moved. The Guizhou poverty rate in 1998 exceeded the Yunnan rate by 11 percentage points (58.3 vs. 47.3 percent). Moreover, whereas the Yunnan poverty rate by 1995 declined 1.7 percentage points to 45.6 percent, the Guizhou rate increased 3.5 percentage points to 61.8 percent. This pattern is strikingly different from that in the World Bank data and the other sources described previously.

What explains these differences? Khan and Riskin's survey corrects some problems in the calculation of income by incorporating income sources that the NBS survey excludes, including rental value of housing[13] and in-kind and subsidy income sources. Overall, its estimates of rural income exceed those of the NBS surveys by 39 percent (for 1988) and 46 percent (for 1995). These sources of income, in any case, should be proportionally similar for Yunnan and Guizhou; however, the average rural income for the two provinces reported in Khan and Riskin's 1995 survey exceeds the NBS survey estimates by 11.6 percent for Guizhou and 49 percent for Yunnan.

13. It is difficult to understand why the rental value of housing is included in surveys of Chinese rural areas because housing is not a liquid asset. Although it might make a difference for inequality, it should not make a difference in poverty rates because poor people do not live off of it and they cannot borrow against this asset.

It is difficult to explain why the results of Khan and Riskin's survey are inconsistent with the puzzle. One possible source of the discrepancy is the fact that this survey uses a subsample of the NBS sample that the World Bank used to calculate poverty rates in 1991 and 1996. Thus, the potential for bias identified by Park and Wang (2001) is the same as or worse than in the World Bank survey. Moreover, as Khan and Riskin (2001, 10, 47) state in several places, their survey sample is much smaller than that of NBS, and for some measures, the sample is too small to draw conclusions at the provincial level. The conclusions that they do make regarding these two provinces contradict other sources, including, as we have seen, one using a larger sample of data from the same source. Because Khan and Riskin themselves warn that their data do not permit blanket conclusions at the provincial level, their findings do not invalidate the puzzle.

The Degrees-of-Freedom Problem

One final issue related to methodology needs discussion. My research project tested the power of nearly three dozen candidate factors to explain the puzzling pattern of poverty reduction and economic growth experienced in two provinces. Does the degrees-of-freedom problem apply to this research?

Methodologists argue that, unless the number of observations exceeds the candidate explanations being tested, alternative explanations cannot be ruled out. As Gary King, Robert Keohane, and Sidney Verba state the problem, "one fact (or observable implication) cannot give *independent* information about more than one other fact" (1994, 119). Detailed case studies, in which a single case study contains a multitude of relevant facts, however, do not fall victim to the degrees-of-freedom problem. As one early critic, Donald Campbell, in qualifying his previous criticism of case studies based on the degrees-of-freedom problem, admits,

> I have overlooked a major source of discipline.... In a case study done by an alert social scientist who has thorough acquaintance, the theory he uses to explain the focal difference also generates prediction or expectations on dozens of other aspects of the culture, and he does not retain the theory unless most of these are confirmed. In some sense, he has tested the theory with degrees of freedom coming from the multiple implications of any one theory. (1975, 181–82)

Therefore, the degrees-of-freedom problem does not pertain to this study, even though it explores numerous factors in only two cases. Each candidate factor in the study is associated with poverty and growth through multiple causal linkages, each of which had to be verified before a factor was accepted as explaining part of the puzzle. Few factors affect poverty and growth rates directly, but many do so through sometimes lengthy strings of connections. The factor was considered invalid if any of the expected links in this chain was inconsistent with the expected pattern. As Andrew Bennett and Alexander George note, "Within a single case there are many possible process-tracing observations along the hypothesized causal paths between independent and dependent variables.... As long as competing theories make different predictions on the causal processes thought to have taken place in a... case study researchers may have the means to reject many of the possible alternative explanations of a case" (2005, 29). Because these two mechanisms collect far more observations than variables, this comparative case study, like most cases studies, has sufficient degrees of freedom.[14]

14. One way to think of this is as a murder case, in which detectives generally have but one case (a victim) and many candidate factors (multiple suspects). Fortunately, detectives have multiple independent facts, including alibi, motive, means, and so forth, which in many cases allow them to determine "who done it." In frustrating cases, detectives lack sufficient evidence to determine who actually committed the crime. Thus, this degrees-of-freedom problem is probabilistic. In much social science research, explanations are rarely definite, and there always remains the possibility that even conclusions supported by plenty of reliable evidence are incorrect.

References

Adelman, Irma. 1986. "A Poverty-Focused Approach to Development Policy." In *Development Strategies Reconsidered,* edited by John P. Lewis and Valeriana Kallab. New Brunswick, N.J.: Transaction Books.

Albouy, Yves. 1991. "Coal Pricing in China: Issues and Reform Strategy." *World Bank Discussion Paper no. 138.* World Bank, Washington, D.C.

Amin, Galal A. 1974. *The Modernization of Poverty: A Study in the Political Economy of Growth in Nine Arab Countries, 1945–1970.* Leiden: Brill.

Amsden, Alice H. 1985. "The State and Taiwan's Economic Development." In *Bringing the State Back In,* edited by Peter Evans, Dietrich Rueschemeyer and Theda Skocpol. Cambridge, UK: Cambridge University Press.

Amsden, Alice H. 2001. *The Rise of "The Rest": Challenges to the West from Late-Industrializing Economies.* Oxford: Oxford University Press.

Auty, Richard M. 1995. *Patterns of Development: Resources, Policy and Economic Growth.* London: Edward Arnold.

Balisacan, Arsenio M., and Ernesto M. Pernia. 2002. "Probing Beneath Cross-National Averages: Poverty, Inequality, and Growth in the Philippines." ERD Working Paper no. 17. Asian Development Bank, Manila.

Balisacan, Arsenio M., Ernesto M. Pernia, and Abnza Asra. 2002. "Revisiting Growth and Poverty Reduction in Indonesia: What Do Subnational Data Show?" ERD Working Paper no. 25. Asian Development Bank, Manila.

Bannister, Geoffrey J., and Kamau Thugge. 2001. *International Trade and Poverty Alleviation.* Washington, D.C.: International Monetary Fund.

Bartke, Wolfgang. 1981. *Who's Who in the People's Republic of China.* Brighton: Harvester Press.

Bates, Robert H. 1981. *Markets and States in Tropical Africa: The Politics Basis of Agricultural Policies.* Berkeley: University of California Press.

Bauer, Peter T. 1984. *Reality and Rhetoric: Studies in the Economics of Development.* Cambridge, Mass.: Harvard University Press.

Bennett, Andrew, and Alexander L. George. 2005. *Case Studies and Theory Development in the Social Sciences.* Cambridge, Mass.: MIT Press.

Bennett, Andrew, Joseph Lepgold, and Danny Unger. 1994. "Burden-Sharing in the Persian Gulf War." *International Organization* 48(1): 39–75.

Benziger, Vincent. 1993. "China's Rural Road System during the Reform Period." *China Economic Review* 4(1): 1–17.

Berry, R. Albert, and William R. Cline. 1979. *Agrarian Structure and Productivity in Developing Countries.* Baltimore: Johns Hopkins University Press.

Bezemer, Dirk, and Derek Headey. 2008. "Agriculture, Development, and Urban Bias." *World Development* 36(8): 1342–64.

Bhagwati, N. Jagdish. 1985. *Essays in Development Economics.* Edited by Gene Grossman. Cambridge, Mass.: MIT Press.

——. 1988. "Poverty and Public Policy." *World Development* 16(5): 539–654.

Bigsten, Arne, and Jorgen Levin. 2001. "Growth, Income Distribution, and Poverty: A Review." Paper presented at the WIDER Development Conference on Growth and Poverty, Helsinki, May 25–26.

Black, Dan A., Terra G. McKinnish, and Seth G. Sanders. 2003. "Does the Availability of High-Wage Jobs for Low-Skilled Men Affect Welfare Expenditures?: Evidence from Shocks to the Steel and Coal Industries." *Journal of Public Economics* 87(9–10): 1921–42.

Bo, Zhiyue. 1996. "Economic Performance and Political Mobility: Chinese Provincial Leaders." *Journal of Contemporary China* 5(12): 135–54.

——. 2002. *Chinese Provincial Leaders: Economic Performance and Political Mobility Since 1949.* Armonk, N.Y.: M. E. Sharpe.

Bramall, Chris. 2001. "The Quality of China's Household Income Surveys." *China Quarterly* 167: 689–705.

Breslin, Shaun Gerard. 1996. *China in the 1980s: Centre-Province Relations in a Reforming Socialist State.* New York: St. Martin's Press.

Britton, Stephen. 1980. "The Spatial Organization of Tourism in a Neo-Colonial Economy: A Fiji Case Study." *Pacific Viewpoint* 21(2): 144–65.

——. 1991. "Tourism, Capital, and Place: Towards a Critical Geography of Tourism." *Environment and Planning D: Society and Space* 9(4): 451–78.

Brundtland, Gro Harlem. 1995. "Statement." Paper presented at the United Nations World Summit for Social Development, Copenhagen, March 11.

Bryceson, Deborah, Annabel Bradbury, and Trevor Bradbury. 2008. "Roads to Poverty Reduction?: Exploring Rural Roads' Impact on Mobility in Africa and Asia." *Development Policy Review* 26(4): 459–82.

Campbell, Donald. 1975. "'Degrees of Freedom' and the Case Study." *Comparative Political Studies* 8(2): 178–93.

Cardoso, Fernando Henrique, and Enzo Faletto. 1979. *Dependency and Development in Latin America.* Translated by Marjory M. Urquidi. Berkeley: University of California Press.

Chambers, Robert, Arnold Pacey, and Lori Ann Thrupp, eds. 1989. *Farmer First: Farmer Innovation and Agricultural Research.* London: Intermediate Technology Publications.

Chan, Hon S. 2004. "Cadre Personnel Management in China: The Nomenklatura System, 1990–1998." *China Quarterly* 179: 703–34.

Chen, Shaohua, and Martin Ravallion. 2007. "Absolute poverty measures for the developing world, 1981–2004." Policy Research Working Paper no. 4211. World Bank, Washington, D.C.

——. 2008. "The Developing World Is Poorer than We Thought, but No Less Successful in the Fight against Poverty." Policy Research Working Paper no. 4703. World Bank, Washington, D.C.

Chen, Weixing. 2007. "Statecraft in an Era of Change: Building a Harmonious Society." In *China in the Twenty-First Century: Challenges and Opportunities,* edited by Shiping Hua and Sujian Guo. New York: Palgrave Macmillan.

Chenery, Hollis, Richard Jolly, Montek S. Ahluwalia, Clive L. Bell, and John H. Duloy. 1974. *Redistribution with Growth: Policies to Improve Income Distribution in Developing Countries in the Context of Economic Growth.* London: Oxford University Press.

Cheng, Tun-Jen. 2001. "Transforming Taiwan's Economic Structure in the 20th Century." *China Quarterly* 165: 19–36.

Cheung, Peter T. Y., Jae Ho Chung, and Zhimin Lin, eds. 1998. *Provincial Strategies of Economic Reform in Post-Mao China: Leadership, Politics, and Implementation.* Armonk, N.Y.: M. E. Sharpe.

China Research Society of Urban Development. Various Years. *Zhongguo Chengshi Nianjian* [Almanac of China's Cities]. Beijing: China Research Society of Urban Development Press.

Chinese Academy of Social Sciences, ed. Various years. *Zhongguo Renkou Nianjian* [Almanac of China's population]. Beijing: Chinese Academy of Social Sciences Press.

Choi, Eun Kyong. 2006. "Building the Tax State in China: Center and Region in the Politics of Revenue Extraction, 1994–2003." PhD diss., Princeton University.

Chung, Jae Ho. 1995. "Studies of Central-Provincial Relations in the People's Republic of China: A Mid-Term Appraisal." *China Quarterly* 142: 487–508.

——. 2000. *Central Control and Local Discretion in China: Leadership and Implementation during Post-Mao Decollectivization.* Oxford: Oxford University Press.

Chung, Jae Ho, and Tao-Chiu Lam, eds. 2009. *China's Local Administration: Traditions and Changes in the Sub-National Hierarchy.* London: Routledge.

Chung, Walter, and Karina Yuen. 2003. "Management Succession: A Case for Chinese Family-Owned Business." *Management Decision* 41(7): 643–55.

Cimadamore, Alberto, Erika Vidal, Fabiana M. Werthein, and Michel Flament. 2002. "Best Practices in Poverty Reduction in Argentina: Towards the Identification of a Selection Method." In *Best Practices in Poverty Reduction: An Analytical Framework,* edited by Else yen. New York: St. Martin's Press.

Coal Industry Ministry. 1985. Meitan Gongyebu Guanyu Banfa "Xiangzhen Meikuang Guanli" de Tongzhi [Coal Industry Ministry Announcement on the Issuing of the "TVE Coal Mining Management Arrangements"]

Collier, David, and James Mahoney. 1996. "Insights and Pitfalls: Selection Bias in Qualitative Research." *World Politics* 49(1): 56–91.

Collier, Paul. 2007. "The Natural Resource Trap." In *The Bottom Billion: Why the Poorest Countries Are Failing and What We Can Do about It.* Oxford: Oxford University Press.

Commission on Growth and Development. 2010. Website. http://www.growthcommission.org/ [accessed June 15 2010].

Conway, Tim, and Andy Norton. 2002. "Nets, Ropes, Ladders and Trampolines: The Place of Social Protection within Current Debates on Poverty Reduction." *Development Policy Review* 20(5): 533–40.

Cooper, Marc. 2003. "Behind Globalization's Glitz: In 'The Other' Cancun, Tourist-Industry Workers Live in Poverty and Squalor." *The Nation,* September 22, 17–20.

Davin, Delia. 1999. *Internal Migration in Contemporary China.* New York: St. Martin's Press.

De Brauw, Alan, and Scott Rozelle. 2008. "Migration and Household Investment in Rural China." *China Economic Review* 19(2): 320–335.

DeLong, J. Bradford, and Jeffrey G. Williamson. 1994. "Natural Resources and Convergence in the Nineteenth and Twentieth Centuries." Unpublished paper, Harvard University.

Demurger, Sylvie. 2001. "Infrastructure Development and Economic Growth: An Explanation for Regional Disparities in China?" *Journal of Comparative Economics* 29(1): 95–117.

DeNavas-Walt, Carmen, Bernadette D. Proctor, and Jessica C. Smith. 2008. "Income, Poverty, and Health Insurance Coverage in the United States: 2007." In *Current Population Reports.* Washington DC: US Census Bureau.

Deng, Xiaoping. 1993. *Deng Xiaoping Wenxuan* [Collected Works of Deng Xiaoping], vol. 3. Beijing: Renmin Chubanshe.

Devereux, Stephen. 2002. "Can Social Safety Nets Reduce Chronic Poverty?" *Development Policy Review* 20(5): 657–75.

d'Hooghe, Ingrid. 1994. "Regional Economic Integration in Yunnan." In *China Deconstructs: Politics, Trade, and Regionalism,* edited by David S. G. Goodman and Gerald Segal. London and New York: Routledge.

Dollar, David, and Aart Kraay. 2000. "Growth *Is* Good for the Poor." *World Bank,* Washington, D.C.

——. 2001. "Trade, Growth, and Poverty." World Bank, Washington, D.C.

——. 2002. "Growth Is Good for the Poor." *Journal of Economic Growth* 7(3): 195–225.

Donaldson, John A. 2007. "Tourism, Development and Poverty Reduction in Guizhou and Yunnan." *China Quarterly* 190: 333–351.

——. 2008. "Growth Is Good for Whom, When, How?: Economic Growth and Poverty Reduction in Exceptional Cases." *World Development* 36(11): 2127–43.

——. 2009. "Provinces: Paradoxical Politics, Problematic Partners." In *China's Local Administration: Traditions and Changes in the Sub-National Hierarchy,* edited by Jae Ho Chung and Tao-chiu Lam. London: Routledge.

Dorward, Andrew, Jonathan Kydd, Jamie Morrison, and Ian Urey. 2004. "A Policy Agenda for Pro-Poor Agricultural Growth." *World Development* 32(1): 73–89.

Du, Yang, Albert Park, and Sangui Wang. 2005. "Migration and Rural Poverty in China." *Journal of Comparative Economics* 33(4): 688–709.

Dunbabin, John P. D. 1974. *Rural Discontent in Nineteenth-Century Britain.* London: Faber and Faber.

Duncan, Tyrrell, Keith Jefferis, and Patrick Molutsi. 1997. "Botswana: Social Development in a Resource-Rich Economy." In *Development with a Human Face: Experiences in Social Achievement and Economic Growth,* edited by Santosh Mehrotra and Richard Jolly. Oxford: Clarendon Press.

Eastwood, Robert, and Michael Lipton. 2001. "Pro-Poor Growth and Pro-Growth Poverty Reduction: What Do they Mean? What Does the Evidence Mean? What Can Policymakers Do?" Paper presented at the Asia and Pacific Forum on Poverty: Reforming Policies and Institutions for Poverty Reduction, Asian Development Bank, Manila, February 5–9.

Eckholm, Erik. 2002. "Chinese Power Company Chief Flees the Country and Scrutiny." *New York Times*. http://query.nytimes.com/gst/fullpage.html?res=9C01E1D6113DF933A15753C1A9649C8B63&n=Top/Reference/Times%20Topics/Subjects/E/Ethics.

Editorial Board of *Who's Who in China*. 1989. "Zhong guo ren ming da ci dian" bian ji bu [*Who's Who in China: Current Leaders*]. Beijing: Foreign Language Press.

——. 1994. "Zhong guo ren ming da ci dian" bian ji bu [*Who's Who in China: Current Leaders 1994 Edition*]. Beijing: Foreign Language Press.

Eng, Irene. 1999. "Agglomeration and the Local State: The Tobacco Economy of Yunnan, China." *Transactions of the Institute of British Geography* 24(3): 315–29.

Estache, Antonio. 2004. "Emerging Infrastructure Policy Issues in Developing Countries: A Survey of the Recent Economic Literature." Policy Research Working Paper no. 3442. World Bank, Washington, D.C.

Evans, Peter B. 1979. *Dependent Development: The Alliance of Multinational, State, and Local Capital in Brazil*. Princeton: Princeton University Press.

——. 1995. *Embedded Autonomy: States and Industrial Transformation*. Princeton: Princeton University Press.

Ewing, Richard Daniel. 2003. "Hu Jintao: The Making of a Chinese General Secretary." *China Quarterly* 173: 17–34.

Falkenheim, Victor. 1969. "The Cultural Revolution in Kwangsi, Yunnan and Fukien." *Asian Survey* 9(8): 580–97.

Fan, C. Cindy. 1997. "Uneven Development and Beyond: Regional Development Theory in Post-Mao China." *International Journal of Urban and Regional Research* 21(4): 620–39.

——. 1999. "Migration in a Socialist Transitional Economy: Heterogeneity, Socioeconomic and Spatial Characteristics of Migrants in China and Guangdong Province." *International Migration Review* 33(4): 950–83.

——. 2002. "The Elite, the Natives, and the Outsiders: Migration and Labor Market Segmentation in Urban China." *Annals of the Association of American Geographers* 92(1): 103–24.

——. 2005. "Interprovincial Migration, Population Redistribution, and Regional Development in China: 1990 and 2000 Census Comparisons*." *Professional Geographer* 57(2): 295–311.

——. 2006. "China's Eleventh Five-Year Plan (2006–2010): From 'Getting Rich First' to 'Common Prosperity.'" *Eurasian Geography and Economics* 47(6): 708–23.

Fan, Shenggen, and Connie Chan-Kang. 2004. *Road Development, Economic Growth, and Poverty Reduction in China*. Research Monograph no. 138. Washington, D.C.: International Food Policy Research Institute.

——. 2008. "Regional Road Development, Rural and Urban Poverty: Evidence from China." *Transport Policy* 15: 305–18.

Fan, Shenggen, Linxiu Zhang, and Xiaobo Zhang. 2002. *Growth, Inequality, and Poverty in Rural China: the Role of Public Investments*. Research Monograph no. 125. Washington, D.C.: International Food Policy Research Institute.

Fan, Shenggen, and Xiaobo Zhang. 2004. "Infrastructure and Regional Economic Development in Rural China." *China Economic Review* 15: 203–14.

Felloni, Fabrizio, Thomas Wahl, Philip Wandschneider, and John Gilbert. 2001. "Infrastructure and Agricultural Production: Cross-Country Evidence and Implications for China." Unpublished paper, Washington State University.

Fitzgerald, John, ed. 2002. *Rethinking China's Provinces*. New York: Routledge.

Frank, Andre Gunder. 1969. *Capitalism and Underdevelopment in Latin America: Historical Studies of Chile and Brazil.* New York: Monthly Review Press.

Franke, Richard W., and Barbara H. Chasin. 1992. *Kerala: Development through Radical Reform*. New Delhi: Promilla.

Freeman, Donald G. 2003. "Poverty and the Macroeconomy: Estimates from U.S. Regional Data." *Contemporary Economic Policy* 21(3): 358–71.

Gan, Qiaolin, Dajin Yao, and Zexiang Yang. 2001. "Yunnan Fuping Gongjian Xiang Tezheng yu Yinsu Fengxi" [Analysis of the Factors and Characteristics of Yunnan's Poor Counties]. *Yunnan Caimao Xueyuan Xuebao* [Journal of Yunnan Finance & Economics University] 17(5): 78–82.

Gelb, Alan H. 1988. *Oil Windfalls: Blessing or Curse?* New York: Oxford University Press.

General Organization of Rural Social-Economic Survey of National Bureau of Statistics, and Foreign Capital Project Management Center of State Council Leading Group Office of Poverty Alleviation and Development. 1999. *Poverty Monitoring Report, 1999*. Beijing: Jingji Kexue Chubanshe [Economic Social Science Press].

George, Alexander L. 1979. "Case Studies and Theory Development: The Method of Structured, Focused Comparison." In *Diplomacy,* edited by Paul Lauren. New York: Free Press.

George, Alexander L., and Andrew Bennett. 2005. *Case Studies and Theory Development in the Social Sciences*. Cambridge, Mass.: MIT Press.

Gerring, John. 2007. *Case Study Research: Principles and Practices*. Cambridge, UK: Cambridge University Press.

Gilbert, Geoffrey. 1997. "Adam Smith on the Nature and Causes of Poverty." *Review of Social Economy* 55(3): 273–91.

Goertz, Gary. 2006. *Social Science Concepts: A User's Guide*. Princeton: Princeton University Press.

Goldstein, Avery. 1994. "Trends in the Study of Political Elites and Institutions in the PRC." *China Quarterly* 139: 714–30.

Gong, Xiaokuan. 1996. "Guizhou Jichu Sheshi Jianshe yu Zhongguo 'T' xing Kaifang Zhanlue" [The Construction of Guizhou's Basic Infrastructure and China's "T"-shaped Development Strategy]. *Guizhou Shehui Kexue* [Social Science in Guizhou] 139(1): 25–30.

Goodman, David S. G. 1986. *Centre and Province in the People's Republic of China: Sichuan and Guizhou, 1955–1965*. Cambridge, UK: Cambridge University Press.

——. 1989. *China's Regional Development*. London and New York: Routledge.

——, ed. 1997. *China's Provinces in Reform: Class, Community, and Political Culture*. London and New York: Routledge.

Guizhou Nianjian Bianjibu, ed. Various years. *Guizhou Nianjian* [Guizhou Yearbook]. Beijing: China Statistics Press.

Guizhou Provincial People's Government. 1986. "Guizhousheng Xianzheng Jiti Kuangshan Qiye he Geti Caikuang Zhanxing Guanli Banfa" [Yunnan

Provincial TVE Collective Mining Area Enterprise and Individual Mining Management Temporary Regulation].

Guo, Baogang. 2008. "Beyond Technocracy: China's Quest for Legitimacy in the Era of Hu Jintao." In *China in the Twenty-First Century: Challenges and Opportunities,* edited by Shiping Hua and Sujian Guo. New York: Palgrave Macmillan.

Guo, Zhengsheng, Dezheng Yuan, and Houchen Zhao, eds. 1990. *Yunnan Sheng 41 ge Pinkunxian Tuopin Zhifu Zhanlue Yanjiu* [Research into the Strategy of Poverty Alleviation of Yunnan's 41 Poor Counties]. Kunming: Yunnan Renmin Chubanshe.

Haq, Mahbub ul. 1995. *Reflections on Human Development.* New York: Oxford University Press.

Hare, Denise. 1999. "'Push' versus 'Pull' Factors in Migration Outflows and Returns: Determinants of Migration Status and Spell Durations among China's Rural Population." *Journal of Development Studies* 35(3): 45–72.

Hemmer, Hans-Rimbert, and Rainer Wilhelm. 2000. *Fighting Poverty in Developing Countries: Principles for Economic Policy.* Frankfurt: Peter Lang.

Hendrischke, Hans J., and Chongyi Feng, eds. 1999. *The Political Economy of China's Provinces: Comparative and Competitive Advantage.* New York: Routledge.

Herrold-Menzies, Melinda. 2006. "Integrating Conservation and Development: What We Can Learn from Caohai, China." *Journal of Environment and Development* 15(4): 382–406.

Hillman, Ben. 2003. "Paradise under Construction: Minorities, Myths and Modernity in Northwest Yunnan." *Asian Ethnicity* 4(2): 175–88.

Hills, Theo L., and Jan Lundgren. 1977. "The Impact of Tourism in the Caribbean: A Methodological Study." *Annals of Tourism Research* 4: 248–67.

Holsti, Kalwei J. 1999. "The Coming Chaos?: Armed Conflict in the World's Periphery." In *International Order and the Future of World Politics,* edited by T. V. Paul and John A. Hall. Cambridge, UK: Cambridge University Press.

Howe, John. 1984. "The Impact of Rural Roads on Poverty Alleviation: A Review of the Literature." In *Rural Roads and Poverty Reduction,* edited by John Howe and Peter Richards. London: Intermediate Technology Publications.

Hu, Kaimei, ed. 2001. *Du Fu Selected Poems.* Beijing: Foreign Languages Press.

Huang, Yasheng. 1996. *Inflation and Investment Controls in China: The Political Economy of Central-Local Relations during the Reform Era.* Cambridge, UK: Cambridge University Press.

International Labour Organization. 1976. *Employment, Growth and Basic Needs: A One-World Problem.* Geneva: ILO.

Jalan, Jyotsna, and Martin Ravallion. 2000. "Is Transient Poverty Different?: Evidence from Rural China." *Journal of Development Studies* 36(6): 82–99.

——. 2002. "Geographic Poverty Traps?: A Micro Econometric Model of Consumption Growth in Rural China." *Journal of Applied Econometrics* 17(4): 329–46.

Jalilian, Hossein, and John Weiss. 2004. "Infrastructure, Growth and Poverty: Some Cross Country Evidence." Paper presented at the conference on Infrastructure and Development: Poverty, Regulation and Private Sector Investment, November 2004.

Johnson, D. Gale. 2003. "Provincial Migration in China in the 1990s." *China Economic Review* 14: 22–31.

Johnston, Louis and Samuel H. Williamson, "What Was the U.S. GDP Then?" MeasuringWorth, 2010. http://www.measuringworth.org/usgdp/

Kanbur, Ravi. 2000. "Income Distribution and Development." In *Handbook of Income Distribution,* edited by Anthony B. Atkinson and François Bourguignon. Amsterdam: Elsevier Science.

——. 2002. "Economics, Social Science and Development." *World Development* 30(3): 477–86.

Kanbur, Ravi, and Lyn Squire. 1999. "The Evolution of Thinking about Poverty: Exploring the Interactions." World Bank, Washington, D.C.

Khan, Azizur Rahman, and Carl Riskin. 2001. *Inequality and Poverty in China in the Age of Globalization.* New York: Oxford University Press.

Khandker, Shahidur R., Victor Lavy, and Dean Filmer. 1994. "Schooling and Cognitive Achievements of Children in Morocco: Can the Government Improve Outcomes?" World Bank, Washington, D.C.

Killick, Anthony 1989. *A Reaction Too Far: Economic Theory and the Role of the State in Developing Countries.* London: Overseas Development Institute.

King, Gary, Robert O. Keohane, and Sidney Verba. 1994. *Designing Social Inquiry.* Princeton: Princeton University Press.

Klasen, Stephan. 2001. "In Search of the Holy Grail: How to Achieve Pro-Poor Growth?" Working Paper. University of Munich, Strategic Partnership with Africa (SPA).

Knight, John, Lina Song, and Huaibin Jia. 1999. "Chinese Rural Migrants in Urban Enterprises: Three Perspectives." *Journal of Development Studies* 35(3): 73–104.

Kohli, Atul. 2004. *State-Directed Development: Political Power and Industrialization in the Global Periphery.* Cambridge, UK: Cambridge University Press.

Krueger, Anne O. 1995. "Policy Lessons from Development Experience since the Second World War." In *Handbook of Development Economics,* vol. 3, edited by Jere R. Behrman and T. N. Srinivasan. Amsterdam: North Holland.

Kuznets, Simon. 1955. "Economic Growth and Income Inequality." *American Economic Review* 45(1): 1–28.

Kwon, Eunkyung K. 2000. "Infrastructure, Growth, and Poverty Reduction in Indonesia: A Cross-sectional Analysis." Asian Development Bank, Manila.

Lai, Hongyi Harry. 2002. "China's Western Development Program: Its Rationale, Implementation and Prospects." *Modern China* 28(4): 432–66.

Lal, Deepak. 1985. *The Poverty of "Development Economics."* Cambridge, Mass.: Harvard University Press.

Lal, Deepak, and Hla Myint. 1996. *The Political Economy of Poverty, Equity, and Growth: A Comparative Study.* New York: Oxford University Press.

Lam, Willy Wo-Lap. 2006. *Chinese Politics in the Hu Jintao Era: New Leaders, New Challenges.* New York: East Gate.

Lan, Daju. 1997. "An Investigative Report on the Migrant Population of Caitang Village, Xiamen Special Economic Zone." In *Farewell to Peasant China: Rural Urbanization and Social Change in the Late Twentieth Century,* edited by Gregory E. Guldin. Armonk, N.Y.: M. E. Sharpe.

Landry, Pierre. 2000. "Controlling Decentralization: The Party and Local Elites in Post-Mao Jiangsu." PhD diss., University of Michigan, Ann Arbor.

Lardy, Nicholas. 1992. *Foreign Trade and Economic Reform in China, 1978–1990*. Cambridge, UK: Cambridge University Press.

Lasswell, Harold Dwight. 1936. *Politics: Who Gets What, When, How*. New York and London: McGraw-Hill.

Lew, Alan A., Lawrence Yu, John Ap, and Guangrui Zhang. 2003. *Tourism in China*. New York: Haworth Hospitality Press.

Lewis, Oscar. 1968. "The Culture of Poverty." In *On Understanding Poverty: Perspectives from the Social Sciences*, edited by Daniel P. Moynihan. New York: Basic Books.

Lewis, W. Arthur. 1954. "Economic Development with Unlimited Supplies of Labour." *Manchester School of Economic Studies* 22: 139–91.

Li, Cheng. 2001. *China's Leaders: The New Generation*. Lanham: Rowman and Littlefield.

——. 2005. "Hu's Policy Shift and the Tuanpai's Coming-of-Age." *China Leadership Monitor* 15(6).

Li, Cheng, and Liang Fook Lye. 2005. *Hu Jintao's Power Consolidation (I): Moving with Ease and Skill*. Singapore: East Asian Institute.

Li, Fan. 1994. "Waichu Dagong Renyuan Guimo, Liudong Fanwei: Zhongguo Nongcun Laodongli Yanjiu Zhi Er" [The Volume, Scope of Mobility, and Other Aspects of Labor Migrants: Research on the Problem of Rural Labor Mobility in China, Part Two]. *Zhongguo Nongcun Jingji* [China's Agricultural Economy] 9: 31–35.

Li, Linda Chelan. 1997. "Provincial Discretion and National Power: Investment Policy in Guangdong and Shanghai, 1978–1993." *China Quarterly* 152: 778–804.

——. 1998. *Centre and Provinces: China 1978–1993: Power as Non-Zero-Sum*. Oxford: Clarendon Press.

Li, Qiang. 2001. "Zhongguo Waichu Nongmin jiqi Huikuan zhi Yanjiu" [Research on China's Migrant Farmers and Remittances]. *Shehuixue Yanjiu* [Sociological Research] 4.

Liang, Zai, and Michael J. White. 1997. "Market Transition, Government Policies, and Interprovincial Migration in China: 1983–1988." *Economic Development and Cultural Change* 45(2): 321–39.

Lieberthal, Kenneth, and Michel Oksenberg. 1990. *Policy Making in China: Leaders, Structures, and Processes*. Princeton: Princeton University Press.

Lijphart, Arend. 1971. "Comparative Politics and the Comparative Method." *American Political Science Review* 65: 682–93.

Lin, Justin Yifu. 1995. "Can China's 'Mini-Bang' Succeed?" *Contemporary Economic Policy* 13(1): 10–14.

Lin, Justin Y., Gewei Wang, and Yaohui Zhao. 2004. "Regional Inequality and Labor Transfers in China." *Economic Development and Cultural Change* 52(3): 587–604.

Lin, Kun-Chin. 2007. "Politics of Highway Construction in Rural China: A Case of Mismatching Central-local Interests." Paper presented at the In *Association for Asian Studies Annual* Meeting, Boston, March 22–25.

Lipton, Michael. 1977. *Why Poor People Stay Poor: A Study of Urban Bias in World Development.* Cambridge, Mass.: Harvard University Press.

Lipton, Michael, and Martin Ravallion. 1995. "Poverty and Policy." In *Handbook of Development Economics,* vol. 3, edited by Jere Behrman and T. N. Srinivasan. Amsterdam: North Holland.

Litzinger, Ralph. 2004. "The Mobilization of 'Nature': Perspectives from North-West Yunnan." *China Quarterly* 178: 488–504.

Liu, Alan P. L. 1992. "The 'Wenzhou Model' of Development China's Modernization." *Asian Survey* 32(8): 696–711.

——. 1996. "Beijing and the Provinces: Different Constructions of National Development." *Issues and Studies* 32(8): 28–53.

Lu, Deming. 2004. "Subei Fuming Gongcheng yu Xinxing Gongyehua Daolu" [The Northern Jiangsu Poverty Alleviation Project and the Road to a New Type of Industrialization]. Paper presented at the Subei Fumin Gongcheng he Xinxing Gongyehua Dalu Yantaohui [Conference on the Northern Jiangsu Poverty Alleviation Project and the Road to a New Type of Industrialization], July 2.

Lv, Jianjun. 1995. "Nongye Fazhan Yu Guizhou Xianxiang" [Agricultural Development and the Guizhou Phenomenon]. *Guizhou Caijing Xueyuan Xuebao* [Journal of Guizhou College of Finance and Economics] no. 4: 4–8.

Lyons, Thomas P. 1994. *Poverty and Growth in a South China County: Anxi, Fujian, 1949–1992.* Cornell East Asia series no. 72. Ithaca: Cornell University Press.

Ma, Laurence J. C., and Biao Xiang. 1998. "Native Place, Migration and the Emergence of Peasants Enclaves in Beijing." *China Quarterly* 155: 546–81.

Ma, Ling. 2006. *Hu Jintao Xin Zhuan* [A New Biography of Hu Jintao]. Taibei: Taidian Dianye Gongsi [Taidian Electronics Company].

Ma, Zhongdong. 1999. "Temporary Migration and Regional Development in China." *Environment and Planning A* 31: 783–802.

Martinussen, John. 1997. *Society, State, and Market: A Guide to Competing Theories of Development.* London: Zed Books.

Mayhew, Bradley, Korina Miller, and Alex English. 2002. *Southwest China.* Victoria, Australia: Lonely Planet Publications.

Max-Neef, Manfred. 1991. *Human Scale Development: Conception, Application and Further Reflections.* New York: Apex Press.

McCulloch, Neil, and Michele Calandrino. 2002. "Poverty Dynamics in Rural Sichuan between 1991 and 1995." Institute of Development Studies, University of Sussex, Brighton.

McMahon, Gary, and Felix Remy, eds. 2001. *Large Mines and the Community—Socioeconomic and Environmental Effects in Latin America, Canada and Spain.* Washington D.C.: World Bank, International Development Research Center.

McMahon, Gary, Elly Rasdiani Subdibjo, Jean Aden, Aziz Bouzaher, Giovanna Dore, and Ramanie Kunayagam. 2000. "Mining and the Environment in Indonesia: Long-Term Trends and Repercussions of the Asian Economic Crisis." EASES Discussion Paper. World Bank Environment and Social Development Unit, Washington D.C.

Mehrotra, Santosh. 1997. "Human Development in Cuba: Growing Risk of Reversal." In *Development with a Human Face: Experiences in Social Achievement and*

Economic Growth, edited by Santosh Mehrotra and Richard Jolly. Oxford: Oxford University Press.

——. 2002. "Some Methodological Issues in Determining Good Practices in Social Policy: The Case of High-Achieving Countries." In *Best Practices in Poverty Reduction: An Analytical Framework,* edited by Else yen. New York: St. Martin's Press.

Mellor, John W. 1995. *Agriculture on the Road to Industrialization.* Baltimore: Johns Hopkins University Press.

Meng, Xin, Robert Gregory, and Guanhua Wan. 2007. "Urban Poverty in China and its Contributing Factors, 1986–2000." *Review of Income and Wealth* 53(1): 167–89.

Mertha, Andrew C. 2005. "China's 'Soft' Centralization: Shifting *Tiao/Kuai* Authority Relations." *China Quarterly* 184: 791–810.

——. 2008. *China's Water Warriors: Citizen Action and Policy Change.* Ithaca: Cornell University Press.

Miller, S. M. 1996. The Great Chain of Poverty Explanations. In *Poverty: A Global Review: Handbook on International Poverty Research,* edited by Else yen, S. M. Miller and Syed A. Samad. Oslo and Paris: Scandinavian University Press and UNESCO Publishing.

Ministry of Finance. 1997. *Difang Caizheng Tongji Ziliao* [Local Government Finance Statistical Materials]. Beijing: Zhongguo Caizheng Jingji Chubanshe [China Government Finance Economic Press].

Minten, Bart, and Steven Kyle. 1999. "The Effects of Distance and Road Quality on Food Collection, Marketing Margins, and Traders' Wages: Evidence from Former Zaire." *Journal of Development Economics* 60: 467–95.

Mowforth, Martin, and Ian Munt. 2003. *Tourism and Sustainability: Development and New Tourism in the Third World.* 2nd ed. London and New York: Routledge.

Narayan, Swati, Jo Walker, and Kim Trathen. 2009. *Who's Really Fighting Hunger?* Johannesburg: ActionAid.

National Bureau of Statistics. 2004. *Poverty Statistics in China.* Beijing: Rural Survey Organization, National Bureau of Statistics.

Naughton, Barry. 1988. "The Third Front: Defence Industrialization in the Chinese Interior." *China Quarterly* 115: 351–86.

——. 1993. "Deng Xiaoping: The Economist." *China Quarterly* 135: 491–514.

Nolan, Peter. 2001. *China and the Global Economy: National Champions, Industrial Policy and the Big Business Revolution.* Basingstoke: Palgrave.

Nurkse, Ragnar. 1953. *Problems of Capital Formation in Underdeveloped Countries.* Oxford: Blackwell.

Oakes, Tim. 1998. *Tourism and Modernity in China.* London and New York: Routledge.

——. 2004. "Building a Southern Dynamo: Guizhou and State Power." *China Quarterly* 178: 467–87.

Obama, Barack. 1995. *Dreams from My Father.* New York: Random House.

Oi, Jean. 1995. "The Role of the Local State in China's Transitional Economy." *China Quarterly* 144: 1132–49.

Oxfam. 2007. "Growth with Equity is Good for the Poor." In *The Globalization Reader,* edited by F. J. Lechner and J. Boli. Malden, MA: Wiley, John & Sons.

Parayil, Govindan, ed. 2000. *Kerala: The Development Experience—Reflections on Sustainability and Replicability.* London: Zed Books.

Park, Albert, Scott Rozelle, Christine P. W. Wong, and Changqing Ren. 1996. "Distributional Consequences of Fiscal Reform on China's Poor Areas." *China Quarterly* 147: 1001–32.

Park, Albert, and Sangui Wang. 2001. "China's Poverty Statistics." *China Economic Review* 12(4): 384–98.

Park, Albert, Sangui Wang, and Guobao Wu. 2002. "Regional Poverty Targeting in China." *Journal of Public Economics* 86(1): 123–53.

Parris, Kristen. 1993. "Local Initiative and National Reform: The Wenzhou Model of Development." *China Quarterly* 134: 242–63.

Patterson, Rev K. 1992. "Aloha for Sale." *Focus* 4: 4–5.

Piazza, Alan, Julia Li, Su Guoxia, Terry McKinley, Enjiang Cheng, Claude Saint-Pierre, Terry Sicular, Bruce Trangmar, and Robert Weller. 2001. *China: Overcoming Rural Poverty.* Report no. 22137. Washington, D.C.: World Bank.

Pierson, David. 2010. "Plenty of New Airports but Few Passengers in China." *Los Angeles Times,* March 13.

Prebisch, Raul. 1950. *The Economic Development of Latin America and Its Principal Problems.* Lake Success, N.Y.: United Nations Department of Economic Affairs.

Przeworski, Adam. 2003. *States and Markets: A Primer in Political Economy.* Cambridge, UK: Cambridge University Press.

Przeworski, Adam, and Henry Teune. 1970. *The Logic of Comparative Social Inquiry.* New York: Wiley-Interscience.

Qian, Wenbao. 1996. *Rural-Urban Migration and Its Impact on Regional Development in China.* Aldershot, UK: Averbury.

Ran, Xiwen, and Xuesong Lie. 2000. "Guizhou Fupin Gongjian Chengxiao, Pinkun Tezheng, ji Duice Cuoshi" [The Effectiveness of the Attack on Poverty, the Special Characteristics of Poverty, and Implementation of Countermeasures in Guizhou]. *Guizhou Minzu Yanjiu* [Guizhou Ethnic Study] 83(3): 44–49.

Ravallion, Martin. 2001. "Growth, Inequality and Poverty: Looking beyond the Averages." *World Development* 29(11): 1803–15.

——. 2009. "A Comparative Perspective on Poverty Reduction in Brazil, China and India." Policy Research Working Papter no. 5080. World Bank, Washington, D.C.

Remick, Elizabeth J. 2004. *Building Local States: China during the Republican and Post-Mao Eras.* Cambridge, Mass.: Harvard University Press.

Rodrik, Dani. 2000. "Growth Versus Poverty Reduction: A Hollow Debate." *Finance and Development* 37(4): 4–5.

Root, Hilton, C. S. Shaijumon, and Ramya Ghosh. 2005. "Making Infrastructure Work for the Poor: Infrastructure and Governance." Paper presented at International Studies Association Annual Meeting, Honolulu, March 5.

Rosen, Stanley. 1988. "China in 1987: The Year of the Thirteenth Party Congress." *Asian Survey* 28(1): 35–51.

Rosenstein-Rodan, Paul N. 1957. *Notes on the Theory of the "Big Push."* Cambridge Mass.: MIT Press.

Rostow, Walt W. 1960. *Stages of Economic Growth: A Non-Communist Manifesto.* Cambridge, UK: Cambridge University Press.

Rozelle, Scott, Guo Li, Minggao Shen, Amelia Hughart, and John Giles. 1999. "Leaving China's Farms: Survey Results of New Paths and Remaining Hurdles to Rural Migration." *China Quarterly* 158: 367–93.

Rozelle, Scott, Linxiu Zhang, and Jikun Huang. 2000. "China's War on Poverty." Working Paper no. 60. Stanford Institute for Economic Policy Research, Stanford University.

Rui, Huaichuan. 2004. "The Rise and Fall of China's TVE Coalmines." *Minerals and Energy—Raw Materials Report* 19(1): 2–15.

——. 2005. *Globalization, Transition and Development in China: The Case of the Coal Industry.* London: RoutledgeCurzon.

Sachs, Jeffrey D., and Andrew M. Warner. 1995. "Natural Resource Abundance and Economic Growth." NBER Working Paper no. 5398. National Bureau of Economic Research, Cambridge, Mass.

Saich, Tony. 1992. "The Fourteenth Party Congress: A Programme for Authoritarian Rule." *China Quarterly* 132: 1136–60.

——. 2006. "China in 2005: Hu's in Charge." *Asian Survey* 46(1): 37–48.

——. 2007. "China in 2006: Focus on Social Development." *Asian Survey* 47(1): 32–43.

Samad, Syed Abdus. 1994. "Poverty Research/Asian Chapter." Paper presented at UNESCO/CROP Scientific Symposium on the Regional State-of-the-Art Review on Poverty Research, Paris, December.

Sathiendrakumar, Rajasundram, and Clement Allan Tisdell. 2001. "Tourism and the Economic Development of the Maldives." In *Tourism Economics, the Environment and Development: Analysis and Policy,* edited by Clement A. Tisdell. Cleltenham, UK: Edward Elgar.

Schumacher, Ernest F. 1973. *Small Is Beautiful: Economics as If People Mattered.* New York: Harper & Row.

Scott, James C. 1985. *Weapons of the Weak: Everyday Forms of Peasant Resistance.* New Haven: Yale University Press.

Sen, Amartya. 1981. *Poverty and Famines: An Essay on Entitlement and Deprivation.* New York: Oxford University Press.

——. 1999. *Development as Freedom.* New York: Knopf.

Shah, Tushaar, Ashok Gulati, Hemant P, Ganga Shreedhar, and R. C. Jain. 2009. "Secret of Gujarat's Agrarian Miracle after 2000." *Economic and Political Weekly* 44(52): 45–55.

Shambaugh, David. 2008. "Training China's Political Elite: The Party School System." *China Quarterly* 196: 827–44.

Sheng, Yumin. 2005. "Central-Provincial Relations at the CCP Central Committees: Institutions, Measurement and Empirical Trends, 1978–2002." *China Quarterly* 182: 338–55.

Sheng, Yumin, and Yasheng Huang. 2006. "Political Federalism and Inflation: Subnational Evidence from China." Paper presented at the Annual Meeting of the American Political Science Association, Philadelphia, August 31–September 3.

Shi, Xianmin. 2005. "Zhongguo Yanhai Jingji Zhongxin Chengshi Laodongli Liudong yu Tizhi Xuanze" [Urban Labor Migration and Choice of Systems in China's Coastal Economic Central Cities]. http://www.usc.cuhk.edu.hk/wk_wzdetails.asp?id=570 [accessed March 29 2005].

Shirk, Susan. 1992. "The Chinese Political System and the Political Strategy of Economic Reform." In *Bureaucracy, Politics, and Decision Making in PostMao China,* edited by Kenneth Lieberthal and David M. Lampton. Berkeley: University of California Press.

——. 1993. *The Political Logic of Economic Reform in China.* Berkeley: University of California Press.

Sinclair, M. Thea 1991. "The Tourism Industry and Foreign Exchange Leakages in a Developing Country: The Distribution of Earnings from Safari and Beach Tourism in Kenya." In *The Tourism Industry: An International Analysis,* edited by M. Thea Sinclair and M. J. Stabler. London: C.A.B. International.

Singh, Prerna. Forthcoming. "We-ness and Welfare: A Longitudinal Analysis of Social Development in Kerala, India." *World Development.*

Skinner, G. William. 1964. "Marketing and Social Structure in Rural China." *Journal of Asian Studies* 24(1): 3–44.

Skocpol, Theda. 1979. *State and Social Revolutions: A Comparative Analysis of France, Russia and China.* Cambridge, UK: Cambridge University Press.

——. 1985. "Bringing the State Back In: Strategies of Analysis in Current Research." In *Bringing the State Back In,* edited by Peter B. Evans, Dietrich Rueschemeyer and Theda Skocpol. Cambridge, UK: Cambridge University Press.

Solinger, Dorothy J. 1977a. "Minority Nationalities in China's Yunnan Province: Assimilation, Power and Policy in a Socialist State." *World Politics* 30(1): 1–23.

——. 1977b. *Regional Government and Political Integration in Southwest China, 1949–1954: A Case Study.* Berkeley: University of California Press.

——. 1995. "The Chinese Work Unit and Transient Labor in the Transition from Socialism." *Modern China* 21(2): 155–83.

——. 1996. "Despite Decentralization: Disadvantages, Dependence and Ongoing Central Power in the Inland: The Case of Wuhan." *China Quarterly* 145: 1–34.

——. 1999. *Contesting Citizenship in Urban China: Peasant Migrants, the State, and the Logic of the Market.* Berkeley: University of California Press.

Songco, Jocelyn A. 2002. "Do Rural Infrastructure Investments Benefit the Poor? Evaluating Linkages: A Global View, a Focus on Vietnam." Policy Research Working Paper no. 2796. World Bank, Washington, D.C.

Spencer, Joseph E. 1940. "Kueichou: An Internal Chinese Colony." *Pacific Affairs* 13: 162–72.

State Council LGPAD, ed. 2003. *An Overview of the Development-Oriented Poverty Reduction Program for Rural China.* Beijing: Zhongguo Caijing Jingji Chubanshe [China Financial and Economic Publishing House].

State Council Population Census Office. 2002. *Zhongguo 2000 Nian Renkou Pucha Ziliao* [Tabulation of the 2000 population census of the People's Republic of China]. Beijing: China Statistics Press.

State Statistical Bureau. Various years-a. *China Western Rural Statistics.* Beijing: China Statistics Press.

——, ed. Various years-b. *Guizhou Tongji Nianjian* [Guizhou Statistical Yearbook]. Beijing: China Statistics Publishers.

——, ed. Various years-c. *Yunnan Tongji Nianjian* [Yunnan Statistical Yearbook]. Beijing: China Statistics Publishers.

Streeten, Paul. 1982. *First Things First: Meeting Basic Needs in Developing Countries.* New York: Oxford University Press.

——. 1993. "Markets and States: Against Minimalism." *World Development* 21(8): 1281–98.

Swain, Margaret. 2002. "Looking South: Local Identities and Transnational Linkages in Yunnan." In *Rethinking China's Provinces*, edited by J. Fitzgerald. New York: Routledge.

Taylor, J. Edward, Scott Rozelle, and Alan de Brauw. 2003. "Migration and Incomes in Source Communities: A New Economics of Migration Perspective from China." *Economic Development and Cultural Change* 52(1): 75–101.

Thomson, Elspeth. 2003. *The Chinese Coal Industry: An Economic History.* London: RoutledgeCurzon.

Tilly, Charles. 1978. *From Mobilization to Revolution.* Reading, Mass.: Addison-Wesley.

Tisdell, Clement Allan. 1998. "A Review of Tourism Economics with Some Observations on Tourism in India." In *Tourism and Development: Economic, Social, Political, and Environmental Issues*, edited by Clement A. Tisdell and Kartik Roy. Commack, N.Y.: Nova Science.

——, ed. 2001. *Tourism Economics, the Environment and Development: Analysis and Policy.* Cheltenham, UK: Edward Elgar.

Tkacik, John. 2002. "A Biographical Look at Vice President Hu Jintao." In *Who's Hu?: Assessing China's Heir Apparent, Hu Jintao.* Washington D.C.: Heritage Foundation.

Todaro, Michael P. 1969. "A Model of Labor Migration and Urban Employment in Less Developed Countries." *American Economic Review* 59(1): 138–48.

Toye, John. 1987. *Dilemmas of Development: Reflections on the Counter-Revolution in Development Theory and Practice.* Oxford: Oxford University Press.

Tsui, Kai-Yuen, and Youqiang Wang. 2004. "Between Separate Stoves and a Single Menu: Fiscal Decentralization in China." *China Quarterly* 177: 71–90.

Uitto, Juha I. 2006. "Hollis B. Chenery." In *Fifty Key Thinkers on Development*, edited by David Simon. London and New York: Routledge.

Unger, Jonathan. 2002. "The Kaleidoscopic Politics of Rural China." In *Transformation of Rural China*, edited by Jonathan Unger. Armonk, N.Y.: M. E. Sharpe.

United Nations Development Programme (UNDP). 1999. *China Human Development Report.* New York: Oxford University Press.

United Nations Economic and Social Commission for Asia and the Pacific (UNESCAP). 2005. "Poverty Statistics in China." www.unescap.org/stat/meet/povstat/pov7_chn.asp [accessed February 1, 2005].

United Nations Educational, Scientific and Cultural Organization (UNESCO). 2005. "Analyses and Recommendations on Ecotourism in China's Nature Reserves." http://www.cashq.ac.cn/~mab/bb2–11.html.

——. 2009. "Old Town of Lijiang." http://whc.unesco.org/pg.cfm?cid=31&id_site=811 (accessed October 6, 2009).

United Nations World Tourism Organization (UNWTO). 2002. *Tourism and Poverty Alleviation.* Madrid: United Nations World Tourism Organization.

——. 2010. *UNWTO World Tourism Barometer.* Madrid: United Nations World Tourism Organization.

van de Walle, Dominique. 2002. "Choosing Rural Road Investments to Help Reduce Poverty." *World Development* 30(4): 575–89.

Varley, Robert C. G. 1978. *Tourism in Fiji: Some Economic and Social Problems.* Cardiff: University of Wales Press.

Vogel, Hans Ulrich, and Sabine Hieronymus. 1993. "Cowry Trade and Its Role in the Economy of Yunnan: From the Ninth to the Mid-Seventeenth Century." *Journal of the Economic and Social History of the Orient* 36(3): 211–52.

Wang, Renlian. 2001. "Yunnan Pinkun Diqu Luyou Kaifa Fupin de Tantao" [A Discussion of Poverty Alleviation through Tourism in Yunnan's Poor Areas]. *Journal of Chuxiong Teachers' College* 16(3): 99–102.

Wang, Shaoguang. 2001. "For National Unity: The Political Logic of Fiscal Transfer in China." Chinese University of Hong Kong, unpublished report.

Wang, Shaoguang, and Angang Hu. 1999. *The Political Economy of Uneven Development: The Case of China.* Armonk, N.Y.: M. E. Sharpe.

Wang, Shijie, and Duanfa Zhang. 2003. *Guizhou Fanpinkun Xitong Gongcheng* [Guizhou's Anti-poverty System Project]. Guiyang: Guizhou Renmin Chubanshe [Guizhou People's Press].

Wang, Xiaoqiang, and Nanfeng Bai. 1991. *The Poverty of Plenty.* Translated by Angela Knox. New York: St. Martin's Press.

Wang, Yuzhao. 2002. *Employment of Farmers and Poverty Alleviation in China.* Beijing: China Foundation for Poverty Alleviation.

Weber-Fahr, Monika, John E. Strongman, Ramani Kunanayagam, Gary McMahon, and Christopher Sheldon. 2002. "Mining and Poverty Reduction." In *Poverty Reduction Strategy Sourcebook,* edited by Jeni Klugman. Washington, D.C.: World Bank.

Webster, Neil, and Lars Engberg-Pedersen, eds. 2002. *In the Name of the Poor: Contesting Political Space for Poverty Reduction.* New York: St. Martin's Press.

Wei, Liqun. 2005. *Kexue Fazhan Guan he Xiandaihua Jianshe* [The Scientific Development Concept and Modern Construction]. Beijing: Renmin Chuban She [People's Publishing House].

Weisbrot, Mark, Dean Baker, Robert Naiman, and Gila Neta. 2000. "Growth May be Good for the Poor—But are IMF and World Bank Policies Good for Growth?" Center for Economic and Policy Research, Washington, D.C.

Wen, Julie Jie, and Clement Allan Tisdell. 2001. *Tourism and China's Development: Policies, Regional Economic Growth and Ecotourism.* Singapore: World Scientific.

Wen, Siyong, and Zhichu Ren. 2002. *Hu Jintao Zhuan* [Biography of Hu Jintao]. Carle Place, N.Y.: Mirror Books.

White, Lynn. 1998. *Unstately Power.* Armonk, N.Y.: M. E. Sharpe.

Wilkinson, Steven I. 2005. "Elections in India: Behind the Congress Comeback." *Journal of Democracy* 16(1): 153–67.

Wolfensohn, James D. 2005. "Transportation Can Help in the Fight against Poverty." *Economic Perspectives* 5(3): 35–37.

Wong, Christine P. W. 1997. *Financing Local Government in the People's Republic of China.* Hong Kong: Oxford University Press.

——. 2002. "China, National Development and Sub-National Finance: A Review of Provincial Expenditures." Report no. 22951-CHA. World Bank, Washington, D.C.

Wong, Linda. 1994. "China's Urban Migrants—the Public Policy Challenge." *Pacific Affairs* 67(3): 335–55.

Woo-Cumings, Meredith. 1999. *The Developmental State.* Ithaca: Cornell University Press.

World Bank. 2009. *World Development Report 2009: Reshaping Economic Geography.* Washington, D.C.: World Bank.

Wright, Daniel B. 2003. *The Promise of the Revolution.* Lanham: Rowman and Littlefield.

——. 2005. "The Politics of Private Education in Rich and Poor China." PhD diss., Johns Hopkins University.

Wright, Tim. 2004. "The Political Economy of Coal Mine Disasters in China: 'Your Rice Bowl or Your Life?'" *China Quarterly* 179: 629–46.

Wu, Harry Xiaoying, and Li Zhou. 1996. "Research on Rural-to-Urban Labour Migration in the Post-Reform China: A Survey." Working Paper no. 96/4. Chinese Economy Research Unit, University of Adelaide, Australia.

Xia, Xiaogong. 2005. "Zhongxin Zhetongxun: Zhili Puzhu Zhongguo—Dongmenglu Datongdao de Ren" [China Xinhua News Agency: A Man Dedicated to Building a Overland Route between China and ASEAN]. http://cafair.newgx.com.cn/staticpages/20050117/newgx41ebdbed-12778.html [accessed March 31, 2005].

Xiao, Honggen. 2003. "Leisure in China." In *Tourism in China,* edited by Alan A. Lew, Lawrence Yu, John Ap, and Guangrui Zhang. New York: Haworth Hospitality Press.

Xing, Li, Shenggen Fan, Xiaopeng Luo, and Xiaobo Zhang. 2008. "Community Poverty and Inequality in Western China: A Tale of Three Villages in Guizhou Province." *China Economic Review* 20(2): 338–49.

Xinhua News Agency. 2010. "Chinese Premier Calls for Improving Migrant Workers' Living Conditions in Cities." June 14. http://news.xinhuanet.com/english2010/china/2010-06/15/c_13350414.htm.

Xu, Gang. 1999. *Tourism and Local Economic Development in China.* Richmond, UK: Curzon Press.

Xu, Gang, and Claudia Kruse. 2003. "Economic Impact of Tourism in China." In *Tourism in China,* edited by Alan A. Lew, Lawrence Yu, John Ap, and Guangrui Zhang. New York: Haworth Hospitality Press.

Yang, Dali. 1997. *Beyond Beijing: Liberalism and the Regions in China.* London and New York: Routledge.

Yang, Xuishi, and Fei Guo. 1999. "Gender Differences in Determinants of Temporary Labor Migration in China: A Multilevel Analysis." *International Migration Review* 33(4): 929–53.

Yao, Shujie, Zhongyi Zhang, and Lucia Hanmer. 2004. "Growing Inequality and Poverty in China." *China Economic Review* 15(2): 145–63.

Ye, Q., and B. M. Zhang, eds. 1998. *China's TVE Coalmines.* Beijing: Coal Industrial Publishing House.

Yunnan Nianjian Bianjibu, ed. Various years. *Yunnan Nianjian* [Yunnan Yearbook]. Beijing: China Statistics Press.

Yunnan Provincial Population Census Office. 2002. *Yunnansheng 2000 Nian Renkou Pucha Ziliao* [The Reference of Population Census on Yunnan in 2000]. Kunming: Yunnan Science and Technology Press.

Yunnan Provincial People's Government. 1987. "Yunnansheng Xiangzhen Jiti Kuangshan Qiye he Geti Caikuang Guanli Zhanxing Tiaoli" [Yunnan Provincial TVE Collective Mining Area Enterprise and Individual Mining Management Temporary Regulation].

Zeng, Xiaowei. 1991. "Provincial Elite in Post-Mao China." *Asian Survey* 31(6): 512–25.

Zhang, Guangrui. 2003. "China's Tourism since 1978: Policies, Experiences and Lessons Learned." In *Tourism in China,* edited by Alan A. Lew, Lawrence Yu, John Ap, and Guangrui Zhang. New York: Haworth Hospitality Press.

Zhang, Guoliang. 2003. *Who's Who: Current Chinese Leaders.* Hong Kong: Wen Wei Publishing.

Zhang, Linxiu, Jikun Huang, and Scott Rozelle. 2003. "China's War on Poverty: Assessing Targeting and the Growth Impacts of Poverty Programs." *Journal of Chinese Economics and Business Studies* 1(3): 301–17.

Zhang, Mei. 2000. "Internal Migration and Poverty: A Case Study in a Rural Region in China." PhD diss., University of Cambridge.

Zhang, Nana. 2006. "Social Networks in Women's Rural-Urban Migration in China." *Labour, Capital and Society* 39(2): 105–25.

Zhao, Mingfang. 2006. "Luoshi Kexue Fazhan Guan Xuyao Guannian 'Liu Biange'" [To Achieve Scientific Viewpoints of Development Requires a Notion of "Six Transformations"]. *Guangming Ribao.* http://xmxh.smexm.gov.cn/2006–8/20068291546l3.htm.

Zhao, Shukai. 2000. "Criminality and the Policing of Migrant Workers." *China Journal* 43: 101–10.

Zhao, Youlang, ed. 2003. *Kaifa Fupin, Shengtai Jianshe: Bijie Shiyanqu Shiwu Nian Huigu yu Zhanwang* [Poverty Reduction, Environmental Conservation: A Review and Outlook on the 15 Years of the Bijie Experimental Zone]. Guiyang: Guizhou Renmin Chubanshe [Guizhou People's Publishing House].

Zheng, Yisheng, Minying Yang, and Zhen Shao. 2002. "The Rural Energy Policy in China." Chinese Academy of Social Sciences, Beijing.

Zheng, Yongnian. 1999. "China's Politics of Power Succession: The Rise of Hu Jintao." EAI Background Brief no. 45. East Asian Institute, National University of Singapore.

——. 2007. "Hu Jintao's Road Map to China's Future." EAI Background Brief no. 355. East Asian Institute, National University of Singapore.

Zheng, Yongnian, Zhengxu Wang, and Sow Keat Tok. 2006. *Hu Jintao at the Helm: Major Issues in the Aftermath of the 6th Party Plenum.* Singapore: East Asian Institute.

Zhongguo Jiaotong Nianjian Bianjibu, ed. Various years. *Zhongguo Jiaotong Nianjian* [China Transportation Yearbook]. Beijing: China Statistics Press.

Zhongguo Lvyou Nianjian Bianjibu, ed. Various years. *Zhongguo Luyou Nianjian* [China Tourism Yearbook]. Beijing: China Statistics Press.

Zhou, Daming. 1997. "Investigative Analysis of 'Migrant Odd-Job Workers' in Guangzhou." In *Farewell to Peasant China: Rural Urbanization and Social Change in the Late Twentieth Century,* edited by Gregory E. Guldin. Armonk, N.Y.: M. E. Sharpe.

Zhu, Ling, and Zhongyi Jiang. 1995. "'Yigong-Daizhen' in China: A New Experience with Labour-Intensive Public Works in Poor Areas." *Development Policy Review* 13(4): 349–70.

——. 1996. *Public Works and Poverty Alleviation in Rural China*. New York: Nova Science.

Zhu, Nong, and Xubei Luo. 2008. "The Impact of Remittances on Rural Poverty and Inequality in China." Policy Research Working Paper no. 4637. World Bank, Washington, D.C.

Zhu, Nong, and Sandra Poncet. 2003. "Provincial Migration Dynamics in China: Borders, Centripetal Forces and Trade." ERSA Conference Paper no. 03p148. European Research Science Association, Vienna.

Index

Page numbers followed by *f, t,* or *m* indicate figures, tables, and maps.

CPSIA information can be obtained
at www.ICGtesting.com
Printed in the USA
LVHW080735291118
598542LV00007B/171/P

9 780801 449680